OXFORD STUDIES IN MODERN LEGAL HISTORY

GENERAL EDITOR

A.W. Brian Simpson
Professor of Law, University of Michigan

OXFORD STUDIES IN MODERN LEGAL HISTORY

The series aims to publish monographs of high quality and originality on legal history covering the period from 1750 onwards.

Advocacy and the Making of the Adversarial Criminal Trial 1800–1865

DAVID J. A. CAIRNS

CLARENDON PRESS · OXFORD
1998

Oxford University Press, Great Clarendon Street, Oxford OX2 6DP
www.oup.co.uk
Oxford New York
Athens Auckland Bangkok Bogota Buenos Aires Calcutta
Cape Town Chennai Dar es Salaam Delhi Florence Hong Kong Istanbul
Karachi Kuala Lumpur Madrid Melbourne Mexico City Mumbai
Nairobi Paris São Paolo Singapore Taipei Tokyo Toronto Warsaw
and associated companies in Berlin Ibadan

Published in the United States
by Oxford University Press Inc., New York

First published 1998

British Library Cataloguing in Publication Data
Data available

Library of Congress Cataloging in Publication Data
Cairnes, David J. A. (David John Adams), 1961–
Advocacy and the making of the criminal trial, 1800–1865
David J. A. Cairns.
p. cm. — (Oxford studies in modern legal history)
Includes bibliographical references.

1. Adversary system (Law)–Great Britain–History. 2. Trial practice–Great Britain–History. 3. Criminal procedure–Great Britain–History. 4. Defense (Criminal procedure)–Great Britain--History. I. Title. II. Series.
KD8364.C35 1998
345.41'05—dc21 98–26754

ISBN 0–19–826284–1

1 3 5 7 9 10 8 6 4 2

Typeset in Great Britain
by J&L Composition Ltd, Filey, North Yorkshire
Printed in Great Britain on acid-free paper by
Bookcraft Ltd., Midsomer Norton, Somerset

For Alethea

Contents

General Editor's Preface

The Oxford University Press decided, some little time ago, to establish a new series of studies in legal history. The emphasis was to be on relatively modern legal history, a field which is attracting a growing number of able and imaginative scholars. This is the first contribution to the new series. Its subject matter is particularly appropriate. For it deals with an institution which is central to the common law system, yet one whose history has never been fully told – the adversarial criminal trial. This is viewed by many to be amongst the chief glories of the common law system; to others it appears to represent nothing so much as an obscene game, through which cynical lawyers profit from their disregard for the pursuit of truth. The institution remains a focus of controversy, and will no doubt continue to do so. Its importance is such that it deserves to be understood; understanding a legal institution necessarily involves understanding its historical evolution.

Until relatively recent times the more general history of common law criminal trials had been very imperfectly investigated. But since the 1970s a distinguished literature has greatly enhanced understanding of the eighteenth and early nineteenth century trial, and, in the process, raised new problems of interpretation and areas of controversy. Attention has been concentrated on the era of the bloody code, and the period before the adversarial trial, in something like its modern idealised form, had come to be established. Dr Cairns' book builds on this work but breaks quite new ground. For it is concerned with the era of reform, and deals in detail with the procedural changes of the early Victorian period, and the climate of opinion which underlay them. Thereby it provides the first full explanation of how the common law system of criminal trial was changed into an adversarial system. Although there have been important changes since this period the basic structure of the trial, and the role of lawyers in it, have remained much the same, and the ethical issues raised have, indeed, a timeless quality. This a pioneering study; I hope that it will, over the coming years, be joined by others as fascinating.

A. W. Brian Simpson

General Editor's Preface

Preface

This is a history of advocacy, professional ideals, and the criminal trial. The history of advocacy, presented here from the perspective of the evolving adversarial criminal trial, perhaps requires some introduction as no more sophisticated or significant expression of the art of the lawyer has been studied less. Whatever the reasons for this neglect, the result is a want of even the most rudimentary framework for the study of advocacy. No common law advocate or teacher has explained advocacy as Aristotle or Quintilian did classical rhetoric and, lamentably, none has ever tried. There has been some useful writing on aspects of common law advocacy but never any comprehensive scholarly treatment of the subject.

In my experience, even the most accomplished advocates suffer from an inability or reluctance to explain their skills in an abstract or theoretical way. At the same time, scholarly investigation is discouraged by the scale of the task and the lingering prejudice that advocacy is essentially a practical skill developed through trial experience. In fact, the skills of advocacy may be understood or developed only through reflection—which may be stimulated equally by study, experience, or exercises.

The neglect of advocacy seems to me to exemplify the continuing gulf between the worlds of legal scholarship and legal practice. I have divided my last eighteen years almost equally between these two worlds, and over three jurisdictions, and see their disparate perceptions of law as a source of considerable intellectual weakness to jurisprudence. Harmony between legal theory and judicial administration, between law in books and law in action, seems as remote as ever.

It is particularly hoped, therefore, that this book will stimulate further scholarly research and writing on advocacy and the other features of the trial process which prepare the messy facts of domestic and commercial life for the application of the law.

I have many debts to acknowledge. The first of these is to Pembroke College, Cambridge, for the research scholarship which enabled me to pursue uninterrupted research for four years. I will be forever grateful to this delightful place, rich with the spoils of time, for the gifts of opportunity, inspiration and friends.

I acknowledge with much gratitude the assistance and encouragement of Professor W. R. Cornish. I derived considerable insight and even more pleasure from his deep knowledge of ninteenth century legal history and his subtle, often ironic, appreciation of the nature of the common law. I also thank Professor A. W. B. Simpson and Mr Stephen Hedley for their many helpful suggestions and enthusiasm to see this work published, and Professor Raymond Cocks for directing me to the surviving nineteenth century circuit mess records.

I have since early 1996 had to juggle the completion of this book with the demands of professional practice. I was fortunate to meet, and subsequently join in partnership, Mai Chen and the Rt Hon Sir Geoffrey Palmer, whose support I have always enjoyed. I also wish to thank Mrs Priscilla Mitchell (née Wakefield), whom I understand has generously supported many scholars, like myself, connected by intellectual inclination and nationality with the endeavours of her famous family, and also the F. W. Maitland and Yorke Funds for assistance with my research expenses.

My debts to family, friends and colleagues during the seven-year gestation of this work are too varied and numerous adequately to recall or explain here. I appreciate all their friendship and assistance, without which I could not have completed this book.

I thank the staff of the many libraries and archives visited during my research, particularly University College London Library, where I made extensive use of the *Brougham Papers*. The portrait of Lord Brougham by James Lonsdale on the front cover is reproduced by courtesy of the National Portrait Gallery; references to the mess records of the Oxford and Midland Circuits, held by the Bodleian Library, are by permission from the Midland and Oxford Circuit and the Court Service. Finally, I am grateful to the staff of Oxford University Press for their unfailing courtesy and professionalism.

David J.A. Cairns
June, 1998
Wellington, New Zealand

Table of Trials

1

The Context of Upheaval

On 7 February 1828 Henry Brougham delivered a six-hour speech on law reform to the House of Commons, recognised in retrospect as one of the masterful speeches of the age. Jeremy Bentham assisted in the preparation of this speech, adding his extraordinary vision of the perfectability of law to Brougham's formidable talents as an orator and agitator. Brougham could not, however, allow the philosopher to dictate as the speech was addressed to a pragmatic audience and was to be a catalyst for action. Within two days it was derided by Bentham. 'Mr Brougham's mountain is delivered', Bentham wrote, 'and behold!—the mouse. The wisdom of the reformer could not overcome the craft of the lawyer'.[1]

The speech bore immediate fruit in the appointment of royal commissions to investigate civil procedure and real property. It also announced the magnitude of the reform that would shortly overtake the common law. Within two years the Tory Government which had ruled Britain with only one short interruption since the beginning of the century was out of office, and the country was in the hands of Lord Grey's Whig administration with Henry Brougham, now Lord Brougham, elevated to the woolsack.[2] Forty years of progressive rationalisation of law and procedure were to follow, culminating in the Judicature Acts of 1873 and 1875. A. V. Dicey, writing in the early years of this century, identified a major shift of public opinion around the time of Brougham's speech

[1] 'Memoirs of Bentham: including Autobiographical Conversations and Correspondence' in 10 Bentham (1843) 588.

[2] The public career of Henry Brougham (1778–1868) spans almost exactly the period of this work. He was one of the original founders of the *Edinburgh Review* in 1802 and in 1864 he was still making provocative comments on the duties of the advocate. He moved from his native Edinburgh to London in 1805, was called to the English bar in 1809, first returned to the House of Commons in 1810, and was Lord Chancellor from 1830 to 1834. His political influence effectively ended in 1834 but he remained an active member of the House of Lords and a tireless proponent of law reform. There is a recent biography of Brougham but the most insightful review of his character and career probably remains Walter Bagehot's essay: see Bagehot (1889) 40–83; and Stewart (1985). The *Brougham Papers* held by University College London are a rich resource for the study of law reform at this time, and have been used extensively throughout this work.

which laid to rest what he called 'old Toryism' and ushered in a new era of Benthamism, individualism and utilitarian reform.[3]

Law reform was to be almost exclusively the preserve of lawyers, and Bentham's juxtaposition of the wisdom of the reformer and the craft of the lawyer recognised its potential to divide the legal profession. The common lawyer's innate respect for existing institutions and his appreciation of the subtleties of the status quo made novelty, particularly in the early years of reform, an object of suspicion. The means and scope of amendment were a further cause for division, even after its need was established. There was a disturbing element of self-examination in law reform to which some lawyers found it difficult to respond with enthusiasm. The status quo would always find friends in influential positions, particularly in respect of criminal law reform amongst the judiciary.

As the pace and scale of law reform increased it became an intense preoccupation of the legal profession. It is the dominant theme of professional literature of the period. The debate over the role of counsel and advocacy in the criminal trial, considered in this work, can be traced in parliamentary debates, select committee minutes, the evidence and reports of the Criminal Law Commissioners, periodical and professional journals, biographies and other professional literature, pamphlets, newspaper editorials and letters, and the private correspondence of barristers and judges. The need to exchange and propagate ideas fostered the establishment of professional journals—most importantly the *Law Magazine* in 1828, the *Law Times* in 1843, and the *Law Review* in 1845—and professional associations devoted to the improvement of the law like the Law Amendment Society and Chancery Reform Association. The success of the *idea* of law reform in the 25 years between 1825 and 1850 was overwhelming, so that while at the beginning of this period reformers praised the common law as they tried to change it, at its end reform had to be praised even by those who sought to resist it.[4]

The criminal trial achieved its modern adversarial shape during this period of reform. It assumed this new shape to a significant degree through the common law's ubiquitous technique of adaptation, but there was also a decisive legislative intervention in the form of the Prisoners' Counsel Act.[5] The immediate impact of this Act was the introduction into criminal trials of speeches by defence counsel, but the major intellectual and forensic adjustments that accompanied this change, encour-

[3] Dicey (1905) Lectures IV and VI.

[4] Cf. Best (1858) at 430: 'Generations seem to have their fashions and faults in legislation. The peculiarity of those immediately preceding our own was an unwillingness to legislate on legal subjects, assuming our laws so perfect that interference with them must be injurious. The present generation is rather inclined to err in the opposite direction'.

[5] 6 & 7 Will. 4, c. 114. The Prisoners' Counsel Act is reproduced in Appendix 1.1.

aged by the spirit of the age, guaranteed the acceptance of adversarial procedure.

The Significance of the Prisoners' Counsel Act

The medieval common law prohibited the assistance of counsel to persons accused of capital crimes. This prohibition was eroded in the later Middle Ages, when counsel were allowed to appear for prisoners for the purpose of arguing questions of law. It was further reduced during the eighteenth century when counsel were permitted to examine and cross-examine witnesses. Its residue was abolished by the Prisoners' Counsel Act of 1836, which authorised defence counsel to address the jury on behalf of prisoners in felony trials.[6]

Until the eighteenth century ordinary criminal trials were almost invariably conducted without counsel. During the early decades of that century prosecution counsel began to appear in a small number of cases, especially in murder trials, and their appearance stimulated the employment of defence counsel by prisoners. By the end of the century counsel had had an immense impact on the conduct of criminal trials. They had ushered into criminal procedure the divisions between examination-in-chief and cross-examination and between evidence and argument, nourished the growth of the law of evidence, changed the nature of the judicial involvement in the trial, and supplemented the haphazard efforts of prisoners to defend themselves with professional advocacy.[7]

Nevertheless, the vestige of the medieval prohibition persisted until 1836, restricting the scope for defence advocacy in felony trials to matters of law and the examination and the cross-examination of witnesses. The restriction of defence counsel first to one and then to both of these duties, and the exclusion of the address to the jury from his functions, is called in this book 'the felony counsel restriction'. The felony counsel restriction was an important distinction between the trial of felonies and those of misdemeanors, where defence counsel had always been able to address the jury.[8] It meant that in felony trials the prosecution counsel, who laboured under no such restriction and could make an opening address to the jury, enjoyed a forensic advantage over defence counsel.

[6] The history and rationale of the felony counsel restriction are explored in Chapter 2.

[7] The first appearance of counsel in criminal trials and their impact during the eighteenth century is considered in Langbein (1978) 307–16; Langbein (1983a) *passim*; and Beattie (1986) ch. 7; and discussed in Chapter 2.

[8] 'Felonies' included all the most serious offences, but by the nineteenth century it was impossible to give a precise meaning to the term. Felonies were enumerated rather than defined: see 2 Pollock & Maitland (1898) 466.

The solicitude of the judge and jury for the prisoner, the latitude allowed to his counsel in cross-examination, and the development in the early nineteenth century of a duty of restraint on prosecution counsel in addressing the jury counterbalanced this prosecution advantage.

The struggle to replace 'restricted' with 'full' defence by counsel in felony trials began in the House of Commons in 1821. There were major debates in the Commons in 1824 and 1826 on proposals to allow full defence by counsel in felony trials, but on each occasion these proposals were rejected. Reform was more favourably received in the 1830s, and was achieved when the Prisoners' Counsel Act passed both Houses in 1836. The first section of this Act entitled persons accused of felonies 'to make full Answer and Defence thereto, by Counsel', meaning that the felony counsel restriction disappeared and for the first time defence counsel were able to address the jury on behalf of prisoners in felony trials.

The merits of advocacy, and particularly its effect on the discovery of the truth in criminal trials, was a major question in the Prisoners' Counsel Act debate. The opponents of full defence by counsel, which included the majority of barristers and judges, argued that there was no need for speeches from prisoners' counsel in criminal trials because juries were able to discern the truth from the examination and the cross-examination of witnesses and from the statements that prisoners made in their own defence. Full defence by counsel would only enable counsel to distort the truth with sophistical and emotive arguments. The supporters of reform, by contrast, argued that juries would be assisted by the comments of counsel on the evidence. They saw the zealous advocacy of counsel as the best means to ensure that juries were fully informed of all the facts, and all the possible interpretations of the facts, in reaching their verdicts. The enactment of the Prisoners' Counsel Act and the rationalisation of vigorous advocacy which accompanied it meant that by the middle of the century the criminal trial had largely achieved its adversarial form familiar today.

The criminal law of the late eighteenth century prescribed the death penalty for all serious offences, and for many minor and obsolete crimes. This prevalence of capital punishment had a major impact on the conduct of felony trials. It affected the procedure of the trial in the survival of the life-saving device of benefit of clergy, and in the strict rules for the formal correctness of indictments and the construction of penal statutes. It meant the regular review of judicial sentences by the Crown, and their frequent commutation through the exercise of the royal prerogative. It invested the impressive ceremony and symbolism of the trial with meaning as part of a philosophy of the prevention of crime through awe and selective terror. On a day-to-day basis the possibility of the death sentence, irrelevant to the guilt or innocence of prisoners, influenced the decisions of prosecutors to appear in support of indictments, grand juries to find true bills, petty juries to convict and, in cases of larceny, juries' valuations of the property stolen. I have adopted the expression 'capital felony process' as a collective term for the trial of capital felonies, the review of death sentences with a view to the exercise of the prerogative of mercy, and the execution of prisoners. This collective term recognises the ideological and functional interdependence of the judicial, executive and punitive phases of capital punishment. The felony counsel restriction was a distinctive feature of the capital felony process.

The rationale of the capital felony process was that widespread capital penalties, selectively enforced, were an effective deterrent of crime. In the early decades of the nineteenth century a new penal logic, which advocated the use of milder punishments certainly enforced, emerged to challenge the capital felony process. The supporters of the new penal logic, initially led by Sir Samuel Romilly, aimed at the amelioration of capital punishment, but their emphasis on certainty necessitated improvements to criminal procedure. The elimination of the anomalous devices and discretions that disfigured the capital felony process was a prerequisite to certainty, and so the repeal of capital statutes, particularly during the 1820s and the early 1830s, was accompanied by a rationalisation of criminal procedure. The felony counsel restriction, a procedural anomaly closely associated with the capital felony process, was heavily criticised during this time, and eventually repealed by the Prisoners' Counsel Act.

New penal ideas, procedural reform, the duties of counsel, the development of advocacy and the emergence of the adversarial trial cluster together in the history of the Prisoners' Counsel Act. The Act, however, has received only passing attention from scholars of the criminal law. Recent studies of the historical role of counsel in the criminal trial have concentrated on the eighteenth century, and often reduced the Act to a postscript. There is an artificial division in modern scholarship between the trial and punishment, the former largely the preserve of lawyers and the latter of criminologists, which applied retrospectively has meant the neglect of trial procedure in accounts of the amelioration of capital punishment in the 1820s and 1830s.[9] The history of advocacy, as explained below, has never been a subject for scholarly consideration. One objective of this work is to redress these oversights. It examines the influence of the new penal ideas on procedural reform, and argues that

[9] Foucault has argued that a critical element in the rise of imprisonment during the nineteenth century was the claim of the prison to autonomy from the judge, which he calls the 'Declaration of Carceral Independence'. The modern scholarly separation of the trial and punishment is perhaps a descendant of this development: see Foucault (1977) 246–8.

the supersession of punitive severity with mild and certain punishment gave a strong impetus to full defence by counsel. It demonstrates that the shift from restricted to full defence by counsel had a dramatic effect on the development of advocacy and adversarial procedure in the criminal trial. The relationship of the Prisoners' Counsel Act to contemporary penal reform, its importance to the development of advocacy, and its contribution to adversarial procedure justifies a major place for the Act in the history of the modern criminal trial.

The Study of Advocacy

Advocacy has eluded theory, abstraction and speculation more than perhaps any other element of the common law. It is, and always has been, acquired not learnt, the reward of experience not study, and an exclusive preserve of practitioners. It requires an apprenticeship of watching, waiting, searching, serving and, not infrequently, humiliation. Its rudimentary attainment is a rite of passage and an induction into the fraternity of the Bar. It is inevitably termed an art not a science, and sometimes seems most to resemble a professional mystery.

There is, of course, considerable literature on various aspects of trial practice but a systematic treatment of English advocacy, and especially its historical development, is wanting. Advocacy manuals command the field, a genre aimed at junior practitioners and largely composed of basic precepts, practical advice, and illustrations from the cases and careers of great advocates. They are usually for digestion by rote and have not, in William Twining's phrase, 'evolved much beyond the cookbook stage'.[10] The common law still awaits a scholarly and comprehensive explanation of its advocacy. Its Aristotle or Quintilian is long overdue.

The purposes of advocacy are proof and persuasion and as proof and persuasion are crowned by favourable decision, so advocacy has a strong affinity with the decision-making of judge and jury. Advocacy and forensic decision-making both operate within the framework of the trial established by the rules of law, procedure and evidence. These rules direct the skills of judge and advocate but considerable personal discretion remains, and while these rules might ensure the identities of the forensic actors are irrelevant to the outcome of a trial, the manner the outcome is reached—the evidence called, the questions asked, the arguments made—will reflect individual choices.

The foundations for the analysis of advocacy in this book are the ideas about advocacy of nineteenth century barristers themselves, for which

[10] Twining (1984), quotation at 38.

the period offers a wealth of sources. The Prisoners' Counsel Act debate was dominated by judges and barristers whose contributions to parliamentary debates, periodical articles, and to the evidence and reports of the Criminal Law Commissioners, contain considerable information about the conduct of criminal trials, the effect on counsel and judge of the felony counsel restriction, and the expectations and fears of speeches by defence counsel. The complaints in the press in the 1830s and 1840s of the abuse of forensic licence generated a number of articles and books defending advocacy, which give particular attention to the privileges and duties of the advocate. 'Great man' biographies of the bar and bench, immensely popular with the early Victorian Bar, often included discussions of the skills of the advocate. Forensic speeches, a form of legal literature which enjoyed a short *vogue* in the early nineteenth century, inspired a secondary literature of review articles which are also a useful source of contemporary opinions on advocacy.

The history of the role of counsel in the felony trial, first admitted to argue questions of law, then allowed to examine and cross-examine witnesses, and finally enabled to address the jury, suggests a basic threefold division of advocacy. A similar functional division appears in the writings of Lord Brougham, discussed in Chapter 6, who divided the skills of the advocate into legal argument, advocacy, which included examination and cross-examination, and oratory or the art of addressing the jury. It is preferable to reserve the term 'advocacy' as an all embracing one, and to recognise the examination and cross-examination of witnesses as a distinct division of the skills of the advocate.

The techniques of legal argument, the analysis and application to a set of facts of principles and precedents, is the most easily understood department of advocacy, for similar skills are the staple of the academic study of law today. There is also a sophisticated body of theory available to assist the study of the jury address in the principles of classical rhetoric. The principles of Greek and Roman oratory were familiar to many of the successful advocates of the early nineteenth century—James Scarlett, Henry Brougham, and John Williams, for example, maintained an interest in the subject throughout their professional careers—and are drawn upon, in a small way, in the analysis of prosecution speeches in Chapter 2. Their potential contribution to the systematic study of advocacy is largely unappreciated today and 'contemporary legal scholarship and legal education have, with some notable exceptions, recognised neither [their] historical nor [their] contemporary significance'.[11]

The examination and cross-examination of witnesses is the division of advocacy most bereft of a theoretical superstructure to assist a study of

[11] Twining (1980) 13.

its historical development. The problem is compounded by a long standing fascination with cross-examination, which has contributed to inflated perceptions of its importance. This fascination is exploited in popular works on advocacy and in advocacy manuals, which prefer dramatic extracts from 'classic' cross-examinations to the more difficult task of relating a painstaking examination of an honest witness to the issues and other evidence, and exploring its subsequent use by counsel in the jury address.[12] Lord Brougham addressed this fascination in an 1844 article on William Garrow. Garrow was a successful criminal barrister of the late eighteenth and early nineteenth centuries, rising to the office of Attorney-General in 1813 and to a position on the bench of the Court of Exchequer in 1817. His aggressive cross-examinations and his power to 'annihilate' adverse witnesses were much admired by bystanders, even when they lacked merit. 'Those bystanders', Brougham wrote, '—and the profession...are not to be excepted from the number—never failed to commit the mistake of supposing a loud and angry examination of a witness to be a successful one; and they constantly supposed that the credit of a witness had been demolished when his person had only been scolded'. The excessive admiration for Garrow's cross-examination meant his more subtle forensic skills were overlooked. 'Mr. Garrow's real forte', Brougham continued, 'was in truth his examination in chief, which was unrivalled, and which is, indeed, a far more important and not less difficult attribute than the cross-examination which so captivates the ignorant'.[13] This fascination with cross-examination mars two recent studies of late eighteenth and early nineteenth century Old Bailey advocacy, which are considered in Chapter 2.

The history and literature of advocacy during the first half of the nineteenth century suggests two further elements must be added to the basic threefold division of advocacy. There were *norms of forensic morality* which guided the advocate in his use of legal argument, the jury address, and the examination and the cross-examination of witnesses, and which sometimes had a major effect on the conduct of trials. The first half of the nineteenth century saw the emergence of a duty on prosecution counsel in addressing the jury to restrain his advocacy within narrow limits, and considerable discussion of the duties of defence counsel in cross-examination and, after the Prisoners' Counsel Act, in his jury address. These developments, the forerunners of modern professional ethics, are discussed in Chapters 2 and 6.

[12] Cf. the comments on the literature of cross-examination in Rutter (1960–61) 312–16.

[13] Brougham (1845b) quotations at 320 and 321. For Brougham's authorship of this article see Stewart to Brougham, November 1844, *Brougham Papers No. 23*, 878.

The final element of advocacy is a skill that was particularly associated with James Scarlett, who had a long career at the bar before his elevation to the office of Chief Baron of the Exchequer, as Lord Abinger, in 1834. Scarlett's legal argument, speeches, and handling of witnesses were competent but unexceptional, yet he was the most successful 'verdict-getter' of his generation. Barristers in periodical articles puzzled over the secret of his forensic mastery, and it received fanciful explanations in circuit anecdotes. It was a skill, commentators agreed, that related to the conduct of the whole cause rather than any particular stage of it, and it guided the barrister in his inaction—the selection of matters to omit or to be silent upon—as much as in his action. 'Common sense, carried to genius' was one description, but the preferred term was tact. *Tact in the management of a cause* was the quintessence of advocacy. 'Of this' wrote Thomas Noon Talfourd, 'a by-stander sees but little; if the art be consummate, nothing; and he is, with difficulty, made to comprehend its full value'.[14]

A skill so important yet so elusive poses great problems for the historian of advocacy. It often leaves no trace in the records of the trial, and its intuitive nature means that even the advocate himself may be unaware of its exercise.[15] It might be most exemplified by silence, as appears in the following anecdote from Brougham's article on Garrow:[16]

> going on a special retainer to defend a gentleman charged with a capital offence (it was murder indeed), he [Garrow] sat in court during the whole trial, and of course watched each word, look, and gesture of each witness, as well as of the prosecuting counsel, and the judge, and the jury, with the eyes of an eagle, *and never once uttered a word from the beginning to the end of the proceeding.*

Brougham tells us that this anecdote demonstrates Garrow's 'discretion, his perfect judgment and entire self command' and so gives an insight into advocacy and Garrow's success that no amount of analysis of trial records alone could give. In this way the reflections of contemporary lawyers cast light on the more sophisticated aspects of advocacy, including the tactical management of prosecutions and defences.[17]

[14] Brougham (1845a); Talfourd (1825) 334 and 336; 'The Late Lord Abinger' (1845) 33 *Law Magazine* 152, especially at 154. For anecdotes of Scarlett's forensic mastery see Scarlett (1877) at 78–9; Brougham (1845a) 83; Stewart (1985) at 161.

[15] Talfourd (1825) 334. Talfourd's writings on advocacy are considered in Chapter 6.

[16] Brougham (1845b) 322, emphasis added. At the time of this anecdote, before the Prisoners' Counsel Act, Garrow was permitted to argue questions of law and to examine and cross-examine witnesses, but not to address the jury.

[17] Cf. Cocks (1983) 34: 'It is a simple thing to say...but it has to be said because historians of the professions themselves usually ignore it: it is impossible to understand a profession without understanding the ideas which it has about itself...Any useful analysis has at least to attempt to come to terms with the ideas about technical expertise which are of central interest to professional men'.

Contemporary literature also adds value to the use of trial transcripts in the study of advocacy. Transcripts or partial transcripts of trials come in many forms: newspaper reports, pamphlets, books about sensational crimes, published speeches, and in serial reports such as the *Old Bailey Sessions Papers* and the *State Trials.* Their accuracy and completeness is always questionable, and was a matter of complaint amongst contemporary lawyers.[18] It is commonplace to find in these accounts translations from the first to the third person, the confused use of tenses, the juxtaposition of names, jumbled sense, and references to matters that do not appear elsewhere in the report but, more importantly, the comparison of alternative accounts of trials, where this is possible, often reveals disturbing levels of mistakes, omissions or amendments in one or both accounts. Transcripts are an indispensable resource in any study of the practice of advocacy and changes within the trial during the first half of the nineteenth century, but are best used selectively and in conjunction with other contemporary sources.[19]

This work considers four trials in some detail: *Patch* in 1805, *Corder* in 1828, *Courvoisier* in 1840 and *Palmer* in 1856. *Corder* serves in the final section of this chapter as an illustration of the characteristics of the capital felony process, and in Chapter 2 of the restrained style of prosecution advocacy.[20] *Patch* and *Courvoisier* were often referred to as examples of the abuse of advocacy, respectively by prosecution and defence counsel, and are so used to explore the norms of forensic morality. *Courvoisier* also provides a convenient illustration in Chapter 5 of some of the problems of the tactical management of defences in the aftermath of the Prisoners' Counsel Act.[21] *Palmer,* discussed in Chapters 6 and 7, settled the role of counsel's personal beliefs in criminal advocacy, and demonstrates the sophistication of the new adversarial

[18] See, for example, Lord Loughborough's comments cited in 'The Life of Lord Loughborough' (1835) 13 *Law Magazine* 59 at 65, and Erskine's complaint to the editor of the *State Trials* referred to in 9 Campbell (1856–57) 78n.

[19] Cf. the discussions of the advantages and problems of the use of trial reports and secondary accounts of *causes célèbres* in modern legal studies in Twining (1984) 38–9 and Twining (1986).

[20] I rely primarily upon Curtis (1828) for the crime, trial and punishment of William Corder, which combines a competent report of the trial with a comprehensive description of surrounding events, and includes a wealth of detail obtained from spectators, witnesses, gaolers and even Corder's legal advisers.

[21] There is a full report of *Patch* by Joseph Gurney, a highly respected shorthand writer. Newspapers provide the only reports of *Courvoisier,* and their inexactness is highlighted by the wrangling after the trial over the expressions used by defence counsel, Charles Phillips, in his controversial speech. Phillips eventually endorsed the accuracy of *The Times* report, which is reproduced in Appendix 3. In Chapter 5 occasional extracts from other reports that do not contradict and appear to supply omissions in *The Times* report are used.

procedure shortly after the mid-century.[22] A number of other trials are also referred to as illustrations of specific problems or developments.

It is not suggested that these trials are representative of contemporary criminal advocacy; indeed the very attention which created the records that enables them to be studied with confidence makes them anomalous. They are selected because of the debate they aroused and the references to them in contemporary discussions of procedure and advocacy. The history of advocacy requires such analyses of trials, but the degree of care with which the evidence and speeches must be examined to make sense of their forensic dynamics means that, by the nineteenth century at least, it is impossible to examine a meaningful sample of cases. The historical study of advocacy is not only novel, but raises major methodological difficulties as well.

I do not attempt in this work to undertake a comprehensive survey of early and mid-nineteenth century advocacy, but rather to explain the complementary changes in procedure and advocacy that created the adversarial criminal trial. The major event in this process was the shift from restricted to full defence by counsel, so there is an emphasis in my analysis of advocacy on counsel's address to the jury. The shift from restricted to full defence by counsel had important implications for forensic morality, and the debate surrounding the Act also gives some rare insights into the tactical management of defences—particularly respecting counsel's decision whether or not to call evidence and the significance of retaining the last word to the jury—so that these matters also feature prominently in this study. The examination and cross-examination of witnesses received less attention from contemporaries and the same is true of this work.

My concern with procedure and advocacy might appear to some to deprecate developments in substantive law and in evidence. I have been surprised by the relative absence in nineteenth century sources of an explicit connection between developments in procedure and advocacy on the one hand, and in evidence on the other.[23] There are many points of contact, but the acknowledged influence of one on the other appears to have been relatively weak. The removal of the major restriction on defence counsel by the Prisoners' Counsel Act, for example, did not stimulate any proposal that the major restriction on prisoners—the

[22] The evidence and cross-examination in *Palmer* are comprehensively recorded in (1855–56) 44 *Central Criminal Court Sessions Papers* 5–225. There are many accounts of this famous trial and I have used Knott and Watson (1952) for the texts of counsel's speeches and the Chief Justice's summing-up.

[23] The Criminal Law Commissioners, for example, excluded as far as possible the rules of evidence from their draft code of criminal procedure in 1845: See *Eighth Report of Her Majesty's Commissioners on the Criminal Law* (1845) Parl. Papers XIV 161 at 178.

inability to give evidence in their own defences—might also require reconsideration. The history of the nineteenth century law of evidence is another subject that requires and deserves a full analysis of its own.

The Capital Felony Process

During the eighteenth and early nineteenth centuries capital punishment dominated the criminal process. There were nominally over two hundred capital felonies, ranging from the most serious crimes against the person and property to species of poaching, pickpocketing and shoplifting. This prevalence of the death penalty distracted prosecutors, witnesses, counsel, judges and jurors from a strict investigation of the facts and application of the law, and hindered the rational development of criminal law and procedure. When the widespread repeal of capital statutes began in the early 1820s this influence of punishment on the trial slackened, and created the opportunity for procedure to develop in an adversarial way and indeed, as Chapters 3 and 4 will show, pressed it in that direction. Accordingly, the history of advocacy and adversarial procedure during the nineteenth century must begin with the theory and practice of the capital felony process. The remainder of this chapter considers the operation of the capital felony process at the assizes, and for illustrative purposes concentrates upon the summer assize of 1828 at Bury St. Edmunds, where the trial and execution of William Corder for the murder of his lover has left an unusually good historical record of events.[24]

The trial of felonies took place at the Old Bailey in London and at the assizes which were usually held twice a year in every county in England. The Lent assizes were held in the Spring, during March and April, and the Summer assizes were held in July and August. They meant a large influx of people into the county assize town, because the assizes were an important social and administrative, as well as judicial, event. The county assize towns were arranged in six circuits and two judges usually rode each circuit, followed from assize to assize by the barristers of the circuit.[25] The responsibility for ensuring the county was ready for the assizes lay with the High Sheriff who notified the many county

[24] The capital felony process began to weaken after the first decade of the nineteenth century and its disintegration was well under way by the time of *Corder* in 1828. However, reform had not reached the crime of murder, nor the felony counsel restriction, so does not affect the use made of *Corder* here.

[25] The six circuits were the Home, Midland, Norfolk, Oxford, Northern and Western Circuits. Each had a circuit mess which informally enforced the circuit etiquette: see Duman (1983) 40–7; Shaw Lefevre (1863) 16–35. For the character and personnel of the Norfolk Circuit Bar around this time see Cocks (1983) ch. 1, and Cock (1976).

officers—the justices of the peace, mayors, coroners, chief constables and the like—who were obliged to attend the assizes in person. He summoned leading members of the county for grand jury service, men of lesser rank, such as merchants, tradesmen and yeomen, for the petty jury panel, and prepared the civil and criminal calendars. The records and the clerical organisation of the assize were in the hands of the clerk of the assize and his associates who travelled with the judge. The judges were also attended by their marshals and criers, who took oaths, made proclamations, and kept order in court, and by trumpeters and javelinmen, provided by the county, 'from twelve to twenty in number, all dressed in full liveries'.[26]

The assize began with the public proclamation of the commissions held by the judges from the sovereign. It included an official church service, where the sheriff's chaplain delivered the assize sermon. This was one of a number of judicial and clerical addresses during the assize where authority and duty were usually emphasised. Similar opportunities were the judicial charge to the grand jury, the passing of sentences of death, and the clergyman's address from the scaffold. The text of the assize sermon of the 1828 Bury St. Edmund's Summer assize, for example, was from 1 Peter 2:13, 'Subject yourselves to every ordinance of man for the Lord's sake'.[27]

The trial began with the arraignment, when prisoners were called by name to the bar and asked to raise one hand to identify themselves. The arraignment was followed by the pleadings, which in criminal trials, unlike civil trials, retained their ancient oral form. The clerk of the assize read the indictment and demanded of the prisoner whether he be guilty or not guilty. The usual plea to an indictment for a capital offence was not guilty, to which, Blackstone explains, the clerk of assize 'on behalf of the crown replies, that the prisoner is guilty, and that he is ready to prove him so. This is done by two monosyllables in the...spirit of abbreviation, *'cul. prit'*...This is therefore a replication on behalf of the king *viva voce* at the bar; which was formerly the course in all pleadings, as well in civil as in criminal causes...By this replication the king and the

[26] Cottu (1820) 25. Charles Cottu was a French judge who travelled the Northern circuit for the summer assizes of 1819. His *On the Administration of the Criminal Code in England and Wales and the Spirit of English Government,* published in France in 1820 and quickly translated into English, is the record of his observations and inquiries, and his suggestions based upon them for improvements to French procedure. He enjoyed high favour on circuit; the two judges, he said, 'paid me the greatest attention themselves, but likewise gave orders that whatever proceedings I might wish to examine, should be laid before me'. The members of the bar were equally helpful and hospitable, including Cottu in their circuit mess, explaining procedure, answering his queries and reviewing the manuscript of his book (*ibid,* 2–3, 75). The result is an account rich in detail, but also rather laudatory of the system of justice of Cottu's hosts.

[27] Hay (1975) 28–30; Curtis (1828) 77.

prisoner are therefore at issue'.[28] The clerk now asked the prisoner how he would be tried and, if necessary, instructed him in his only reply 'by God and the country', that is by jury. 'When the prisoner has thus put himself upon his trial, the clerk answers in the humane language of the law, which always hopes that the party's innocence rather than his guilt may appear "God send thee a good deliverance".'[29]

Where the prisoner pleaded guilty judgment and sentence of death followed without trial. A plea of guilty was a confession of the indictment, but this was a confession that judges were very reluctant to hear, and 'out of tenderness to the life of the subject' usually advised the prisoner to retract it and plead not guilty.[30] Cottu described the anxiety of the court, of 'the utmost sincerity', to convince the prisoner to plead not guilty:[31]

> When the prisoner pleads *guilty* (which often happens on account of the great probability of his punishment being commuted), the judge admonishes him that the crime of which he is accused is of a capital nature, and it is to his interest for him to stand upon his defence; the clerk, the gaoler, nearly all the counsellors, even the prosecutor himself, beg him to give himself the chance of an acquittal.

The chance of an acquittal was always a real one, even though the jurors who would try the case were most probably in the courtroom and heard the prisoner change his plea. At the Bury St. Edmunds assizes, for example, William Key pleaded guilty to the theft of some bread and cheese. Sir William Alexander convinced him to change his plea and then, after hearing the evidence, instructed the jury to acquit as an element of the offence had not been proved.[32]

The arraignment over, the next step was the impanelment of the jury. The jurors selected to serve had to swear to well and truly try and a true verdict give 'between our sovereign lord the king and the prisoner at the bar', and kiss the New Testament. The clerk of the assize then told the prisoner to raise his hand while he read the indictment again, this time to the jury. He concluded by telling the jury the prisoner had been arraigned on this indictment, 'and thereunto has pleaded not guilty;

[28] 4 Blackstone (1765–69) 333. For the failure of pleading to develop in the criminal law and the impoverishment of the criminal law as a result see Milsom (1981) 42–52 and 413. Note that the issue was between the king and the prisoner. The enforcement of a criminal law in the eighteenth and early nineteenth centuries relied upon private individuals, commonly the complainant or victim. They were referred to during trials as the 'prosecutor' but, in legal theory, prosecutions were in fact public and the prosecutor was the king: cf. Maitland (1885) 141 n. 1.

[29] 4 Blackstone (1765–69) 335; Cottu (1820) 47. The exchanges subsequent to the not guilty plea were abolished in 1828 by 7 & 8 Geo. 4, c. 28, s. 1, which deemed a prisoner put himself upon the country by pleading not guilty.

[30] 4 Blackstone (1765–69) 324.

[31] Cottu (1820) 41, emphasis original.

[32] *The Bury and Norwich Post*, 20 August 1828.

and for his trial has put himself upon God and his country, *which country you are.* Your charge is to enquire whether he be guilty of [the crime] as he stands indicted, or not guilty'.[33]

The prisoner often arrived in court 'squalid and depressed from his confinement', and in chains.[34] The spectator would notice a contrast between the prisoner's condition and his considerate treatment during the arraignment and the impanelment of the jury. First, the leg irons were removed. If the prisoner pleaded guilty then the court, as noted earlier, went to anxious lengths to make him change his mind. If the prisoner pleaded not guilty the clerk immediately wished him well: 'God send thee a good deliverance!' The prisoner was asked how he wished to be tried and was instructed in his right of challenge, which the spectator perhaps watched him exercise. These courteous preliminaries established, first, that the prisoner consented to be tried and chose trial by jury. This consent was real, despite the severe consequences to the prisoner of a refusal, for until 1827 a prisoner who would not plead or select trial by God and country could not be tried.[35] Secondly, the prisoner was to be tried by 'the country', the men of his or her county. The names of potential jurors were called out, and from amongst the people—the country—gathered in the courtroom they walked to the jury box. The spectator might not have considered these respectable jurors to be the 'equals and neighbours' of the prisoner eulogised by Blackstone, but there was no doubt that the prisoner's guilt or innocence was to be decided by local people and not the lawyers from London.[36]

We are accustomed today to the separation of spectators from the working body of the court, but during the eighteenth and nineteenth centuries it was usual for privileged spectators, especially women, to sit on the bench as guests of the judge. Cottu described the appearance of the bench during a criminal trial in the following terms:[37]

> In England every thing breathes goodness and indulgence; the judge seems like a father in the midst of his family, called upon to judge one of his children. His countenance has nothing terrific in it. His desk, according to an ancient custom, is covered with flowers, as is also the table of the officers. The sheriff, likewise, and other persons connected with the court, each wear a bouquet. The judge himself, with a condescension which is really surprising, suffers the space allotted to him to be intruded upon by the crowd of spectators, and in this

[33] Cottu (1820) 48, emphasis original.

[34] Smith (1826–27) 77.

[35] At common law the uncooperative prisoner was induced to plead or select his mode of trial by *peine forte et dure,* and pressed to death if he remained obstinate. Between 1772 and 1827 such a prisoner was convicted without trial. In 1827, by 7 & 8 Geo. 4, c. 28, a refusal to plead became a not guilty plea, and for the first time prisoners could be tried by jury without their consent.

[36] 4 Blackstone (1765–69) 343–4.

[37] Cottu (1820) 56.

manner he may often be seen surrounded by the prettiest women in the county, the wives, sisters, or daughters of the grand jury, who, coming to the balls and the public amusements which are given at the assizes, likewise make it either a point of duty, or a pleasure to attend the court. They appear in the most elegant morning dresses, and a singular contrast is afforded by the venerable head of the judge, covered, as it is, with a large wig, elevated above so many youthful female heads, adorned with all of beauty that nature can give, and of attraction that art can add.

Cottu identifies, and probably idealises, the image conveyed by the appearance of the bench: goodness, indulgence, and the judge as a father, with the women and flowers, the blooms of youth and beauty, conspicuously suggesting life. Cottu's description is partially confirmed by Corder's trial, where on the first day of the trial the judge enjoyed the company of four ladies, including the High Sheriff's wife, on the bench. The impact of this feminine presence surrounding the judge must have been heightened by the exclusion on the first day of the trial, by order of the Sheriff, of women from the courtroom.[38]

Cottu was struck by the publicness of English criminal procedure, and other foreign visitors made similar observations.[39] Publicness comprised two characteristics. First, access, which enabled spectators to see the law in action. The public's right of access to a criminal trial was enhanced by conducting the trial as a single and fast event. The English trial was not a process of interrogations and investigations completed over time; instead the arraignment, the selection of the jury, all the evidence and the verdict usually occurred in a single sitting. Preliminaries were of minor importance because all evidence had to be presented at the trial. Still, in cases involving death the coroner's inquest was in public, as was often the taking of depositions before a justice of the peace. The execution and the dissection of the corpse were in public. The second feature of publicness is orality, by which the audience in court could follow every step of the trial. Orality served the simultaneous purposes of informing the selected doomsmen of the jury, and the county generally. The prisoner was arraigned and pleaded, witnesses were examined, counsel made their submissions, the prisoner addressed the court, the judge summed up, the jury delivered their verdict, sentence was passed, oaths were taken and proclamations were made, orally. The indictment, prolix, technical and repetitive, and documents produced in evidence were read aloud by the clerk of the assize. Plea bargaining, Cottu noted, did not 'take place secretly, or in a corner, but, incredible

[38] Curtis (1828) 82, 143, and 147–8.
[39] Cottu (1820) 61; 1 Radzinowicz (1948–86) 717.

as it may appear, in open court, in the face of the public, the jury, and the judge'.[40]

Prisoners who pleaded or were found guilty of capital crimes were entrusted, between the sentence of death and its execution, to the minor and anonymous figures in the capital felony process of the gaoler, his wardens and the prison chaplain. Most convicted felons, except murderers and forgers, had reasonable prospects of a commutation of sentence, but had to endure the wait, in the shade of the gallows, for news of their petitions of mercy. They might live in this purgatory for over two months, with the anxiety of the wait reflected in their faces and bodies:[41]

> In several instances I have seen brown hair turned gray, and gray white, by a month of suspense such as most London convicts undergo. In the same short period the face of a man of twenty-five becomes often marked with decided wrinkles on the forehead and about the mouth; and, in certainly three cases out of four, one month of the [condemned] cells of Newgate causes a great diminution of flesh over the whole body. 'How thin he grows!' is the common remark.

The prisoners selected to die had to prepare themselves for their lives' most intensely personal moment, and perhaps the entry into another world. Prisoners died in many fashions: defiance, merriment, protestation of innocence, resignation, fear and penitence. The prison visitors and clergymen taught them to repent, confess and admit the justice of their sentences. This advice derived force from a scriptural story of supreme significance to condemned felons, for it showed that a man *like them* might be saved. This is the story of the thieves executed with Christ, one of whom on the cross confessed the justice of his sentence and asked Jesus to remember him. Jesus replied 'Verily I say unto thee, Today thou shalt be with me in paradise'.[42]

The condemned were very susceptible to religious instruction. The church had an accustomed role in the preparation for death, as natural as in baptism and marriage. It was an obvious source of consolation for prisoners bewildered or terrified by the vision of their own sudden deaths. This latent susceptibility was often tirelessly worked upon by prison clergy and administrators. The persistent pressure to confess applied to an unhappy prisoner is well illustrated by Corder's final hours, documented in detail by Curtis, and by John Orridge, the governor of Bury St. Edmunds gaol, in a statement to the local newspaper. The prison chaplain was constantly with Corder, the governor repeatedly hinted at the need to confess, his grief-stricken wife urged him to die a true penitent, the

[40] Cottu (1820) 52, speaking of forgery cases, where the 'daily' practice of banks was to call no evidence on an indictment for uttering forged notes, a capital felony, if the prisoner pleaded guilty to the lesser and non-capital offence of possession of forged notes.

[41] Wakefield (1831) 147–8. [42] 23 Luke 32–43.

sheriff's chaplain paid a special visit; even his warden gave an opinion on the necessity for a public confession. By the time of his condemned sermon 24 hours before his execution Corder appears to have been approaching nervous collapse. He groaned, shuddered and sobbed uncontrollably through an acutely personal service, which paraded his crime, guilt and jeopardy before him, but also offered hope through faith, repentance, and public confession.[43] The chaplain continued his unwearied attendance on Corder throughout his final day. Late that night the sympathetic, almost fatherly, figure of Mr Orridge obtained a written confession of guilt from Corder, which promptly appeared in the local and national newspapers.[44]

Corder died an exemplary death on the scaffold, though not without the prompting of Mr Orridge. As the executioner drew the cap over Corder's face Orridge reminded him that 'if he had any declaration to make, that was the time'. Corder then said, in broken accents, 'I am guilty—my sentence is just—I deserve my fate—and may God have mercy on me!' 'Mr Orridge then advanced to the front of the platform, and in a loud voice exclaimed—"The prisoner acknowledges his sentence to be just, and declares that he dies in peace with all mankind!"'.[45] With his final words Corder fulfilled his duty to the divine and the living, to God and the country.

It seems that a significant proportion of prisoners died such penitent deaths. Edward Gibbon Wakefield was a prisoner for three years in Newgate in the late 1820s, where he watched the condemned come and go after each of the eight annual Old Bailey sessions. He estimated that about 50 per cent of executed prisoners fully embraced their religious instruction, and that only one in four was prepared to reject the consolations of religion outright. Religious fervour, he thought, sustained the bodily health of the condemned by enabling them to eat, sleep, and remain calm.[46] Newspaper accounts of executions at this time confirm the regular penitence and confession of the condemned.[47]

[43] Cf. Wakefield's description of condemned sermons at Newgate: 'crimes, punishment, bonds, shame, ignominy, sorrow, sufferings, wretchedness, pangs, childless parents, widows and helpless orphans, broken and contrite hearts, and death tomorrow morning for the benefit of society': Wakefield (1831) 164.

[44] Curtis (1828) 210–31; *The Bury and Norwich Post*, 13 August 1828. Cf. Thackeray's discussion of the confession of Courvoisier in Thackeray (1840). For a discussion of the role of religion in the seventeenth century execution see Sharpe (1985).

[45] Curtis (1828) 235.

[46] Wakefield (1831) 154–6.

[47] Newspaper reports of executions at this time varied from lengthy descriptions to a few lines, which might omit this type of information. In London and Middlesex during 1828, 20 persons were executed, and the reports of these executions in *The Times* record that two prisoners addressed the crowd and acknowledged the justice of their sentences (27 March, p. 3, Weedon; 9 December, p. 3, James), two displayed intense religious devotion (15 April, p. 3, Welch; 9 December, p. 3, Hunton) and two are reported as displaying more subdued religious feelings such as prayer or taking the sacrament (May 14, pp. 3–4, Roberts; 9 December, p. 3, Mahoney).

Religious teaching neatly complemented secular authority by making the condemned passive on the scaffold and prepared to admit that their deaths were deserved, and so to vindicate publicly the capital felony process. The frequent publication of confessions and scaffold declarations indicate authorities were not blind to the secular advantages of encouraging the concern of prisoners for their souls, but the system could not depend on the cooperation of its victims. The function of the execution in the ideology of the capital felony process was to give substance to the threat of death, for which the prisoner had to be seen to die. The violence was important; the prisoner's behaviour while alive was simply convenient or inconvenient.

The execution was a shabby event in comparison with the judicial business of the assize. There were not the manifestations of royal or state power which Foucault identifies in contemporary French executions, except perhaps in cases of treason.[48] The judges and their train of barristers and officials left the county before any executions took place, their javelinmen and trumpeters had returned to their normal occupations, jurors and county officers had dispersed to their homes, and the High Sheriff usually did not attend. Instead the crowd saw the insignificant figures of the under-sheriffs, gaolers, prison chaplain, hangman and, in murder cases, the county surgeon. A routine execution of a sheep-stealer or a highwayman might involve no more state ritual than a procession to the edge of town, the fixing of ropes, and a prayer and a psalm before the hangman released the drop or pushed the prisoner off the back of the cart. The well-attended execution of a notorious criminal might require special arrangements for the location and the procession, but state and royal authority were no more evident.[49]

The crowds for some executions were enormous, especially in the nineteenth century as executions became less common. For Corder's execution nearly ten thousand people came from all over the county and beyond, on foot, 'by six, chaises, gigs and vehicles of every description', filling Bury St. Edmunds' stables and inns, and exhausting supplies of food in the town. After the hanging, Corder's corpse stayed suspended on the gallows for an hour before being cut down and taken in a wagon to the shirehall for dissection.[50] The county surgeon first

[48] Foucault (1977) 42–54. The prominence Foucault gives to retribution and royal revenge as objectives of punishment in France is not supported by contemporary English discussions, such as that of Paley considered *infra*.

[49] 'The state seemed to show a perverse lack of interest in the solemnity of hangings, and in making its presence decently manifest. On the contrary, it perpetrated the shabbiest of rituals with the minimum of authorial control': Lacquer (1989) 309–23.

[50] The Murder Act 1752 (25 Geo. 2, c. 37) provided that the punishment for murder include dissection after hanging: see generally Linebaugh (1975).

made a longitudinal incision down the chest, as far as the abdominal parts, and folded back the skin so as to display the muscles of the chest to public view. The corpse was then returned to *the courtroom* and placed upon a large table. 'The public were now admitted by one door, and passing by one end and along one side of the table, made their egress at the other, constables having been stationed to cause the visitors to keep moving. Many thousands of persons, and some of high respectability, and of both sexes, availed themselves of this last opportunity of seeing the remains'.[51]

The next day there was another dissection at the Suffolk General Hospital where the body had been conveyed 'in pursuance of the Special Directions of the Judge's Warrant'. This was the first dissection at the local hospital, and it attracted a large attendance of physicians, surgeons and students. This was a comprehensive dissection, including the removal and individual anatomisation of organs. A 'zealous phrenologist who attended', the local newspaper reported, 'was unable to discover any peculiar development of the "organ of destructiveness" in the cranium; but casts were taken which we believe are to be submitted to the highest authorities'. Mr. John Dalton, a hospital surgeon, was entrusted with the preparation of the skeleton 'for the purpose of aiding the objects of surgical knowledge'. Corder was thus dissected twice; first carved as a dish for public consumption, his carcass was then hewed for the advancement of learning.[52]

A feature of the capital felony process was that most prisoners escaped the death prescribed by law for their crimes. At the Bury St. Edmunds assize, for example, six persons were convicted of capital crimes, but Corder alone hanged.[53] The legislative enthusiasm for the death penalty during the eighteenth century was never matched by a willingness to execute all those convicted. The proportion of capital sentences executed did at times reach 60 per cent, but by the early years of the nineteenth century was in rapid decline.[54] By the year of Corder's execution, in the twilight of the capital felony process, only 58 of the 1,165 prisoners capitally convicted were executed, a ratio of one in 20.[55] The prisoners who did not hang were saved by the royal prerogative of mercy, and were usually transported instead. In the scales of early nineteenth cen-

[51] Curtis (1828) 130, 142–3, 225 and 236. *The Bury and Norwich Post*, 13 August 1828, estimated that five thousand persons passed through the courtroom to view the corpse.

[52] *The Bury and Norwich Post*, 13 and 20 August 1828; Curtis (1828) 210. Corder's scalp is still on public display today, in the local museum at Bury St. Edmunds.

[53] *Judges' Report, Norfolk Summer Circuit 1828* (PRO, HO 13/6).

[54] For the incidence of executions in the eighteenth century see 1 Radzinowicz (1948–86) ch. 5, and Hay (1975) 23. For an explanation of the decline in execution rates in the early nineteenth century see Gatrell (1994) 19–21.

[55] *Criminal Offenders. England and Wales. Summary Statements* (1830–31).

tury justice punitive severity and the horror of the execution were counterbalanced by the routine commutation of sentence through the prerogative of mercy.

The leading contemporary rationalisation of this system of many capital crimes and few executions came from William Paley. Paley saw the objective of the criminal laws to be the prevention of crime, and not the satisfaction of justice through the retribution of pain for guilt. 'The fear', he wrote, 'lest the escape of the criminal should encourage him, or others by his example, to repeat the same crime, or to commit different crimes, is the *sole* consideration which authorizes the infliction of punishment by human laws'.[56] The paramountcy of prevention was accepted by many writers of this period, from Madan to Bentham, but Paley is distinguished by his use of it to justify the status quo. He saw the terrors of capital punishment as necessary to reach the soul of a villain, and it was best that these terrors hung over a wide range of crimes. However, only a small proportion of the convicted needed to be executed. These 'fit examples of public justice' had to be singled out on the basis of character and the aggravating circumstances of their crimes. The power of choosing prisoners to die was properly exercised by the Crown 'as a judicial act' and not as a matter of favour.[57] Too many executions would be counterproductive because excessive familiarity with 'barbarous spectacles of human agony' would harden and deprave the public feeling. The importance of the manipulation of executions was not to be underestimated, as is strikingly shown by Paley's reflections on their possible improvement.[58]

Douglas Hay's modern interpretation of the eighteenth century criminal law in *Albion's Fatal Tree* also stresses selective terror. Hay, following Paley, argues Parliament did not intend its capital statutes to be strictly enforced.[59] The purpose of this selective use of capital punishment is the theme of Hay's essay. Instead of Paley's objective of the prevention of crime, Hay begins his argument from another section of Paley's same

[56] *The Principles of Moral and Political Philosophy,* in 4 Paley (1820) 419, emphasis added. William Paley (1743–1805), archdeacon of Carlisle, was a popular, commonsense moral philosopher, with a long interest in the criminal law. *The Principles of Moral and Political Philosophy* first appeared in 1785 and went through numerous editions during his lifetime.

[57] *Ibid,* 419–42, especially 425–7.

[58] 'if a mode of execution could be devised, which would augment the horror of the punishment, without offending or impairing the public sensibility by cruel or unseemly exhibitions of death, it might add something to the efficacy of the example: and, by being reserved for a few atrocious crimes, might also enlarge the scale of punishment...Somewhat of the sort we have been describing, was the proposal, not long since suggested, of casting murderers into a den of wild beasts, where they would perish in a manner dreadful to the imagination, yet concealed from the view': *ibid,* 437–8.

[59] Hay (1975) 22–3 and 56–7 rejecting Radzinowicz's contrary view. For Sir Samuel Romilly's opinion on Parliament's intention in this matter see Chapter 3.

work, entitled *How Subjection to Civil Government is Maintained*. In this section Paley observes that in all cases of civil government *'the physical strength resides in the governed'*.[60] How government is nevertheless maintained, he goes on, 'by what motives the many are induced to submit to the few, becomes an inquiry which lies at the root of almost every political speculation'.[61] It is Hay's argument that the objective of the selective implementation of capital punishment was to 'mould the consciousness by which the many submitted to the few'. The criminal law, he asserts, was an ideological instrument of the ruling class which 'helped to create the spirit of consent and submission, the "mind-forged manacles" which Blake saw binding the English poor'.[62]

Hay distinguishes three aspects of the law as an ideological instrument to mould consciousness: majesty, justice and mercy. The majesty of the law was manifested through the imagery and spectacle of the assize. The justice of the law was suggested by a superficial impartiality, such means as a punctilious attention to forms, and the occasional execution of a man of property or position, or the victory in the courts of a labourer or cottager. The mercy of the law was most obvious in the widespread commutation of capital sentences, something presented as mysterious, sacred and absolute, an act of grace from an exalted height. '[T]hese repeated acts of goodness coming immediately from his own hand, endear the sovereign to his subjects, and contribute more than anything to root in their hearts that filial affection, and personal loyalty, which are a sure establishment of a prince.'[63]

In Paley's analysis the pardon power was exercised judicially. Hay argues that 'class favouritism and games of influence' played a decisive role in the granting of pardons. Mercy 'was part of the currency of patronage', with petitions 'passed up through increasingly higher levels of the social scale, between men bound together by the links of patronage and obligation'. An employer, clergyman, or local gentleman with good connections could start the process which might save a petty thief 'and then command his gratitude, or at least the approval of the neighbourhood as a man of compassion'. The influence of the respectable on the prerogative of mercy complemented their power over prisoners as prosecutors, justices of the peace and character witnesses, and helped maintain a 'fabric of obedience, gratitude and deference'.[64] At the higher levels of this process the rulers of eighteenth century England, in Hay's view, blended executions and pardons, terror and mercy, to sustain the belief in the justice of their rule. He describes their private manipulation

[60] 4 Paley (1820) 319–25, quotation at 320, emphasis original.

[61] 4 Paley (1820) 319–20, cited in Hay (1975) 25–6.

[62] Hay (1975) 26 and 49.

[63] 4 Blackstone (1765–69) 391 quoted in Hay (1975) 48.

[64] Hay (1975) 40–9.

of the criminal law as 'a ruling-class conspiracy' to maintain power through the deference of the governed.

Hay's analysis has been challenged, most importantly by Peter King and John Langbein, and cannot be accepted without qualification.[65] There was substantial participation and discretion in the capital felony process for non-elite groups such as farmers, tradesmen and artisans who were the primary victims of crime, and who prosecuted and sat on the petty juries at the assizes. Indeed, as will be discussed, their discretion was perceived as a major problem. Further, mercy involved the good faith consideration of the circumstances of the prisoner and the crime and was not exercised in the calculated, almost venal, manner implied by Hay. Nevertheless, Hay captures the intimate interaction of terror and mercy in the capital felony process, and the significance of their images to the maintenance of authority. Only a tiny proportion of prisoners indicted needed to be executed, so the authorities were able to be just, even magnanimous, at the trial and mercy phases of the capital felony process and save many more than they condemned. Here the authoritative figures in the process—the king, the judges, the county elite, the jurors and the church—displayed themselves, and were glorified by ceremony and symbolism. Justice and mercy were claimed by the rulers, while terror remained anonymous.

The prosecution was public, the trial was public, the execution and dissection were public and the public attended the assize in large numbers, especially at the punitive phase. The assize conducted in private would lose its benevolent side and the contrast with the terror. The robes, the flowers, and the scaffold; the wigs, the women and the dissection table; the trumpets, the proclamations and the black cap were a statement to the people about authority and obedience to the laws. However, the reaction of the spectators to this message was ambiguous and complex,[66] and here lay the great weakness of the capital felony process. It depended upon public cooperation in the detection, prosecution and trial of offences, and an ambivalence amongst ordinary people about the execution of death sentences affected their willingness to

[65] King (1984); Langbein (1983b). See also Green (1985) 310–17.

[66] There has been considerable recent debate over the interpretation of the role and behaviour of the crowd at executions: see Linebaugh (1975); Foucault (1977) ch. 2; Lacquer (1989) and Gatrell (1994) chs. 2 and 3. Gatrell's detailed analysis can in the end only confirm the ambivalence of the crowd's relationship with the law, and warn of the dangers of any generalisations: 'It is foolish to look for uniform postures, "radical" or "deferential" as the case may be. People steered a wavering course between tacit ethical approval, sardonic and transgressive defiance, and mockery, sentimental anguish, or outright voyeurism. But what is clear is that those who assembled at the scaffold did not do so with the empty heads contemporaries ascribed to them...[I]t will be clear by now that their actions always made *sense*...precisely *what* sense can sometimes only be guessed at' (at 196, emphasis original).

cooperate in the enforcement of the law at its earlier stages. At the beginning of the nineteenth century there was already concern, discussed in the next two chapters, at the leniency of prosecutors, witnesses and jurors towards prisoners accused of capital crimes. An efficient criminal law, reformers would argue, required a level of harmony between the law and public feeling which the capital felony process did not achieve.

2

The Early Nineteenth Century Trial

The Felony Counsel Restriction and the Criminal Trial Until 1800

The *Leges Henrici Primi* of the early twelfth century contains a number of references to the circumstances when an accused person was or was not entitled to counsel. At the time this book was written, the jury and the professional counsel had yet to begin their careers in the criminal law. The jury's glorious ascent from an experiment in trial by neighbours after the Fourth Lateran Council to the palladium of English liberties in Blackstone, and counsel's rise from counters to pleaders, and from pleaders to advocates, lay in the future. The word 'felony' had only just emerged as the name for the most serious crimes, and stood in contradistinction to trespass; misdemeanour was a later term. Yet the felony counsel restriction of the early nineteenth century by which the prisoner's counsel on a trial for felony, though not for a misdemeanour, was not permitted to address the jury, is undoubtedly a descendant of the principle confusedly recorded by the author of the *Leges Henrici Primi.*[1]

'In the *Leges Henrici*' says Maitland, 'it is already the peculiar mark of an accusation of felony that the accused is allowed no counsel, but must answer at once; in all other cases a man may have counsel'.[2] By 'counsel' is meant the counsel of relatives and friends, not a professional adviser.[3] The action required of the accused without counsel was simply to answer the accusation, and procedural consequences and punishment by fine might follow for an accused taking counsel without first making a denial or an objection.[4] The crimes to which this rule applied are described in the *Leges Henrici* as *causae capitales*, equated by Maitland in the above passage with 'felonies', by Holdsworth with 'capital crimes' and by Downer with 'capital' and 'more serious' crimes. Even in its early

[1] On the *Leges Henrici Primi* see 1 Pollock and Maitland (1898) 99–101; Downer (1972) *passim.*

[2] 1 Pollock and Maitland (1898) 211.

[3] *Ibid*; Downer (1972) 156–7 and 386; *Leges Henrici Primi* 46,4.

[4] *Leges Henrici Primi* 48,1a and 48,1c.

medieval formulation, the restriction on counsel was related to capital punishment.[5]

The friends or relatives who might in some circumstances confer or even speak for the accused in the *Leges Henrici* had been supplanted by the second half of the thirteenth century by professional legal representatives. During the same period a firm distinction had emerged between criminal proceedings initiated by presentment and by appeal. The written presentment of the grand jury was the indictment, and the future of criminal prosecution lay with this procedure. The appeal of felony was a much used procedure in the Middle Ages, but had almost gone out of use by 1650. Amongst the many procedural differences between the appeal of felony and the indictment was the entitlement of the appellee, the accused under the appeal procedure, to the assistance of counsel. The felony counsel restriction, from an early period, was confined to proceedings by indictment.[6]

The appeal of felony was a truly private form of prosecution, akin to a civil suit, while an indictment was presented in the King's name. As early as the reign of Edward I the royal presence appears as the justification for the denial of counsel, with the court in one case telling the prisoner he could not have counsel 'against the King'.[7] Royal involvement joins capital punishment as an early mark of the felony counsel restriction.

A reflective discussion of the felony counsel restriction appears in the second dialogue of *Doctor and Student* (1530).[8] Already it seems anomalous and requires justification for the Doctor questions its reasonableness, and the student admits:[9]

> it were a great unreasonableness in the law yf it shold prohybyt hym that standeth in Jeopardy of his lyfe that he sholde haue noo counsayle and than to dryue hym to plede after strayte rules and formalytyes of the law that he knoweth not.

The Student does not justify the restriction so much as excuses, or as Blackstone later described it, palliates the rule, by introducing the idea that the judge must help the undefended prisoner as much as justice requires.[10] This means the prisoner is not prejudiced by the absence of

[5] *Ibid*, 46,1a, 47,1, 61,17 and 61,18; 2 Holdsworth (1923) 106–7; Downer (1972) discusses the meaning of *causae capitales* in some detail at 427–30. On the link between the designation 'felony' and the punishment of death see 4 Blackstone (1765–69) 97–8 and 2 Pollock and Maitland (1898) 466.

[6] For the distinction between appeals of felony and indictments, and for appeals generally see Milsom (1981) 406–10; Baker (1977) 15–20; Kaye (1966) xxiv *et seq.*

[7] Y. B. 30 & 31 Edward I (Rolls Series) 529–32; Post (1984) 24.

[8] *Doctor and Student* Second dialogue, ch. 48, in Plucknett and Barton (1974) 284–6.

[9] *Ibid*, 285.

[10] 4 Blackstone (1765–69) 349.

counsel, so the common law is saved from the stain of unreasonableness. The Student neatly connects the judicial assistance to prisoners with the royal involvement in prosecutions by indictment, but does so in a wry, offhand manner that suggests it is a mistake to seek too much logic in the felony counsel restriction:[11]

> but when that a man is Indycted at the kynges sute the kynge intendeth nothyng but iustice with fauour & that that is to the rest & quyetnes of his faythfull subiectes & to pull away mysdoers from among them charytably & therfore he wyll be contented that his iustyces shall helpe forth the offenders as ferre as reasone and Justyce may suffre. And as the kynge wyll be contented therin: yt ys to presume that hys counsale wyll be contented. And soo there is no daunger therby neither to the court ne the party & as I suppose for this reason it began that they shold haue no councell vpon indytementes & that hath so longe contynued that it is now growen into a custome & into a maxym of the law that they shal none haue.

On a more pragmatic level royalty may have had a darker influence on the persistence of the felony counsel restriction. It was convenient for the Bar to be prohibited from speaking against the Crown in the most important criminal trials, and especially in state trials. In the reigns of the Tudors and the early Stuarts juries were sometimes imprisoned or fined for returning verdicts contrary to royal pleasure. Counsel for the prisoner, if permitted, might have received the same treatment. At a time when advancement in the profession depended upon royal favour ambitious lawyers had to display a willingness to serve their royal masters, with an enthusiasm like that displayed by Sir Edward Coke in the prosecution of Sir Walter Raleigh.[12] Prosecution in state trials meant security and preferment, defending would have jeopardised career, property, liberty, and, in the early years of the reformation, not inconceivably the life of counsel.[13]

In *Doctor and Student* the work counsel is not permitted to do on the prisoner's behalf is pleading, rather than advocacy.[14] The difference

[11] Plucknett and Barton (1974) 286.

[12] *The Trial of Sir Walter Raleigh* 1 State Trials (1730) 205.

[13] Coke (1644) 137 records a case of counsel being indicted (he does not specify the offence) for advising a prior not to admit the King's Serjeant at Arms to the priory. The difficulties of defending state prisoners are illustrated by *The Trial of the Seven Bishops* 4 State Trials (1730) 300 at 344 where the Solicitor-General threatened defence counsel with unspecified legal action for their efforts to establish in cross-examination a promise from King James II to the bishops. The bishops were represented by counsel because the offence, seditious libel, was a misdemeanour rather than a felony.

[14] For example, 'in all thynges that perteyne to the ordre of pledynge: the Juges shal so instructe hym & so ordre hym that he shall renne into noo Jeopardye by hys myspleadynge', in contrast to an appeal of felony where the judges might 'byd the party and hys counsayle plede at theyre peryll': Plucknett and Barton (1974) 284–5. See also the first quotation in the text, *supra.*

between pleading and advocacy, in broad terms, is that pleading involves the definition of the issue between the parties, which might be an issue of fact or law, while advocacy involves the proof of the issue, by the examination of witnesses, the production of evidence, or by argument. The joinder of issue was the effective end of the work of the pleader, but the effective beginning of the work of the advocate.[15]

As advocacy rather than pleading became the function of counsel more confusion began to surround the felony counsel restriction. Textbooks of the late sixteenth and early seventeenth centuries, beginning with the first treatise exclusively devoted to the criminal law, Staunford's *Les Plees del Coron*, state that the prisoner is denied counsel only when he pleads the general issue, that is, not guilty. Counsel, it is said, is denied as to 'the fact', and fresh palliatives of the restriction appear to match this new formulation. The absence of counsel is now said to be conducive to the discovery of the truth, for a prisoner might disclose the truth when counsel 'would be so couert in their speeches, and so shadow the matter with words, and so attenuate the proofes and evidence, that it would be hard or long to haue truth appear'.[16] Another palliative, first appearing in Coke's *Third Institute*, was that the prisoner did not require counsel because 'the testimonies and the proofs of the offence ought to be so clear and manifest, as there can be no defence to it'.[17] Finally Christopher St. German's palliative that the judge would assist the prisoner as far as justice requires was sufficiently general to continue in service, and came to be expressed by the pithy maxim that the judge was 'counsel for the prisoner'.[18] The concern of these rationalisations with proof, evidence and speeches show the prohibited activity was now advocacy rather than pleading.

The accumulated history of the felony counsel restriction meant its seventeenth century form was a litany of apparent contradictions. Counsel were prohibited on trials for felonies, but not for misdemeanours; on prosecutions by indictment, but not by appeal; on the general issue, but not questions of law.[19] Counsel were prohibited, yet the judge was said

[15] On the shifts in counsel's role from counter to pleader and pleader to advocate see Milsom (1963) xxv–xxvi. During the same period there was a complementary shift in the role of the trial jury from witnesses of fact to impartial triers of fact.

[16] Pulton (1610) at 184–5; see also Staunford (1557) book 2, ch. 63. The most well-known expression of this rationalisation is in Hawkins (1724) book 2, ch. 39, s.2, quoted in Chapter 4.

[17] Coke (1644) 29; see also 137, and *The Trial of Lord Cornwallis* 2 State Trials (1730) 721 per Lord Nottingham. Other explanations for the restriction on counsel appearing in individual seventeenth century writers are the law's abhorrence of maintenance and the defence of bad causes, and the poverty of prisoners: see Davies (1628) 'A Preface Dedicatorie'; Hawles (1689) 22–5.

[18] Coke (1644) 29 and 137.

[19] As early as the fifteenth century counsel had been permitted in felony trials for purely legal argument: see Milsom (1981) 413; 5 Holdsworth (1924) 192n.

to act as counsel for the prisoner. When the constitutional struggles of the seventeenth century drew attention to the procedural disabilities of prisoners in state trials the felony counsel restriction, not surprisingly, was attacked as arbitrary and unfair.[20] After the Glorious Revolution a proposal was introduced into Parliament to allow full defence by counsel in cases of treason and misprison of treason, which was eventually enacted as the Treason Act of 1696.[21] This increased the protection for prisoners in politically charged state trials, but added another contradiction to the felony counsel restriction. Counsel were prohibited on trials for felonies, except for treasons, the most serious felonies.

During the reigns of Elizabeth I and the Stuarts counsel had a very small role in felony trials. They appeared in the rare appeal of felony, occasionally argued questions of law, and represented the Crown in state trials, but the vast majority of trials were conducted without them. There is no record of any restriction on the prosecution employing counsel but prosecutors, except in state trials, did not do so. The prosecution witnesses were called, sworn, questioned by the judge, and perhaps the accused. Prisoners spoke in their own defence, called any witnesses they could as to the facts and their character, then the judge addressed a few words to the jury, who often delivered their verdict without retiring from the courtroom.[22] During the eighteenth century, however, the criminal trial changed in many respects, and recent scholarly studies have placed the new and expanded role for counsel at the forefront of these changes.[23]

John Langbein's research on trials at the Old Bailey, and John Beattie's work on the Surrey assizes, show similar patterns for the beginnings of the regular appearance of counsel in felony trials. Prosecution counsel began to appear in a small number of cases, especially murder trials, in the second and third decades of the eighteenth century, followed by a more substantial increase in numbers in the 1730s. The impetus towards prosecution counsel might initially have been official anxiety about security and order in the early Hanoverian years, which led the government to engage counsel to prosecute not only in state trials, but in some serious non-political cases as well. 'These initiatives', Beattie suggests,

[20] For example, Hawles (1689) 22–5.

[21] Treason Act (1695–96, 7 & 8 Will 3, c. 3). Parliamentary impeachments were originally excluded from the operation of the Treason Act. This limitation was removed in 1748: see 20 Geo. 2, c. 30. For the full political and legal background to the Treason Act see Rezneck (1930); Phifer (1980); Shapiro (1993); Beattie (1986) 357–9; and Langbein (1978) 307–10.

[22] For a contemporary description of this form of trial see Smith (1583) 75–84. For a modern description see Baker (1977) 32–45.

[23] The leading recent discussions of counsel in the eighteenth century criminal trial are Langbein (1978); Langbein (1983a); Beattie (1986), especially part II; Beattie (1991); Landsman (1990).

'may well have encouraged some private prosecutors to engage lawyers'.[24]

Defence counsel began to appear at the Old Bailey and the Surrey assizes in the 1730s. The increased use of prosecution counsel, Beattie and Langbein suggest, produced a sense of unfairness and imbalance in the criminal trial, and 'this imbalance induced the judges to allow accused felons to engage counsel'.[25] A further adaptation of the felony counsel restriction soon followed. Judges allowed the prisoner's counsel to examine and cross-examine witnesses,[26] which narrowed the felony counsel restriction to a prohibition on counsel addressing the jury on the prisoner's behalf. By the second half of the eighteenth century prisoners at the Old Bailey were engaging counsel more regularly than prosecutors, and this trend continued until the end of the century.[27]

This increasing role of counsel in the felony trial has been identified as a cause or a contributing factor to a number of eighteenth century developments in procedure, evidence and advocacy. Counsel gave more structure to criminal trials, as the 'rambling altercation' between the accused and witnesses was replaced by distinct prosecution and defence 'cases', which in turn encouraged evidential objections and the recognition of burdens of proof.[28] Defence counsel exploited cross-examination and legal arguments to challenge suspect evidence such as hearsay,[29] confessions, and the evidence, often relied upon by London authorities at this time, of thief-takers prosecuting for rewards and accomplices testifying under promises of non-prosecution.[30] These activities altered the dynamic of the jury trial in two ways. First, counsel began to silence the prisoner, for if counsel conducted the cross-examination the prisoner did not need to take any part in his defence until the completion of the prosecution case. If counsel could establish grounds for an acquittal at this stage then the prosecution terminated without a word from the prisoner, and if the prisoner did need to address the jury in his defence, his participation in the trial was at least deferred until the prosecution evidence was fully known. In this development Langbein sees the conception of the trial moving from an older 'accused speaks' theory to the modern 'testing the prosecution' trial.[31] Secondly, Langbein

[24] Beattie (1991) 224–6 (quotation on 225); Beattie (1986) 352–6; Langbein (1978) 311–13.

[25] *Ibid* (quotation Beattie (1991) 226).

[26] Langbein (1978) 313–14.

[27] Sample levels of representation are given in Landsman (1990) 607 and Beattie (1991) 227. Cf. Langbein (1983a) 126 (prosecuting counsel 'appeared less and mattered less'). Counsel appeared in a minority of cases: 'By the end of the century, between a quarter and a third of defendants at the Old Bailey had the benefit of counsel': Beattie (1986) 228 (footnote omitted).

[28] Langbein (1983a) 130–2; Beattie (1991) 248–9 (the presumption of innocence).

[29] Landsman (1990) 564–72.

[30] Beattie (1991) 362–76; Langbein (1983a) 84–114.

[31] Langbein (1983a) 129–31; Langbein (1994) 1048, 1068–71.

shows that in the late seventeenth century, before the arrival of counsel, the judge dominated the criminal trial and could exercise considerable influence over the jury's verdict. During the eighteenth century, he argues, there was a significant shift in power from the judge to the parvenu lawyers.[32] By 1820 these two trends had progressed so far that 'judge and accused—who a century earlier were playing main forensic roles in the criminal trial—were yielding the center stage to the lawyers for prosecution and defense'.[33]

The inability of defence counsel to address the jury by reason of the felony counsel restriction meant counsel were unable to comment on their own cross-examinations or the credibility of witnesses at the conclusion of the evidence. The felony counsel restriction made cross-examination the primary function of the eighteenth century counsel, and forced it to be self-contained. The importance of cross-examination was heightened by the regular testimony of self-interested witnesses such as thief-takers and accomplices, and developing notions of the burden of proof. Beattie and Landsman argue there was a flowering of the art of cross-examination during the eighteenth century. They refer to the growing assertiveness of counsel in cross-examination, an increasing sharpness and use of sarcasm, and a preparedness to persevere in the face of judicial hostility. A new style had emerged by the 1780s, which Landsman demonstrates through a review of a number of 'classic cross-examinations' and Beattie through the cases of William Garrow, the leading Old Bailey practitioner of the time. Garrow's practice, says Beattie, exemplifies 'a more committed advocacy of [defendant's] cases in the courtroom and a new emphasis on their rights'. 'There is no doubt that in his aggressive behaviour, in his insistent and pressing and revealing cross-examinations of prosecution witnesses, in his challenges to the rulings of the bench, in his dominating presence in the courtroom, he represented a new phenomenon'.[34]

A trend towards adversariness links these developments in procedure, evidence and advocacy. It is apparent also in the attitude of counsel who 'clearly pushed harder...became more aggressive, more actively committed to their clients' interests, and more challenging of the rules under which they were allowed to work'.[35] The activities of counsel radically reconstructed the criminal trial, suppressing the prisoner's involvement,

[32] Langbein (1978) 284–300 and 313–16.

[33] Langbein (1978) 307. See also Landsman (1990) *passim,* who also notes a decline in judicial influence (especially at 513–24) but, by identifying counsel more closely with his client than Langbein does, sees increased *party* control in the criminal trial. Nevertheless, Landsman considers that counsel 'became the dominant courtroom force in the last twenty years of the eighteenth century.' (*ibid*, 557).

[34] Beattie (1991) 226–47 (quotations from 238 and 247 respectively); Landsman (1990) 533–64 (expression 'classic cross-examinations' from 548).

[35] Beattie (1991) 229.

and breaking down the traditional judicial mastery of proceedings.[36] 'Over the course of the eighteenth century', says Langbein, 'our criminal procedure underwent its epochal transformation from a predominantly nonadversarial system to an identifiably adversarial one'.[37]

This flourish of research advances but also distorts our understanding of the eighteenth century criminal trial. Two biases of perspective repeatedly appear in the scholarship, the first traceable to an over-reliance on one primary source, and the second to methodological assumptions. The result is too many conclusions have been drawn from events at the Old Bailey, and insufficient attention given to their historical and legal contexts.

The *Old Bailey Sessions Papers* were 'an early species of periodical journalism, purveying a diet of true-life crime stories for the interest and amusement of a nonlawyer readership. They were sold on the streets of London within days of the trials they reported'.[38] These reports are the major source for recent studies of the eighteenth century criminal trial.[39] Langbein has discussed their reliability and shortcomings, tested their accuracy by comparison with the judge's notes of Sir Dudley Ryder, and concluded that they were never fictionalised, but suffered from extensive omissions.[40] It is surprising that there has not been a systematic attempt to trace alternative pamphlet accounts of trials as a cross-check on accuracy and to assess the significance of the omissions. Such pamphlets were sometimes printed after trials which attracted public attention, such as the trial of Eliza Fenning in 1815. Amongst the accounts of this trial is a pamphlet with an express purpose of correcting errors and misrepresentations in the *Old Bailey Sessions Papers* report.[41]

The most distortive feature of the use of the *Old Bailey Sessions Papers* has been to consider these reports as a self-contained and complete resource. The Old Bailey was only one criminal court amongst many, and one common law court amongst many. Its practitioners were members of the professional institution of the Bar and so worked, travelled

[36] Langbein (1994) 1071; Langbein (1978) 314.

[37] Langbein (1983a) 123. Langbein has recently further suggested that 'the example of aggressive adversary procedure in the criminal courts towards the end of the eighteenth century may have set the tone for civil practice as well', and thereby provide a possible explanation for the rise of the modern law of evidence in criminal *and civil* cases around this time: see Langbein (1996) (quotation at 1202).

[38] Langbein (1983a) 4.

[39] The *Old Bailey Sessions Papers* are the major source for Langbein (1978), Langbein (1983a), Landsman (1990), and Beattie (1991). Beattie (1986) often relies on Langbein's work for its analyses of defence counsel and evidence: see, for example, 355, 356–7, 360, 371.

[40] Langbein (1983a) 3–30; Langbein (1978) 267–72.

[41] Watkins (1815). The *Old Bailey Sessions Papers* report omits numerous answers in evidence, parts of the prisoner's statement, the Recorder's summing up, exchanges between the Recorder and the prisoner, and misnames two witnesses and *eight* of the twelve jurymen. On *Fenning's case* see Gatrell (1994) 353–70.

and dined with other barristers, and joined in their membership of chambers, circuits and the Inns of Court. The royal judges were senior members of the same profession, drawn from the ranks of the Bar, who socialised with senior barristers on circuit and with the serjeants in London.[42] The profession demanded certain standards of behaviour from its members, and these rules of etiquette, informally enforced by social pressure, might affect the representation of prisoners. An overzealous barrister on the Midland Circuit, for example, was expelled from the circuit mess in 1790 in respect of his handling of a prisoner's defence.[43] Any study of advocacy must acknowledge this professional context, and preferably draw upon the ideas about advocacy of contemporary barristers themselves.

A particular feature of legal culture neglected in the scholarship is the reputation of the Old Bailey and most of the counsel who practised there. Recent work praises Old Bailey advocacy for its 'high level of forensic art', 'a striking skill and intensity in cross-examination',[44] and the work of William Garrow at the Old Bailey as 'carrying defense advocacy to a new level' and even as 'a new phenomenon'.[45] There are many features of the Old Bailey of the late eighteenth and early nineteenth centuries which, *a priori,* make it unlikely soil for the flowering of advocacy—for example, the speed of the trials, the poverty of the clients, the low level of client representation, and the felony counsel restriction. There was more scope for the display of a full range of forensic talent, and much better fees, for counsel in civil actions. In the 1830s and 1840s there was some scathing criticism of the quality of the counsel at the Old Bailey 'and none of the critics ever suggested that the practices they condemned were novel; on the contrary, it was believed that they stretched back into the distant past'.[46] The *Law Times* in 1844 wrote 'that practices unrecognised by the Bar have existed and do exist to a great extent at the Old Bailey. The world also knows, *and long has known*, that "An Old Bailey Practitioner" is a byword for disgrace and infamy'.[47]

The dangers of using the Old Bailey Sessions Papers without regard to the practice of other courts or legal culture generally can be illustrated by the claims made by Beattie and Landsman for cross-examination. These scholars do not refer to cross-examinations performed in other courts.

[42] Cf. 2 Stephen (1883) 452.

[43] *Midland Circuit Records,* vol. 1, Spring Circuit, 1790, Warwick. The barrister, Henry Hutton, was expelled for writing a letter to a potential witness seeking alibi evidence.

[44] Landsman (1990) 550 and 552.

[45] Beattie (1991) 245 and 247.

[46] Cocks (1983) 21 (footnote omitted).

[47] (1844) 3 L. T. 501 (emphasis added). The problems of the Old Bailey in the 1830s are discussed later in this chapter and those of the 1840s in Chapter 6.

They do not refer to any contemporary discussions of cross-examination or the professional conception at the time of its practice. They do not articulate the standards by which they make their qualitative assessments of cross-examinations. The attention, in many cases admiration, they bestow on simple interrogations or forensic swagger confirms the warnings of experienced advocates of the deceptiveness of cross-examination. A cross-examination can dazzle the audience, or the reader, and not move the jury; in cross-examination not all that glisters is gold.[48]

Under the heading 'the full flowering of the art of cross-examination' Landsman discusses a cross-examination in the trial of a prisoner called William Phillis, which he describes, with two other cross-examinations, as demonstrating 'the high level of forensic art achieved by counsel'.[49] The entire cross-examination reported in the *Old Bailey Sessions Papers* consists of 39 questions, and would have been completed in a few minutes. The facts, as Landsman observes, involved 'one of the oldest confidence schemes in the world' and for that reason had no doubt been seen at the Old Bailey many times before, and the greedy foolishness of the prosecutor was an obvious target for cross-examination. Landsman makes it a matter of comment, presumably as increasing the merit of the cross-examination, that counsel took this brief at the last minute but was able to complete a successful 'unrehearsed and unbriefed interrogation' 'at a moment's notice'.[50] This was, however, unexceptional within the legal culture of the time where appearing without preparation and handling the unexpected were the daily experience of the common law barrister, and well into the nineteenth century it was usual for a criminal brief not to be delivered to counsel until the day of the trial.[51] The cross-examination in *Phillis* is competent and effective, but also routine and lacking in any special skill which makes it worthy of note.

'Garrow', says Beattie, 'was the leading exemplar of aggressive advocacy in the 1780s', and broadened the limits within which defence counsel worked 'by his willingness to do bruising battle with recalcitrant witnesses, to quarrel with judges, and by his sheer skill as an advocate'. His 'capacity for sarcasm and repartee' was a feature of his handling of reluctant witnesses.[52] Landsman also notes the frequency of sarcasm,

[48] Cf. the opinions of some early nineteenth century lawyers on cross-examination: Talfourd (1825) 327–8 ('In most cases, before an intelligent jury, it is mere show'); Scarlett (1877) 75 ('much more mischief than benefit generally results from cross-examination'.); 9 Campbell (1857) 153 (Lord Eldon, who attributed his effectiveness as a prisoner's advocate to his *disinclination* to cross-examine); and Brougham's comments on cross-examination and Garrow's advocacy referred to in Chapter 1.

[49] Landsman (1990) 548–52 (quotation at 550). Phillis' trial appears in the *Old Bailey Sessions Papers*, April 1782, 339.

[50] Landsman (1990) 550.

[51] Brougham (1845a), and see also *infra* p. 37–8.

[52] Beattie (1991) 239; see also 245 and 247.

'brutal and nasty' cross-examination, and the preparedness of counsel to defy the judge.[53] They argue that such behaviour shows an increased aggression in counsel, which perhaps it does, but also that it is indicative of an improvement in advocacy, and an increased commitment to their clients.[54] However, the rough and sarcastic treatment of witnesses and wrangling with the Bench are usually signs of poor advocacy.[55] They are an intrusion of counsel's personality into the conduct of the defence, indicative often of frustration, a loss of control, and a deflection from the best interests of the client. The aggressive Old Bailey style of cross-examination, the *Westminster Review* was to note in 1835, did not usually help the prisoner's defence.[56]

The sarcasm, quarrelling and contentiousness of counsel at the Old Bailey during the late eighteenth century are capable of interpretations other than the flowering of advocacy as a fine art and increased zeal for prisoners. An opposite explanation is perhaps plausible—the 1780s saw the first manifestations of the low standards of advocacy and suspect ethics for which this court became renowned in the 1830s and 1840s. Garrow, it is true, nurtured a successful career at the Old Bailey, but his aggression may have had a negative influence on the advocacy of a court never distinguished for the quality of its practitioners.

The second source of bias in recent scholarship touches the perennial problem in legal historical writing of the different approaches to the past of law and history. Law looks to the past for justification in the doctrine of precedent, but with the purpose of finding a solution to today's problems rather than of understanding the past. 'A lawyer finds on his table a case about rights of common which sends him to the Statute of Merton. But is it really the law of 1236 he wants to know? No,...'[57] Legal method is different from historical method, and the lawyer's use of authorities often appears to the historian as 'a process of perversion and misunderstanding' of history.[58] As part of the recent debate over methodology amongst scholars of the eighteenth century criminal law Hay identifies some of the dangers of 'thinking like a lawyer', which include the fallacy of presentism or 'of working from present concerns to past

[53] For example, Landsman (1990) 536, 539–43, 548–57.

[54] For example, see Beattie (1991) at 234 ('cross-examination was undoubtedly developed as a fine art'), at 245 ('carrying defense advocacy to a new level in the 1780s'), at 229 ('more aggressive, more actively committed to their clients' interests'); Landsman (1990) at 550 ('the high level of forensic art'), at 552 ('the flowering of the art of cross-examination during the late eighteenth century. The skill and intensity of the interrogations is striking').

[55] Cf. Brougham's comments on the superficiality of aggressive cross-examination referred to in Chapter 1; Scarlett (1877) 65 (description of Erskine).

[56] (1835) *Westminster Review* 195 at 203. This passage is quoted *infra* pp. 48–9.

[57] Maitland (1911) 490.

[58] Ibid, 490–2 (quotation from 491); Plucknett (1951) 190–1, who observes that 'legal history is not law, but history'.

origins, [which] is anathema to historians, but necessarily half the lawyer's method. Whatever its merits in finding supporting arguments for a brief, it has the effect in historical work of writing out of the past any developments which did not survive in much the same form into the present'.[59]

The use of modern models of the adversary system and modern rights language introduces present concerns to the analyses of the eighteenth century criminal trial of Langbein, Landsman and Beattie. Langbein, for example, uses 'the adversarial criminal procedure of today's Anglo-American systems', and to a lesser extent modern Continental procedure, to characterise the development of the eighteenth century criminal trial. His repeated modern comparisons mean the origins of today's rules of evidence and procedure dominate his analysis, at the expense of historical perceptions of the trial.[60] He compounds presentism with moralism, for there is a recurring assumption in his work of the inferiority of eighteenth century procedure, which is condemned for falling short of the standards of the late twentieth century.[61] Landsman also has a preoccupation with the modern adversary system, which he suggests is the 'historical purpose' of the labours of the 'judges, lawyers and litigants' of eighteenth century England. His article concludes with an epilogue praising the modern adversarial trial and warning of its need for protection from judicial encroachment.[62] The result is an adversarial bias in the scholarship that simplifies the emergence of the modern trial and gives the impression of an inevitable development rushing to completion.

[59] Hay (1984) *passim* (quotations respectively at 17 and 18–19, footnote omitted); Langbein (1983b) *passim;* Linebaugh (1985) *passim*. For the fallacy of presentism see also Fisher (1971) 135–40.

[60] For example, Langbein (1978) 263, 272–3, 282–4, 289, 292n., 302, 307, 314–16 (quotation from 314); Langbein (1983a) 31, 42–3, 96, 105, 124, 132–4. Sometimes Langbein's choice of expression betrays the use of the present to explain the past as when, for example, he refers to shifts that 'in the full light of hindsight appear to presage the future', or to changes that 'in retrospect, appear to us to foreshadow the rise of adversary procedure', or to a passage of Hawkins that can be understood 'only when we remember that the law of evidence as a counsel-propelled, jury-oriented exclusionary system lay in the future': Langbein (1983a) 96 and 124; Langbein (1978) 310 respectively.

[61] For example, the 'fundamental changes' in eighteenth and nineteenth century procedure are explained by the 'grievous shortcomings' of Old Bailey procedure in the 1730s in comparison with 'either of the two mature twentieth-century procedural models': Langbein (1978) 314. Another example is the condemnation of Sjt. Hawkins' explanation of the felony counsel restriction as 'naive', 'justly ridiculed' and 'preposterous': Langbein (1978) 311 and Langbein (1994) 1053. Moralism is discussed generally in Hay (1984) 19 and Fisher (1971) 78–82, and Langbein's moralism in Linebaugh (1985) 219–28.

[62] Landsman (1990) 502–3, 602–5.

Procedure and Advocacy in the Early Nineteenth Century

It was a regular concern of the circuit messes, the informal guardians of the etiquette of the Bar, to ensure that their members did not demean the Bar and unfairly obtain briefs by currying favour amongst the attorneys of the assize towns, and so professional etiquette included rules to prevent premature contact with attorneys.[63] The members of the circuit were not to enter the assize towns before the commission day, nor to arrive by public transport, as in public transport they might meet attorneys, litigants or witnesses with business at the assizes. The enforcement of these rules can be seen in the Midland and Norfolk Circuits' mess records from an early date. For example, in 1783 three members of the Midland Circuit were fined for being in an assize town before the commission day.[64] In 1827 the Norfolk Circuit mess passed a resolution that 'it is unprofessional in any member of the circuit to travel to any circuit town in any public conveyance'.[65]

These rules of etiquette meant counsel were not usually instructed until the assizes began. An attorney could travel to London to brief counsel before the circuit if the case warranted the expense, but in criminal cases the usual practice was not to brief counsel before the assizes. As late as 1863 Fitzjames Stephen said prosecution briefs were delivered 'to counsel generally speaking (at least in the country) in court on the day of the trial'. The prosecution brief, according to Stephen, was usually no more than copies of the depositions.[66] Prior to the Prisoners' Counsel Act the prisoner was not entitled to copies of the depositions nor, except in cases of treason, to a copy of the indictment. He or she was entitled to be attended by an attorney at the taking of the depositions, whose notes of the evidence might form the basis of a brief. Where the prisoner was poor or the attorney had little time to spend on the defence, the case handed to counsel in court might be in a lamentable state of preparation, as noted by a contemporary journal:[67]

[63] On the character of the circuit messes and the operation of professional etiquette see Cocks (1983) ch. 1; Duman (1983) 37–55 and Dicey (1867).

[64] *Midland Circuit Mess Records*, Warwick, 1783. The commission day was the day the assizes formally began through the public proclamation of the judges' commissions.

[65] *Norfolk Circuit Mess Records*, Bedford, 27 July 1827. A second resolution on this theme passed the same night is discussed in Cocks (1983) 15–16. On the etiquette of arriving in an assize town see Kinghorn (1880) 340–1.

[66] Stephen (1863a) 156.

[67] (1835) *Westminster Review* 195 at 204, speaking of the Old Bailey. Cf. Scarlett's description of his early years in practice, in less serious cases, at the Lancashire Sessions: 'The counsel were accustomed to arrive late in the evening before the sessions, the attorneys on the next day. The magistrates commenced their business at half-past eleven. It was only during the few hours that elapsed from eight to that time that I had to prepare the day's work...I believe I may safely say that I did not read one brief in ten in the most important cases in which I was concerned at quarter sessions': Scarlett (1877) 61–2.

In a majority of prison cases, no care is taken to sift the evidence, or to bring forward witnesses for the prisoner; a slovenly statement is drawn up in the form of a brief, consisting of loose general protestations of innocence, compliments to the great talents of counsel, intimations that policemen are not to be believed upon oath, and a direction to call the prisoner's friends who will give him a good character. The brief is then delivered, and the counsel recognizing the common form, assumes correctly that his instructions are worthless.

It was from such imperfect instructions, and usually without preparation beyond a hasty reading of the brief, that counsel rose to prosecute and defend prisoners on trial for their lives.

Prosecution Counsel

The prosecution case began immediately after the arraignment and impanellment of the jury. The prosecution counsel, if any, might begin with a short address to the jury setting out the case against the prisoner. This address was the privilege of counsel, which meant that a private prosecutor unrepresented by counsel was not permitted to address the jury, except as a witness. A prosecution by indictment was in law the suit of the king, and so a prosecutor could not claim the ordinary privilege of a litigant to speak directly to the court.[68] Prosecution counsel were often referred to as 'counsel for the Crown'.

Where the judge, from his reading of the depositions, considered the facts of a prosecution to be comprehensible to the jury without introduction, he might instruct counsel to dispense with the opening address and simply call the witnesses. The use of the opening address was also loosely regulated by circuit practice. On the Northern Circuit the practice was for counsel 'always' to make an opening address to the jury, though this rarely lasted for longer than quarter of an hour. On the Oxford Circuit counsel 'scarcely ever' began with a speech. On the Midland Circuit there was a strong feeling against opening speeches: counsel only opened in cases of intricate circumstantial evidence.[69] The Midland Circuit mess, in one instance in 1838, fined a member for an unnecessary

[68] *R v Brice* (1819) 2 B & A 606; *R v Stoddart*, October 16 1819 per Abbot C. J., discussed in Dickenson and Talfourd (1829) 81n.–82n. and 350.

[69] *Second Report of His Majesty's Commissioners on Criminal Law* (1836) Parl. Papers xxxvi 183, at 10n. (Northern and Midland); Cottu (1820) 48, and *Prisoners' Defence Bill. Minutes of Evidence taken before the Select Committee of the House of Lords etc.* (1836) Lords' Papers 119, at 7 (Oxford); (1835) 28 P. D. 866 (Northern and Midland); evidence of Tindal L.C.J, Park and Parke JJ. in *Report from the Select Committee on the Receipt and Expenditure of County Rates* (1834) Parl. Papers XIV. 1 at 143 (Midland). For practice at the Old Bailey, where there were few prosecution counsel, see *Lords' Evidence* (*supra*) 3.

opening address when the court was trying to clear a heavy backlog of untried prisoners.[70]

There were also expectations as to the content of prosecution counsel's opening. Counsel in felony trials were not to argue for a conviction, but to restrict themselves to a bare narrative of facts sufficient to enable the jurors to follow the evidence they were about to hear. Counsel had a duty of restraint in opening a prosecution, described in a contemporary textbook in these terms:[71]

When he [prosecution counsel] addresses the jury in a case of felony, he ought to confine himself to a simple detail of the facts he expects to prove; because the prisoner has no opportunity of laying his case before the jury by his counsel; and even the privilege of stating circumstances, however dryly, in such order and direction as may tend most directly to a particular conclusion is, of itself, no small advantage accorded to the prosecutor, and certainly should be exercised with great forbearance and caution. It is especially right for counsel to refrain from stating *any part of the case the proof of which, from his own brief, may appear doubtful*...[H]e should always forbear from stating *confessions*, which often turn out to be inadmissible; and should very rarely detail *conversations*, which are peculiarly liable to be misunderstood...In cases of misdemeanour, the prosecuting counsel is not thus restricted, because here the defendant is allowed to make a real defence by his counsel, and, therefore, here the counsel for the prosecutor may not only state his facts, but *reason upon them*, and *anticipate any line of defence* which his opponent may probably adopt; but, even here, he should refrain from indulging in *invective*, and from *appealing to the prejudices or passions of the jury;* for it is neither in good taste nor in right feeling to struggle for a conviction, as an advocate in a civil cause contends for a verdict.

The duty of restraint was not the same in felony and misdemeanour trials, with more forbearance required from counsel in felony trials where defence counsel were not entitled to address the jury. The italicised phrases in the above passage identify seven matters prosecution counsel were supposed to avoid in opening a felony prosecution: doubtful facts, confessions, conversations, reasoning upon facts, anticipating the defence, invective, and appealing to the prejudices and passions of the jury. Two cruder forms of appeals to prejudice are the gratuitous introduction of patriotism and religious sentiment, the abuse of which are clearly apparent in *R v Vaughan*, another case from the Norfolk Summer Circuit of 1828. In opening this prosecution for the misdemeanour of grave-robbing, counsel dealt with an anticipated defence based on the authority of French science by thanking heaven that the practice of Paris was not the practice of England, which was followed by a

[70] *Midland Circuit Mess Records*, 2 August 1838, Leicester.
[71] Dickenson and Talfourd (1829) 350 (emphasis added).

mawkish description of the decent dead awaiting the resurrection in peace.[72]

The duty of restraint in action is well-illustrated by the opening of Biggs Andrews, senior counsel for the prosecution, in *R v Corder.* Andrews introduces Corder and the victim, Maria Marten, and their relationship in two simple paragraphs, which is followed by a plain chronological account of the circumstances of her disappearance, Corder's subsequent suspicious behaviour, the discovery of the body, medical opinion of the cause of death, and Corder's arrest. He does not add any argumentative or rhetorical superstructure to his bare narrative of the facts. He does not draw inferences, discuss probabilities or reason to any conclusion. Notwithstanding the enormous emotive potential of this case, which was to become a staple of Victorian melodrama, Andrews avoids complex metaphors, amplified descriptions, moralising and pathos. His opening was a model of artlessness.[73]

The prosecution in *Corder* was based on circumstantial evidence, which derives its significance from its interpretation and its connection with other evidence. Andrews' reluctance to reason on the facts meant key inferences and linkages in the prosecution theory of the case were not made in the opening, and were left for the jury to discover for themselves on hearing the evidence. This can be seen in Andrews' handling of motive, inevitably a question of inference. The solicitor for the prosecution, in his brief to Andrews, referred to differences Corder and Maria Marten had over a five pound note sent to her by a former lover, which Corder had intercepted and stolen. The solicitor elaborated the known facts of this matter, drew the inference that Corder feared criminal prosecution, added Corder's oft-repeated promise to marry his victim, and concluded with a plausible motive for the murder: Corder believed 'that he was immediately in the power of the deceased & that if he should not perform the promise he had made to marry her, she might be induced to make such a disclosure as would be inconsistent with his safety'.[74] Andrews in his opening mentions Corder's promise to marry Maria, her cryptic remark in another context that if she should go to prison then Corder would go also, and differences over a five pound

[72] *R v Vaughan,* Norwich, 12 August 1828, reported in *The Times*, 14 August 1828. The duty of restraint was less strict in this case because the offence was a misdemeanour and Vaughan had senior counsel, but two contemporary journals considered the prosecution opening excessive: see *The Lancet,* 23 August 1828, at 659 and 661 ('grovelling submission to the vulgar prejudices of a jury of Norfolk yeoman'), and *The Examiner,* 17 August 1828 ('sycophancy to the rabble prejudice'). Vaughan's career in bodysnatching is discussed in Richardson (1987) 64–5, 69, 77, 84, 86, and 89.

[73] For Andrews' speech see Curtis (1828) 93–103. For the melodrama based on the 'Red Barn' murder of Maria Marten see Slater (1928).

[74] *R v Corder Prosecution Briefs*, ref. 568/2 (Andrews) f.7.

note 'which relates to a circumstance that will hereafter appear in the evidence to be adduced'.[75] He does not explain the relevance of these facts, nor the possible connection between them. He does not introduce topics such as greed, avarice or fear which might lead the jurors to suspect the significance of these facts. He does not mention the subject of motive at all.[76]

Andrews' opening stands in sharp contrast to the opening in *R v Patch*, another murder prosecution based on circumstantial evidence.[77] William Garrow opened this case with a skilful and persuasive demonstration of the prisoner's guilt, cited during the Prisoners' Counsel Act debate as the epitome of the dangerous power of prosecution counsel.[78] Garrow set out to prove the two complementary propositions that Patch had committed the murder, and that it was absolutely impossible for any other person to have committed the murder.[79] Garrow's intention to prove these two propositions was incompatible with the duty of restraint as described above, for the first proposition, in a case of circumstantial evidence, requires detailed factual analysis, and the second proposition involves the anticipation, discussion and rejection of the defences the prisoner might raise.

Garrow proved his two propositions in a virtuoso display of forensic power. He reasoned from facts, doubtful facts and pejorative interpretations of the facts; from suppositions, suspicions, probabilities, and the exclusion of possibilities; from anticipated defences, commonplaces, common experience, anecdotes and the conduct of a hypothetical innocent man; and from his own observation and opinion.[80] This argumentative inventiveness was enhanced by a rich array of rhetorical embellishment. Garrow makes particularly effective use of questions—repeated questions, sequential questions, self-answered questions and rhetorical questions—and figures based upon repetition, especially anaphora and epanados. His highly charged choice of expression exploits

[75] Curtis (1828) 95.

[76] Andrews' bland handling of the five pound note is itself an instance of the duty of prosecution restraint, as his ability to prove the allegations in his brief was doubtful. The defence successfully excluded the letter in which Corder confessed he had stolen this note: *ibid*, 125–6.

[77] Gurney (1806) 7–50.

[78] See (1824) 11 P. D. 210; Calvert (1836) 17; *Lords' Evidence* (*supra* n. 69) at 8; *Second Report* (*supra* n. 69) at 10, and Appendix No. 1, 61 and 95.

[79] Gurney (1806) 9, 23.

[80] For example: doubtful facts: Gurney (1806) 10–13, 93–4 (Patch's impecuniosity, discussed further *infra*); pejorative interpretations of the facts: *ibid*, and 9 (Patch's personal relationship with the deceased); suppositions: 14 ('I take it for granted that she had not far to go'); suspicions: 33–4 (the comments to the maidservant); probabilities and the exclusion of other possibilities: 43–5; anticipated defences: 20–1 (the maidservant's evidence as to time); commonplaces: 28 ('innocence and truth are always consistent'); common experience: 21 ('whether your own constant and hourly experience does not teach you'); anecdotes: 23–5, 41; the conduct of a hypothetical innocent man: 23; his own observation: 15, 42–3; his own opinion: 22, 33, 34, 41.

the dramatic potential of the murder, by turns insinuative, hyperbolic, moralistic, melodramatic and pathetic. Patch is painted in dark murderous tones, the victim in a benevolent light, God and providence are thanked for revealing the murderer, judge and jury are fawned upon, and in one extraordinary passage the victim, Isaac Blight, is introduced to confirm Patch was his murderer:[81]

One should have thought that however painful and distressing to the mind of a dying friend [i.e. Blight] to entertain a suspicion which would attach the crime of base black ingratitude, of an inhuman unnatural attempt against his life, to be executed by deliberate and most unheard-of contrivance and artifices, to one who had been living under his roof and protection [i.e. Patch], and deriving all his benefits from his generous friendship; I say, however painful such a suspicion must have been, and however reluctant the human mind would naturally be to give it reception, yet if Mr. Blight had been left coolly to deliberate upon all the extraordinary circumstances of his most calamitous case, it was next to impossible that a suspicion should not have glanced at the person now accused as his murderer.

Motive can again be used to illustrate counsel's style. Garrow detailed at the beginning of his speech the facts from which he would infer motive, including Patch's impecuniosity on his first introduction to Issac Blight, their complex financial transactions, Patch's agreement to purchase Blight's business, his lack of funds, and Blight's anxiety at the delay in payment.[82] In contrast with *Corder*, motive is explicitly discussed, introduced with typical Garrow pugnaciousness, as if the jury were challenging him to show a motive:[83]

If I have excluded every other hand; if I have shewn you the probability that the Prisoner was the guilty hand, you will ask me another question. You will ask me, *what was, or what could be the motive* for a deed of such complicated atrocity?...There is no motive that can be adequate to make its impression upon a virtuous and good mind to occasion the death of one of his fellow-creatures. We must search into other causes for motives than into the causes which spring out of virtue and morality; but we do know, that those causes are to be found in the

[81] Gurney (1806) 26.
[82] *Ibid*, 10–14, 18–19. The only evidence of Patch's means when he met Blight was to be Mrs Blight (at 93–4). She states that on his introduction to Blight Patch had 'some difficulties respecting some tythes' and was prepared to work for a month or two for victuals only without any salary. Garrow colours these simple facts with the pejorative conclusions that Patch at this time was 'a considerably distressed man', 'glad to enter into the meanest employment' and 'a sort of outcast without any means of subsistence' (at 10–11). From the same facts he infers that *two years later* Patch could not have been able to afford to pay the consideration for the purchase of Blight's business (at 13). Patch's impecuniosity is then connected with other evidence of his dealings with Blight and Blight's widow to infer a financial motive for murder: see 31–2 (quoted in text *infra*). This is an example of the tendency in this speech to multiply conclusions from a few facts.
[83] *Ibid*, 23, emphasis original. A misspelling in 'every' has been corrected.

bad and corrupt passions of the human heart; that envy, jealousy, long-conceived hatred; above all, Gentlemen, I am afraid *the love of inordinate gain*, which can be obtained only by putting another to death, are found in the history of the depravity of the human heart, to be the causes that produce these dreadful events. I shall shew that these causes, up to a most alarming degree, were certainly operating upon the Prisoner at the bar.

The motive is restated a few pages later as a desire for specific property of the victim rather than abstract greed:[84]

observe the motive I attribute to him—You ask me what it is? I answer, it was to possess himself of the business of Mr. Blight, either entirely, for that appears sometimes to have been his object, or at least of one-third of it.

Further evidence of motive is then discussed. Patch had made false representations to the deceased of his possession of a substantial bill of exchange, had made false representations to Blight's widow, and had attempted to obtain from her documents relating to the ownership of the business. The most important circumstantial evidence is then recapitulated and linked together to establish the motive for the murder:[85]

Now, Gentlemen, have I not stated to you motives sufficient to operate, not upon a virtuous mind indeed; you might offer the wealth of the Indies to a moral virtuous man to induce him to engage in a deed of guilt; he spurns your offer, and will not embrue his hands in blood; and therefore, if we are to wait till we can produce to a Jury a consideration for murder adequate to move a moral mind to commit murder, we may shut up all our courts of justice; there is an end to all inquiry. But if you find this man, in a moment of pressure to pay a large sum of money, totally unprovided for it; if you find him fabricating false papers, and producing them as true; if you find him representing to the person interested in the paper, that it is satisfied, and afterwards representing to the representative and executrix of the deceased that the debt is paid; if you find him, at another time, describing that this is a real transaction, for which he paid 2065*l.* as the consideration; do you not find a tissue of lies upon every part of the subject?

Contemporaries called the opening in Patch a 'hanging speech' for its effect was to make the result of the trial a foregone conclusion.[86] Patch

[84] *Ibid*, 27.

[85] *Ibid*, 31–2. One of the many interesting features of this passage rhetorically is the manner the jury are prepared for the conclusion. The passage sets up a moral antithesis between the 'virtuous man' and 'this man' (Patch). A similar antithesis appeared in the first discussion of motive, quoted in the text. The passage assumes the jury might be dissatisfied with the proposed motive, which is met by suggesting their virtue leads them to set their standards too high and warning them of the consequences–the escape of criminals ('shut up all our courts of justice')—if they require a motive 'adequate to move the moral mind'. Having thus fortified the jury with virtue and necessity, the phrase 'if you find him' is repeated (the figure of anaphora) to link the main circumstantial evidence of motive in a compelling, demanding form which sets up—in the final rhetorical question—the conclusion the jury must reach.

[86] (1824) 11 P. D. 210; Calvert (1836) 17.

was on his way to the dissection table before a witness was sworn or a syllable of evidence heard. It is a fine example of the power counsel can exercise over a trial through a speech. Powerful speech-making was a common phenomenon in late eighteenth and early nineteenth century courts, especially in treason, libel, adultery and seduction cases, but only in ordinary felony trials did it threaten the life of a subject without the safeguard of a speech by counsel in reply. The duty of restraint was the professional recognition that a prosecution advocate should not 'struggle for a conviction, as an advocate in a civil cause contends for a verdict'.[87]

The duty of restraint was neglected in *Patch* and respected in *Corder.* This may reflect differences in the personalities of counsel, differences between the Home and the Norfolk Circuits, or the increasing strength of the principle of restraint between *Patch* in 1805 and *Corder* in 1828. The duty of restraint could only develop to the detail of the passage from Dickenson and Talfourd quoted earlier if prosecution counsel were regularly employed, and regularly made opening speeches. These developments were not occurring at a uniform rate throughout the circuits and courts of England during the early nineteenth century. There was never an authoritative expression of the duty of restraint, so it remained a matter of circuit etiquette, judicial discretion, and the 'good taste' and 'right feeling' of counsel in individual cases.[88] Nevertheless, by the time of the Prisoners' Counsel Act debate of the 1820s and 1830s the existence of a duty of restraint was not doubted, though some remarked upon its recent origin,[89] and the opening in *Patch* was generally referred to as an anomaly requiring explanation.[90]

The duty of restraint did not silence criticism of the prosecution opening during the Prisoners' Counsel Act debate. Supporters of full defence by counsel argued that *any* opening gave the prosecution an advantage if the prisoner could not reply by counsel. The mere fact of placing the evidence in a coherent structure impressed on the jury a particular interpretation of the facts, and was likely to impart greater force to the evidence than it would otherwise possess. Some argued that the most deadly type of opening was the restrained one:[91]

What was the kind of speech likely to have the most fatal effect [in capital cases depending upon circumstantial evidence]? It would be the speech of an

[87] Dickenson and Talfourd (1829) 350, quoted *supra.*

[88] (1826) 15 P. D. 627–8 (Brougham); the expressions 'good taste' and 'right feeling' are from Dickenson and Talfourd (1829) quoted *supra.*

[89] (1836) 34 P. D. 765 (Lord Lyndhurst); (1835) 28 P. D. 871 (Sjt. Talfourd).

[90] (1824) 11 P. D. 210; Calvert (1836) 17; *Lords Evidence* (*supra* n. 69) at 8; *Second Report* (*supra* n. 69) at 10 and Appendix No. 1, 61.

[91] (1836) 34 P. D. 766 per Lord Lyndhurst. See also Smith (1826–27) 84; *Second Report* (*supra* n. 69) at 10; (1835) 28 P. D. 871 (Sjt. Talfourd).

ingenious counsel, who would collect all the little facts of the case, and arrange them in such order and manner, interspersing them with occasional observations, as to lead the minds of the jury to the conclusion that the accused was guilty of the offence with which he stood charged. Such a speech as he had described, introduced as it would be with the expression of great mercy towards the prisoner, and of a hope that he would be able to extricate himself from the toils in which he had entangled himself, was likely to produce a much more powerful effect on the jury, unfavourable to the prisoner, than any speech delivered with zeal and passion, which, by creating a revolting impression, would be likely to produce no effect at all...But this was precisely the description of speech which counsel now, under the restrictions they were supposed to be subjected to, addressed to the jury in that class of cases.

Lord Lyndhurst here conceives an opening more detailed than in *Corder*, where Andrews did not examine 'all the little facts of the case', but even the minimalist opening in *Corder* prepared the jury for the prosecution's interpretation of the evidence. The jury knew, for example, that a five pound note was important, that the victim had suggested that the imprisonment of Corder was within her power, and from the arrangement of Andrews' speech might have connected these facts with the promise to marry. They might readily infer, therefore, the prosecution theory of motive when they heard the evidence. The duty of restraint, therefore, could ameliorate but not eliminate the prejudice to the prisoner from the opening speech of prosecution counsel.

The early nineteenth century concern with the opening speech of prosecution counsel is an important development in the growth of the modern adversarial trial. It marks the first recognition in the ordinary criminal trial of the power and the danger of counsel's speech, and the need for some regulation of the advocacy of counsel. The other work of counsel—legal argument, the examination and the cross-examination of witnesses—dealt with specific aspects of the case, and involved counsel in dialogue with the judge and witnesses rather than the jury. The speech offered dramatic potential to counsel to influence the outcome of the trial, enabling, as in *Patch*, the persuasive presentation of an intellectually complex interpretation of the evidence directly to the jury. The professional recognition, in the form of the duty of restraint and circuit practices discouraging opening speeches, of a need to temper prosecution advocacy was a forerunner of developments in professional ethics later in the century. Some contemporaries, however, saw a more effective control on prosecution counsel in the abolition of the felony counsel restriction, which came to pass with the Prisoners' Counsel Act of 1836. The prisoner's counsel was to have the same power to address the jury as prosecution counsel, and their equality would ensure a balanced presentation of the evidence to the jury. The solution to the problems of speech-making in criminal trials was to be more speeches.

At the conclusion of counsel's opening, if any, the prosecution witnesses gave their evidence. It was by this time established that counsel must avoid leading questions in their examination of witnesses, except for introductory questions or questions to a hostile witness.[92] If there were no prosecution counsel then the court reverted to the centuries-old practice of the judicial interrogation of the witnesses. The judge used the depositions to identify the admissible and relevant evidence and to guide his questioning, and in cases where there were no depositions the practice was for the judge 'to consult the person prosecuting as to the manner of bringing his case before the court, and as to the witnesses proper to be examined'.[93] There was increasing judicial distaste in the second quarter of the nineteenth century for the examination of witnesses in this way, indicative perhaps that prosecution counsel were now not only accepted, but expected. There are complaints by judges in the 1830s of the inconvenience and time wasted in having to examine witnesses themselves, and this was followed by concern that the judicial examination of prosecution witnesses might make the judge appear in the unsatisfactory role of prosecutor. By the mid-1840s the practice was described as 'disagreeable and improper' by one judge, while another called it 'indecent' and refused to examine the witnesses, ordering instead that the depositions be given to a barrister in court to conduct the prosecution.[94]

Defence Counsel

The earliest intervention in the trial by the prisoner's counsel might be to raise a question of law. Questions such as the legality of the proceedings, the adequacy of the indictment, or the validity of a special plea would be settled before the prosecution case began. The argument of questions of law was historically the oldest, and until the eighteenth century the only, role for defence counsel in trials of indictments for felony. Originally defence counsel were assigned by the court to argue legal questions rather than engaged by the prisoner. Counsel was assigned, whether requested by the prisoner or not, when the court recognised a legal

[92] Dickenson and Talfourd (1829) 330–1.

[93] *R v Stoddart* (1819) per Abbot C.J., referred to in Dickenson and Talfourd (1829) 81n.–2n.

[94] *Report of the Select Committee on the Receipt and Expenditure of County Rates* (1834) Parl. Papers XIV. 1 at 139, 141 (Tindal L.C.J., Park and Parke JJ.); (1836) 34 P. D. 777 (Lord Denman); *R v Hezell* (1844) 1 Cox C.C. 384 (Cresswell J.); *R v Page* (1847) 2 Cox C.C. 221 (Maule J.); see also 'Prosecuting Judges' (1847) 9 *Law Times* 256; 'Soup System-Prosecution by Magistrates' (1849) 41 *Law Magazine* 103.

question requiring discussion. The legal objection could be raised by the prisoner, the court itself, or *any* barrister present in court. Before the arrival of prosecution counsel defence counsel did not have an adversary, except in state trials. The judge was not an adversary—he, too, was 'counsel for the prisoner'.[95] Such a defence counsel more closely resembles an *amicus curiae* than a representative of a client. Judge and assigned counsel were engaged in a common endeavour. Both men probably hoped the law favoured the prisoner, but their common responsibility was to ensure the objection was properly determined, and not to secure the prisoner's release.

This *amicus curiae* conception of defence counsel must have disintegrated quickly with the developments of the eighteenth century. Defence counsel were engaged, with a brief and a fee, prior to the trial rather than assigned by the court during the hearing. Cross-examination expanded their role beyond a dialogue with the judge. There was the new and hostile voice of prosecution counsel in the proceedings. Defence counsel had to be assertive on the prisoner's behalf, and the trial, as recent scholarship has shown, became increasingly contentious. By the first decades of the nineteenth century there is no doubt that a prisoner's counsel was a representative of the prisoner and not *amicus curiae*. However, old ideas die hard in the common law. The conception of defence counsel as court appointees lingered through the eighteenth century in the axiom that defence counsel appeared at the discretion or 'good pleasure' of the judge,[96] and appeared in the early proposals of the 1820s to allow full defence by counsel.[97] The idea that defence counsel had responsibilities to the court reappears in discussions of forensic morality after the Prisoners' Counsel Act.

The primary function of defence counsel in the early nineteenth century was cross-examination, and counsel here were put under pressure by the felony counsel restriction. The denial of an address to the jury forced counsel to cross-examine for, put bluntly, he had 'either to cross-examine or do nothing'.[98] Counsel was fee'd to cross-examine, he was expected by the prisoner and the attorney to cross-examine, yet to cross-examine might achieve little. It was best avoided if counsel did not have an evidential base from which to challenge the testimony or credit of the prosecution witness, which must have often been the case when, as we

[95] These details of the assignment of counsel to prisoners for legal argument are from Coke's *Third Institute* at 29, 137 and 230. Coke is silent on the point, but it seems unlikely that such an assigned counsel would receive any fee.

[96] 4 Blackstone (1765–69) 349–50; Beattie (1986) 359–60.

[97] For example, the Capital Crimes Defence Bill (1821) Parl. Papers I 171, which provides that persons accused of capital crimes can make their defence by counsel 'who shall be assigned for that purpose by the Court'.

[98] Talfourd (1825) 328. See also *Second Report* (*supra* n. 69) at 15.

have seen, counsel were not entitled to copies of the depositions and his instructions might be inadequate or delivered without time for preparation. There were ways counsel could attempt to meet the expectation to cross-examine and conceal its lack of substance, such as hazarding a speculative line of questioning, or trying to intimidate the witness into admissions. If the witness were honest, had told all he or she knew, and would not be intimidated, then the inevitable result of the cross-examination was to reinforce the prosecution case.[99]

Another difficulty of cross-examining in the shadow of the felony counsel restriction was that counsel lacked a speech to explain to the jury the significance of his questioning. The significance of the question had to be apparent from the question itself, and it has been suggested that this is one of the reasons the practice developed of asking leading questions in cross-examination. 'When they [prisoners] were allowed to have counsel to cross-examine, but not to speak for them', Fitzjames Stephen suggested, 'the cross-examination tended to become a speech thrown into the form of questions, and it has ever since retained this character to a greater or less extent'.[100] Contemporaries saw the felony counsel restriction as responsible for 'a latitude' in cross-examination which would not have been allowed 'if it were not often the only mode of suggesting an important view of the case to the minds of the jury'.[101]

This latitude in cross-examination, like the imperative to cross-examine, was a temptation to speculative and abusive cross-examination in felony trials. Beattie and Landsman have referred to the sarcasm and nastiness to witnesses at the Old Bailey in the late eighteenth century, and in the last section I suggested that their association of these characteristics with good advocacy was misplaced. They are more likely an early indication of the low standards of advocacy in this court, which became a major source of complaint in the 1830s. *The Times* referred to the 'veteran brawlers and bullies' of this court, 'irritable and foul-mouthed', and *The Westminster Review* complained of their insinuations, rudeness to women and insults. *The Westminster Review* also made the obvious point that this style of cross-examination was usually counterproductive:[102]

[99] Talfourd (1825) 327–8. Scarlett (1877) 75, and the discussion of cross-examination at the Old Bailey *infra*.

[100] 2 Stephen (1883) 431. Erskine had to justify his use of leading questions in cross-examination in *The Trial of Thomas Hardy* (1794) 24 State Trials (1809–26) 199 at 659 in an exchange which suggests the practice was a recent development.

[101] Dickenson and Talfourd (1829) 382; *Second Report* (*supra* n. 69) at 10 and 16; (1826) 15 P. D. 624 (Scarlett).

[102] (1835) *Westminster Review* 195 at 203; *The Times*, 4 November 1834, p. 2; see also (1826) 15 P. D. 632 (Denman, who was Common Serjeant at the Old Bailey at this time); 2 Grant (1837) 263–4. On the treatment of women at the Old Bailey see also Charles Dickens' letters to the *Morning Chronicle* of 23 and 29 June 1840, considered in Chapter 6.

This court has a peculiar style of cross-examination, which seems founded on the assumption that every prisoner is falsely accused, and all the witnesses against him are conspiring to obtain his conviction. Thus suspicions are insinuated, and warm tempered witnesses become angry at imputations...This conduct...neither is, nor is intended to be useful to the prisoner on trial. The juries see through it, and are unmoved; but it serves as an advertisement of counsel's strength of lungs and impudence of face, and satisfies the client that though convicted, every thing has been done for him that his case would admit.

The Times hoped the reorganisation of the Old Bailey in the Central Criminal Court Act would improve the behaviour of counsel, but was not sanguine in its expectations.[103] The Prisoners' Counsel Act was also held out by its promoters as likely to improve cross-examinations:[104]

If the Counsel had the opportunity of addressing the Jury, he would be careful after a fact favourable to his client had once been stated, to avoid the risk of weakening its force by cross-examination; the fact being in evidence, he would reserve his comment to the period of his address to the Jury, when he could make it the more directly and forcibly, and without fear of contradiction.

'If the counsel had the privilege of speaking', James Scarlett told the House of Commons, 'he would not waste the time of the Court in cross-examinations'.[105]

The defence case opened with the prisoner's statement to the jury. The prisoner was not at this time permitted to give evidence on oath, and as his counsel was not permitted to address the jury, this unsworn statement from the dock had to satisfy the needs of evidence and speech. The prisoner's statement had, in Langbein's terms, a 'testimonial' and a 'defensive' function. Langbein argues that 'a fundamental premise' of the criminal trial before the arrival of counsel was that 'the defendant should be routinely available as a testimonial resource'.[106] The prisoner's statement enabled the court to hear the prisoner's version of events, and observe his demeanour, notwithstanding the prohibition on the prisoner giving evidence. Prisoners did not require any legal assistance to speak to the facts because, like witnesses, they were simply required to speak the truth. It was accepted, even welcomed, that the prisoner's explanation or manner might betray his or her guilt—the theory was that the prisoner should speak 'either to clear himself or to hang himself'.[107]

[103] (1834) 4 & 5 Will. 4, c. 36; *The Times* (*supra* n. 102).

[104] *Second Report* (*supra* n. 69) at 15.

[105] (1825) 15 P. D. 624; see also (1836) 34 P. D. 776 (Denman).

[106] Langbein (1994) 1053. In a footnote Langbein explains he means by 'testimonial' that the defendant spoke to the merits, even though he was not on oath.

[107] Langbein (1983a) 124; Langbein (1994) 1053. This view of the prisoner's statement is implicit in Sjt. Hawkins' justification of the felony counsel restriction: Hawkins (1724) book 2, c. 39, s. 2, quoted in Chapter 4.

Most prisoners were unable to make a competent statement to the jury. 'The prisoner', said a Yorkshire magistrate, 'comes into court, squalid and depressed from long confinement—utterly unable to tell his own story from want of words and want of confidence'. The prisoner's statement placed impossible demands on the handicapped, the infirm, the ignorant and the foreigner.[108] Prisoners who engaged counsel often believed their counsel would speak for them, and were surprised to find in court that this was not so.[109] The scanty record which survives of prisoner's speeches suggests they were a mixture of statements of fact, protestations of innocence, blank denials of prosecution evidence, mitigating circumstances, and irrelevant digressions.

By the early nineteenth century prisoners with means were having their statements prepared by, or in conjunction with, their legal advisers.[110] This development provides another example of the activities of counsel silencing the prisoner. The prisoner's lawyers reduced the 'testimonial' content of the statement by carefully controlling factual disclosures and, by introducing legal style arguments, gave it a strong 'defensive' flavour. In *Corder*, for example, the prisoner's solicitors discussed prior to the trial whether the jury would more favourably receive a story of suicide or provocation, and during the trial Corder made changes to his statement on legal advice.[111] Such a groomed presentation was a far cry from the unrehearsed explanation of events expected in the pre-counsel trial of the early eighteenth century.

The preparation of a speech by counsel or attorney was not without its dangers for the prisoner. The speech needed to be prepared in advance, on assumed facts, and unexpected developments during the trial might mean either hurried amendments or, as in *Patch*, a statement at cross-purposes with the evidence. In *Patch* someone had prepared for the prisoner a lengthy and intelligent statement, displaying familiarity with legal concepts and coherently examining the complex circumstantial evidence. It argued that only a left-handed man could have committed the murder unseen, and Patch was right-handed. However, counsel did not establish in cross-examination or from defence witnesses the two straightforward propositions of this argument. There are similar discrepancies throughout Patch's statement between the

[108] Smith (1826–27) (quotation at 77); (1824) 11 P. D. 202; (1836) 34 P. D. 765 and 774; (1836) 35 P. D. 177–8; *Second Report* (*supra* n. 69) at 3; Beattie (1986) 350–1; Langbein (1994) 1053.

[109] Smith (1826–27) 85; (1824) 11 P. D. 180–1 (jurymen's petition); (1826) 15 P. D. 610 (Twiss).

[110] 'it is only of late years that written defences have been prepared by Counsel. The practice is not at all general, and doubts have been entertained of its propriety': *Second Report* (*supra* n. 69) at 11.

[111] Curtis (1828) 143–7.

defence conceived by its writer and the case established in evidence by counsel.[112]

Further, Patch did not read the statement himself but gave it to the Clerk of Arraigns to read. How competently this official read a statement with which he was totally unfamiliar is not recorded, but the judge in his summing-up clearly misapprehends the defence. The practice of passing prepared speeches to an officer of the court was a sterile development which stripped the prisoner's statement of testimonial value without achieving the defensive potential of an address to the jury.

At the conclusion of the defence evidence in a felony trial the prosecution counsel could in some circumstances call rebuttal evidence, but was not permitted to address the jury again.[113] Felony trials differed in this respect from trials of civil actions and misdemeanours where the counsel for the plaintiff or prosecution was entitled to a speech in reply to the defence evidence. In such trials defence counsel often chose to close the defence after his opening speech, for by calling no evidence he thereby denied the plaintiff or prosecution counsel a reply. Felony trials, where defence counsel had no speech and prosecution counsel no reply, were spared this tactical jockeying for the last word to the jury. Cottu eulogised this absence of speeches. 'No one', he said, 'is allowed to alter the light of the evidence by showing it through the prism of his own opinion or fancy; it appears to the jury in all its purity, and simply as it was manifested in the course of the examinations. It remains with them alone to judge of it without the help of any other influence'.[114]

The Favours of Judge and Jury

Doctor and Student, we have seen, justified the felony counsel restriction by reference to the help the judge might give the prisoner. The most common expression of this idea from the time of Coke was that the judge was 'counsel for the prisoner', an aphorism which cleverly justified the denial of counsel by implying the prisoner had one. The aphorism suggested that the judge had a responsibility for the prisoner, which was true, and that this responsibility was akin to the duty of counsel to his client, which was false. The judge's responsibility to the prisoner derived from the judicial qualities of impartiality and legality, as is clear from Sjt Hawkins elaboration of this expression:[115]

112 Gurney (1806) *passim.* The preparation of this statement by someone other than Patch, probably a lawyer, is inferred from its style, the evidence of Patch's limited literacy skills (for example, his letter at 97), and his inability to read it himself.

113 Dickenson and Talfourd (1829) 387–8.

114 Cottu (1820) 49.

115 Hawkins (1724) book 2 c. 39 s. 2. The nature of the judicial duty of impartiality is further considered in Chapter 5.

if it be further considered, that it is the duty of the Court to be indifferent between the King and Prisoner, and to see that the indictment be good in Law, and the proceedings regular, and the evidence legal, and such as fully proves the point in issue, there seems no good reason to fear but that, generally speaking, the innocent, for whose safety alone the Law is concerned, have rather an advantage than a prejudice in having the Court their only Counsel.

Impartiality and legal correctness, however, might not be enough to ensure a fair trial for a poor or ignorant prisoner without counsel. The judge might need to assist the prisoner further and the expression 'counsel for the prisoner' encouraged him to do so, though what form this assistance might properly take, compatible with the judicial office, remained ambiguous. Hawkins in the above passage suggests the judge should ensure the proofs were complete, which at least contemplates the judicial cross-examination of witnesses.

In the seventeenth century the judges held office at the pleasure of the Crown, the nominal prosecutor of all indictments, and perhaps needed this robust aphorism to emphasise their responsibilities to the prisoner. During the eighteenth century the independence of the judiciary was assured, their impartiality expected, and counsel began to appear regularly in the criminal courts. Errors in the indictment, evidential objections, and probative inadequacies became matters for counsel to raise and argue, and for the judge to decide rather than detect. By the early nineteenth century counsel had an established role in felony trials, and by sharply distinguishing the office of judge from this role critics of the felony counsel restriction were able to demonstrate that the judge could not possibly be counsel for the prisoner.[116]

The literal discussion of this aphorism during the Prisoners' Counsel Act debate obscured a residue of its original meaning not eroded by the passage of time. Sir John Copley made this point in the Commons in 1826, first disclaiming the troublesome phrase:[117]

although the judge was not to be considered as counsel for the prisoner, it was still his duty to act impartially between the Crown and the prisoner, and to give the latter the benefit of any suggestions which the circumstances of the case might seem to demand.

[116] An elegant demonstration of this impossibility was made by Horace Twiss: 'Did the judge take all advantages to defeat the prosecutor and acquit the prisoner? Then as a judge, he betrayed his oath of office. Did he decline to take those advantages? Then as counsel for the prisoner he deserted his client': (1826) 15 P. D. 610. The Criminal Law Commissioners made a sustained attack on the aphorism: see *Second Report* (*supra* n. 69) at 7–10.

[117] (1826) 15 P. D. 601. Cf. Sir Alexander MacDonald's interpretation of the aphorism: *Report from the Select Committee appointed to consider so much of the Criminal Law as relates to Capital Punishments in Felonies* (1819) Parl. Papers VIII. 1.

The felony counsel restriction, Copley continued, gave the prisoner the advantage of the 'favourable disposition of the judge'. He did not argue that this favourable disposition justified the felony counsel restriction, but that it was likely to be lost if the restriction were removed, a concern discussed further in Chapter 5.

Eighteenth century juries also showed a favourable disposition towards prisoners in their high rates of acquittals and 'partial' verdicts. A partial verdict is the name applied to a conviction for a lesser offence than that for which the prisoner was indicted, which usually meant a non-capital conviction rather than a capital one. Such verdicts were often the result of discomfiture with the severity of capital statutes, a kind of 'pious perjury', Blackstone said, to save the lives of prisoners.[118] It was suggested in the 1820s and 1830s that the felony counsel restriction similarly inclined juries to leniency. The Criminal Law Commissioners stated that the denial of counsel 'appears to the generality of people to be harsh and unreasonable', and that this feeling prejudiced trials by creating 'an additional temptation...to show undue favour to the Prisoner, and this unjustly tends to the escape of the guilty'[119] This perception of pernicious judicial and jury sympathy for the prisoner links the felony counsel restriction with the contemporary capital punishment debate, which is the subject of Chapter 3.

Conclusions

The felony counsel restriction appears in the *Leges Henrici Primi* shortly after the Conquest as a characteristic of capital crimes. Through the seas of change of seven centuries, through rationalisations invented, mutated and discarded, it emerged on the shores of the nineteenth century still firmly attached to crimes punishable by death.

The felony counsel restriction suffered the encroachments of counsel from the late seventeenth century. First it was excluded by Parliament from treason trials, then judges allowed defence counsel to examine and cross-examine witnesses in other felony trials. It survived as a prohibition on defence counsel addressing the jury, and trial procedure adapted to compensate for this inequality of counsel. Prosecution counsel had to be restrained in exercising their advantage of a speech, and on some circuits were obliged to forgo it. Defence counsel, by contrast, were allowed special latitude in their questioning of prosecution witnesses.

[118] 4 Blackstone (1765–69) 239; 1 Radzinowicz (1948–86) 93–7; Beattie (1986) 410–30; Langbein (1983a) 41–55.

[119] *Second Report* (*supra* n. 69) at 17; see also (1826) 15 P. D. 627 (Brougham); (1836) 35 P. D. 282–83 (Abinger); (1824) 11 P. D. 180–1 (jurymen's petition).

Judges and jury recognised the disability of defence counsel and developed a lenient disposition towards prisoners.

The encroachments of counsel were continuing in the early nineteenth century. The prisoner's statement might now be written by counsel, and as a result have a more defensive and less testimonial character. The centuries old practice of the judicial examination of witnesses was questioned by some judges, who saw this as the work of counsel. A need for equality between counsel was most apparent in trials which turned on alternative interpretations of circumstantial evidence. These developments suggest a continuation of the trend identified by Langbein during the eighteenth century of an expanding role for counsel in the criminal trial, at the expense of an increasingly passive judge and silent prisoner.

The early nineteenth century saw concern with forensic morality, a theme which would continue through the 1830s with the Prisoners' Counsel Act debate, and the 1840s with the licence of counsel controversy. The concerns of the early decades of the nineteenth century were the prosecution opening and cross-examination. The potential for abuse of the prosecution opening gave rise to circuit practices discouraging openings and to the duty of restraint, which are perhaps the earliest examples of identifiable rules of professional conduct regulating advocacy in criminal trials. The criticism of cross-examination centred on the Old Bailey, which was outside circuit control and renowned for low standards of judicial and professional behaviour. Some saw the abolition of the felony counsel restriction as a means to improve cross-examination, by removing the need for defence counsel to conduct their entire case through questioning.

Modern scholarship suggests that by the end of the eighteenth century English criminal procedure was substantially adversarial.[120] These accounts tend to look for adversarialism, and to underemphasise the persistence of non-adversarial features of trial procedure, a consequence perhaps of the use of modern adversarial models to study the past. Fitzjames Stephen, writing in 1863, described the adversarial, in his term 'litigious', characteristics of the criminal trial of his day using the model of civil litigation. Similarly, civil procedure was regularly referred to during the Prisoners' Counsel Act debate as a model for criminal procedure. It is suggested that the civil procedure of the early nineteenth century is the most appropriate standard to identify the adversarial and non-adversarial features of the criminal trial. Stephen's analysis of criminal procedure at a later but not too distant date using this model provides invaluable assistance.[121]

[120] For example, Langbein (1983a) 123; Landsman (1990) 502.
[121] Stephen (1863a) ch. 5.

The most obvious departure from the civil model was that in a felony trial defence counsel was not permitted to address the jury. The speech was counsel's most potent opportunity to influence the jury. Here counsel in a civil trial would attack, doubt, interpret, defend and reason upon the evidence; praise, justify, excuse, pity or sympathise with the client; and challenge, cajole, flatter, persuade and lead the jury by their noses to a verdict in his client's favour. The speech was so highly valued in civil trials that defence counsel were often prepared to call no evidence, so as to deprive the plaintiff's counsel of a reply and ensure the defence had the last word. Another important difference between civil and criminal trials was that the opportunities for prosecution counsel to address the jury were more restricted than for his civil counterpart. Circuit practice and the duty of restraint constrained his opening, and he was not entitled to a speech in reply to the defence evidence. Stephen considered the prosecution must have a speech in reply to satisfy the 'fundamental rule of all litigation' that both sides 'be heard on any matter which may be propounded'.[122]

Notwithstanding the advances of the eighteenth century, the role of counsel in the criminal trial in the early decades of the nineteenth century was severely restricted in comparison with contemporary civil trials. At the same time the judge and jury were not as scrupulously impartial as in civil trials, for they were in some circumstances prepared to show a 'favourable disposition' towards the prisoner. The eighteenth century trend towards adversarialism cannot be said to be complete before the Prisoners' Counsel Act restructured the criminal trial in the image of civil litigation, and abolished the disability which was the source of leniency to the prisoner.

[122] Stephen (1863a) 161.

3

The Logic of Reform

During the late eighteenth and early nineteenth centuries a number of commentators doubted whether the capital felony process, as rationalised by Paley, was achieving its objective of the prevention of crime. The Reverend Martin Madan, for example, argued that increased severity, through strict enforcement of the capital statutes and the restriction of the prerogative of mercy to exceptional cases, would better achieve 'the great end of prevention'. Another view, advocated by Samuel Romilly in his reply to Madan, was that deterrence would be increased by repealing capital penalties, except for the most serious offences, and more strictly enforcing lesser punishments.[1] In his subsequent attempts to convince Parliament to accept this view Romilly argued that the capital felony process was arbitrary, ineffective and unfair. Romilly's depiction of the capital felony process and the logic of his proposed reform of punishments are considered in the first section of this chapter. The second section explores the implications of this logic for other phases of the penal process, and concludes that the amelioration of capital punishment required a revision of criminal procedure, which the felony counsel restriction was unlikely to survive.

The Lottery of Justice

The movement for the reform of the criminal law began in Parliament with Sir Samuel Romilly's campaign against capital punishment. Romilly sponsored many bills in the House of Commons in the decade after 1808 in an attempt to abolish obsolete capital felonies and to repeal the death penalty for larcenies. His disinterested advocacy of this and other great causes, his sensibility and his personal integrity gave him an unmatched reputation for public virtue. Henry Brougham thought his

[1] Madan (1785) *passim,* (quotation from 11); Romilly (1786) *passim.* For Paley's rationalisation of the capital felony process see Chapter 1.

character surpassed ancient paragons, and referred to the way unrelaxed sincerity of principle and compassion sat together almost perfectly within him. Sir James Mackintosh said he knew no man 'so deeply and violently affected by the recital of cruelty than Romilly'. This strength of feeling was usually concealed by his grave, reserved manner, but it occasionally bursts through the close reasoning of his speeches in a sublime indignation at the way things are. He enjoyed only a small measure of legislative success before his death in 1818, but his rationalisation of the need for reform and the lustre his character and commitment gave to the cause of reform survived him. It was the inspiration that Romilly passed on, rather than the achievement he left behind which makes him the fountainhead of nineteenth century criminal law reform.[2]

Romilly's first work on the criminal law, published early in his legal career, was the *Observations on a Late Publication Intituled Thoughts on Executive Justice* written in 1786 as a reply to Madan's *Thoughts on Executive Justice*. Six years later, assisted by his friend James Scarlett, he published an idiosyncratic work entitled *Letters Containing an Account of the Late Revolution in France and Observations on the Constitution, Laws, Manners and Institutions of the English*. The second part of the *Letters* was written by Romilly in the form of a series of letters from an imaginary foreign visitor to England describing English laws and institutions. Romilly attempted an ironic social commentary through the puzzled observations of his fictitious foreigner, commenting on many themes which were to appear again in his parliamentary career including capital punishment, compensation to acquitted prisoners, cruelty to animals, the slave trade, and the perniciousness of state lotteries. The *Letters* were published anonymously, but the increasing violence of the French Revolution and the republican sentiments of some passages of the book convinced Romilly to stop its distribution and burn all unsold copies.[3]

Romilly's thought matured between these early works and the period of his parliamentary career. The younger Romilly sometimes had an outspoken sympathy with the poor and scorn for the governing classes which was subsequently lost or suppressed.[4] Again, the youth sweepingly condemned all capital larcenies, for 'death cannot be inflicted for a mere invasion of property, consistently with reason and justice, nor without a gross violation of the laws of nature and the precepts of our religion', but, as will be seen, the politician was more circumspect.[5] Two ideas in these early works, however, illuminate the reasoning of

[2] 1 Brougham (1839–45) 290–8; 2 Mackintosh (1835) 345. For Romilly's life and career see Medd (1968).

[3] Romilly (1792); 1 Romilly (1840) 415, 432–3; Scarlett (1877) 53–5.

[4] For example, Romilly (1786) 42–3, 47–9, 94–5; Romilly (1792) Letters XIII and XXII.

[5] Romilly (1786) 24 (footnote omitted); 32–3.

Romilly's parliamentary speeches, and must be looked at more closely. These ideas are the need for harmony between the criminal law and public feeling, and the psychology of the criminal.

Romilly considered that the effectiveness of the criminal law was contingent upon the approval and the cooperation of the public. 'If laws operate in violation of the feelings and understandings of men', he wrote, 'they are unjust and unwise, by however legitimate an authority they were enacted; if they be repugnant to the character of a nation, they must remain unexecuted'.[6] He believed that the strict enforcement of all capital statutes, as proposed by Madan, would be repugnant to the character of the English people, who would react by taking steps themselves to mitigate the severity of the law. Prosecutors and witnesses would not participate in what they considered 'acts of solemn injustice and cruelty', jurors would refuse to convict on capital indictments, and the result would be fewer convictions and complete impunity for many offenders.[7] Romilly developed these consequences of lack of harmony with public feeling to refute Madan's call for increased severity, but his analysis is an implicit condemnation of the status quo. It was sufficiently well known that prosecutors, witnesses and jurors sometimes frustrated the operation of capital statutes for Blackstone to christen one of their practices in his *Commentaries*. He gave the name 'pious perjury' to the practice of juries of undervaluing stolen property to save prisoners from conviction for capital larcenies.[8]

Romilly also makes some intriguing observations on the criminal mind in the early works. He believed that the criminal, especially the thief, lived for the present, for instant gratification, and believed in luck. The criminal was an opportunist, or to use a modern term a risk-taker, more impressed by the prospects of gain and impunity for a crime, than by the possibilities of punishment. A more severe application of the law, by a policy of fewer pardons and more executions, as Madan had urged, would be ignored by felons of this mind, who would act on the many chances of escape that the capital felony process still offered rather than on the disappearance of the possibility of a pardon:[9]

> If the power of pardoning were abolished, and conviction doomed the convict to inevitable death, the chances against a criminal would be greater undoubtedly than they are at present, but there would still be a very considerable chance in his favour; and a thief, like a deluded gamester, will play on, even though the odds be against him.

[6] Romilly (1786) 38.

[7] Romilly (1786) 87–90. On Madan and his *Thoughts on Executive Justice* see 1 Radzinowicz (1948–86) 239–48.

[8] 4 Blackstone (1765–69) 239.

[9] Romilly (1786) 66.

Romilly saw the gambling mentality as a powerful self-destructive impulse, not restrainable by adjusting the odds. In the *Letters* he considers gambling in the context of state lotteries, where he emphasised its social cost in terms of misery, crime, suicide, and the destitution of families. Lotteries, he said, encouraged crime through financial desperation and by their shared state of mind of rashness and the desire for profit without labour. He compared the atmosphere in a lottery shop to a criminal court, with the gamblers 'waiting in the most anxious suspense to hear their fate, like so many convicted criminals brought to the bar, to hear the sentence which awaits them'.[10] A constant assumption in Romilly's thought on the prevention of crime was to be the need to recognise the gamester in the criminal.

Romilly's election to Parliament in 1806, 20 years after the publication of the *Observations*, gave him the opportunity to fulfil his long-held ambition to attempt to mitigate the criminal law. He expected opposition, and proceeded cautiously. His first concern was capital larcenies, where his original intention was to reduce the severity of the law by raising the value of the property required to make the offence capital. James Scarlett, however, urged Romilly 'to attempt at once to repeal all the statutes which punish with death mere thefts, unaccompanied by any act of violence, or other circumstance of aggravation. This suggestion', Romilly continues in his *Memoirs*, 'was very agreeable to me. But, as it appeared to me, that I had no chance of being able to carry through the House a Bill which was to expunge at once all these laws from the statute book, I determined to attempt the repeal of them one by one'. Romilly began this strategy by moving the repeal in 1808 of the statute making pickpocketing to the value of a shilling a capital offence, and continued this piecemeal approach to reform until his death 10 years later.[11]

A pragmatic assessment of the legislative opposition also appears in the types of arguments Romilly adopted in Parliament to justify his reforms. Romilly's familiarity with Beccaria's writings, his friendship with Bentham, and his own reflections over many years gave him an impressive intellectual arsenal to attack capital punishment. However, he for the most part avoided arguments derived from social theory or the value of human life, and responded with venom to attempts to label him a humanitarian or a theorist.[12] Romilly's humanitarian impulses were

[10] Romilly (1792) Letter XIII (quotation 244). Romilly subsequently opposed state lotteries in parliament, see particularly (1816) 34 P. D. 1091–2. For state lotteries generally see George (1992) 306–7.

[11] 2 Romilly (1840) 239; (1808) 11 P. D. 395.

[12] For example see (1811) 19 P. D. App. 84; (1811) 18 P. D. 1267. Romilly's friends also took pains to deny he was a rash innovator: see, for example, (1819) 39 P. D. 793 (Mackintosh), and Brougham (1812b) 408–15.

beyond doubt, and almost beyond praise, but he realised that the milk of human kindness would never change the law. 'Men cannot be reasoned into humanity'. he once observed to Étienne Dumont.[13] Instead he sought to justify his reforms 'upon the grounds of policy and expediency', and to satisfy 'the coldest and harshest reasoner upon such subjects'.[14]

Policy and expediency meant the prevention of crime and the entrenched opinion, following Paley, was that crime was best prevented by a severe code of laws administered mercifully. Lord Ellenborough, to whose father Paley's *Principles* were dedicated, restated the conventional wisdom in opposing Romilly's Privately Stealing in Shops Bill of 1810:[15]

> Scarcely any crime, my lords, against property can be weighed in the same scales with man's life. But, in all these cases, the end of the law is the prevention of crime, and I am persuaded, no penalty less than the terror of death would amount to any thing like prevention of that offence now under our consideration...[T]he law, as it stands, is but seldom carried into execution, and yet it ceases not to hold out that terror which alone will be sufficient to prevent the frequent commission of the offence.

The primary objective of Romilly's parliamentary speeches on capital punishment was to discredit this reasoning, by showing that capital larcenies did not prevent theft. The key argument was that punishment was not certain under the capital felony process, and effective deterrence required certainty. This reasoning was likely to be treated as mere theory or ingenious speculation by defenders of the status quo, and so Romilly sought to demonstrate the escape of criminals through multiple examples and the novel technique of statistics. He also attempted a lengthy refutation of Paley's rationalisation of the selective enforcement of capital statutes.[16] His thought best appears in his most important speech on capital punishments, on 9 February 1810, in support of the repeal of three capital larcenies. This speech, which Radzinowicz considers 'one of the most brilliant ever delivered in Parliament on the subject of crime and punishment', is a comprehensive indictment of the deficiencies of the capital felony process and an introduction to the new penal logic which was to reverberate through three decades of criminal law reform.[17] The felony counsel restriction was not mentioned in this

[13] 1 Romilly (1840) 433.

[14] (1811) 19 P. D. App. 84. Cf. McGowen (1983) especially at 114 and 124 on the importance to the campaign against capital punishment of claiming the authority of practical experience.

[15] (1811) 19 P. D. App. 89.

[16] (1811) 19 P. D. App. 18–41.

[17] 1 Radzinowicz (1948–86) 504. The content and public reception of this speech are discussed by Radzinowicz at 322–6. The speech was initially reported at (1810) 15 P. D. 366, later appearing more fully in pamphlet form and then as an appendix to the *Parliamentary Debates*: see (1811) 19 P. D. App. 1. On the different versions of the speech see 1 Radzinowicz (1948–86) 323–4. All references in this work are to (1811) 19 P. D. App. 1.

speech, but Romilly's logic would eventually reach and sweep away this ancient rule.

Romilly opens his speech by explaining the non-enforcement of capital statutes. He begins from the premise, contradicting Paley and still contentious amongst modern scholars, that the legislature intended its capital statutes to be strictly enforced.[18] These laws were no longer strictly enforced because they were no longer in harmony with public feeling. There had been a slow change 'in the manners and character of the nation, which are now so repugnant to the spirit of these laws, that it has become impossible to carry them into execution'.[19] Romilly refers to statistics for the number of convictions and the number of executions for London and Middlesex to establish his contention that executions, and thus the enforcement of the law, were declining. Amongst the statistics were figures relating to the three capital larcenies Romilly was attempting to repeal. There had been 1,872 persons committed to Newgate for trial for these crimes in the preceding seven years, of which only one was executed. Romilly used this figure to mediate upon the number of thieves who escaped through the dissatisfaction of 'wise and honest' citizens with the law:[20]

> In how many instances such crimes have been committed, and the persons robbed have not proceeded so far against the offenders as even to have them committed to prison: how many of the 1,872 thus committed were discharged, because those who had suffered by their crimes would not appear to give evidence upon their trial: in how many cases the witnesses who did not appear with-held the evidence that they could have given: and how numerous were the instances in which juries found a compassionate verdict, in direct contradiction to the plain facts clearly established before them, we do not know; but that these evils must all have existed to a considerable degree, no man can doubt.

The evils of non-enforcement were compounded by the arbitrary selection of victims for execution. Prisoners of bad reputation, or whom the evidence suggested were involved in other crimes, might be left for execution for these reasons, rather than the circumstances of their offences. One judge might recommend mercy for the same reason that another would refuse it, such as the former good character of the prisoner or the frequency or novelty of the crime. The unfettered judicial discretion of the mercy phase of the capital felony process meant the law, invariable in theory, was in practice 'continually shifting

[18] (1811) 19 P. D. App. 4–5. Radzinowicz follows Romilly, and Hay takes Paley's view: see 1 Radzinowicz (1948–86) 151–9, and 163–4, and Hay (1975) 23. Romilly once subscribed to Paley's opinion: see Romilly (1786) 80–2.

[19] (1811) 19 P. D. App. 4.

[20] (1811) 19 P. D. App. 7–8. The expression 'wise and honest' is from Romilly's discussion of this theme in the *Observations*: see Romilly (1786) 88.

with the temper, and habits, and opinions of those by whom it is administered'.[21]

The non-enforcement of the law of capital larceny was therefore occurring on a massive scale, but a prisoner was occasionally executed, for reasons probably only known to the presiding judge, as a terrible example of justice. This was Romilly's vision of the capital felony process, and to show this system did not prevent crime, he described how the law might appear to a criminal:[22]

> Let us only reflect how all these fluctuations of opinion and variations in practice must operate upon that portion of mankind who are rendered obedient to the law only by the terror of punishment. After giving full weight to all the chances of complete impunity which they can suggest to their minds, they have besides to calculate upon the probabilities which there are, after conviction, of their escaping a severe punishment; to speculate upon what judge will go the circuit ...As it has been truly observed, that most men are apt to confide in their supposed good fortune, and to miscalculate as to the number of prizes which there are in the lottery of life, so are those dissolute and thoughtless men, whose evil dispositions penal laws are most necessary to repress, much too prone to deceive themselves in their speculations upon what I am afraid they accustom themselves to consider as the lottery of justice.

This passage perfects Romilly's youthful identification of the criminal and the gambler as the capital felony process becomes a state lottery. It also introduces psychological dimensions to the criminal absent from earlier discussions of the capital felony process. In Paley's analysis a criminal experienced the terror of an execution, connected terror with the law, and did not offend the law. Romilly's criminal, intuitively or logically, could perform a cost-benefit calculation, and had a developed attitude to risk. He could disregard the unfortunate wretch on the gallows, and act upon the probability of escape. This psychological profile of the criminal suggested a more effective approach to the prevention of crime:[23]

> It is the desire of a supposed good which is the incentive to every crime; no crime, therefore, could exist, if it were *infallibly certain* that not good, but evil must follow, as an unavoidable consequence to the person who committed it.

The principle of certainty ruled Romilly's new penal order. This principle enjoyed a symbiotic relationship with the amelioration of punishment. Milder punishments were needed to squeeze out the discretion exercised

[21] (1811) 19 P. D. App. 8–11, quotation at 10. McGowen (1983) examines the image of justice projected to the public by punitive severity and judicial discretion, and interprets the campaign against capital punishment as an attempt, motivated by class and political interests, to substitute impersonal for discretionary justice.

[22] (1811) 19 P. D. App. 11–12. Romilly anticipates the jurisprudence of legal realism in many respects, in this passage the 'bad man' perspective of Oliver Wendell Holmes: see Holmes (1897) *passim*.

[23] (1811) 19 P. D. App. 12 (emphasis added).

by prosecutors, witnesses, jurors and judges and so achieve certainty. Once certainty was established no more than mild punishments were needed to prevent crime. Certainty linked mild punishment and crime prevention, and so enabled Romilly to justify his desire for more humane laws in terms which might satisfy the cold, harsh reasoners of Parliament.

The chain of certainty between the crime and the punishment was only as strong as its weakest link, so that certainty has to be perfected at all stages of the punitive process. The opposition in Parliament, especially in the House of Lords, to the repeal of capital larcenies consumed Romilly's attention so that he did not have the chance to develop in legislation the wider implications of the principle of certainty before his suicide in 1818. His speech in 1810, however, shows he realised more was required than milder punishments and the elimination of discretion:[24]

> This absolute certainty, however, is unattainable...All that can be done is, by a vigilant police, by rational rules of evidence, by clear laws, and by punishments proportioned to the guilt of the offender, to approach as nearly to that certainty as human imperfection will admit.

Certainty of detection, certainty of prosecution, certainty of conviction, certainty of punishment. No mercy and no escape. This was the logic of reform.

Consanguineous Vices

Sir Samuel Romilly contemplated wide-ranging reform of the criminal law. He proposed or supported moves to improve secondary punishments, to obtain compensation for innocent persons imprisoned pending trial, and for the repeal of corruption of blood and the aggravated punishments for treason. He composed many essays on criminal subjects, unfortunately never published and since destroyed.[25] After his death his supporters, led by Sir James Mackintosh, concentrated their efforts, as Romilly had done, on the amelioration of capital punishment, but also gradually widened the agenda for reform.

Mackintosh[26] had an early success in carrying a motion on 2 March

[24] (1811) 19 P. D. App. 12.

[25] On these essays see 3 Romilly (1840) 369–76 and 13 Holdsworth (1952) 276, which list their titles. They include an essay *On allowing counsel to Persons accused*.

[26] Sir James Mackintosh (1765–1832) established an intellectual reputation with his *Vindiciae Gallicae*, a response to Burke's *Reflections on the Revolution in France*, and his lectures on the law of nature and nations at Lincoln's Inn Hall in 1799–1800. He was called to the bar in 1795, and was Recorder of Bombay from 1803 to 1812. He entered the House of Commons in 1813.

1819 to appoint a Select Committee 'to consider so much of the Criminal Law as relates to Capital Punishment'. This Committee accumulated a mass of material to prove the disharmony between public feeling and the capital felony process, as manifested in a reluctance to prosecute, to give evidence, and to convict. The Committee proposed the repeal of many capital offences, but most of its recommendations did not pass into law. Mackintosh successfully carried another motion in 1822 on 'the efficacy of the Criminal Laws', which explicitly connected the amelioration of capital punishment, the strengthening of the police, and the reform of secondary punishments. He continued to press the government towards reform, in 1823 proposing nine resolutions to abate the rigour of the criminal laws. These resolutions were not passed, but the Home Secretary, Sir Robert Peel, admitted the necessity for reform of the criminal law, and said the real question between him and Mackintosh 'was only as to degree'.[27] James Scarlett recognised the significance of Peel's commitment to reform, which he welcomed in these terms:[28]

> He [Scarlett] rejoiced that the day had at length arrived when those principles which his late lamented friend, sir Samuel Romilly, had long endeavoured to introduce met with the general concurrence of the government. His majesty's minister had confessed himself a convert to the opinion, that severity of punishment was not the most expedient method of repressing crimes; that punishment ought to be consonant to the feelings and sympathies of mankind; and that those feelings ought to be enlisted on the side of the administration of justice.

Romilly's name, reputation and penal logic were regularly invoked in these debates, and in debates on the criminal law for many years to come. Mackintosh emphasised time after time the need to bring the criminal laws into harmony with public feeling, and the reluctance of prosecutors and witnesses to participate in the criminal process, and of juries to convict, as a result of the severe punishments.[29] The risk-taking psychology of the criminal and Romilly's metaphor of the criminal law as a lottery were reiterated.[30] The principle which Romilly so firmly drew from his perception of the criminal mind of the need for certainty in the criminal law was more subdued in his successors, but is unmistakably present.[31] The movement against capital punishment founded

[27] (1823) 9 P. D. 421. See also (1819) 39 P. D. 777 (1819 motion); *Report from the Select Committee appointed to consider so much of the Criminal Law as relates to Capital Punishments in Felonies* (1819) Parl. Papers VIII. 1: (1822) 7 P. D. 790 (1822 motion); and generally 1 Radzinowicz (1948–86) ch. 17.

[28] (1823) 9 P. D. 430–1.

[29] For example, (1819) 39 P. D. 784, 788–9, 794–5, 797–8; (1823) 9 P. D. 403–4; (1830) 24 P. D. 1034–5, 1038.

[30] For example, (1819) 39 P. D. 794, 820–1, 840; (1830) 24 P. D. 1054–56.

[31] For example, (1819) 39 P. D. 818–20; (1830) 24 P. D. 1057. Reformers tended to concentrate on establishing the ineffectiveness of severity, and so a need for reform, rather than the theoretical advantages of certainty.

on these premises threatened the felony counsel restriction, which Mackintosh spoke against as early as 1821, for two reasons.

First, capital punishment sustained many devices and discretions in other phases of the capital felony process, illogical in themselves but tolerated and defended because they saved lives. The severity of the law of capital larceny was mitigated, Blackstone pointed out, by benefit of clergy and the 'pious perjury' of jurors, although perjury was a peculiar quality to condone in an institution which, in Blackstone's view, sustained the liberties of England and must remain forever 'sacred and inviolate'.[32] The judge, it was said, was counsel for the prisoner, but this too crumbled into nonsense under analysis. Bentham asked why the law needed this aphorism for 'putting a pertinent question, bringing to light the innocence of the innocent, needs no apologies, no adages'. He saw the adage as a mask of virtue worn by judges while they assisted guilty prisoners to an acquittal.[33] The devices and discretions of the capital felony process turned jurors into perjurers, prisoners into clergymen, judges into counsel and allowed the guilty to walk free. Such absurdities flourished because, Bentham observed, the 'more barbarous the punishment, the less disposed is the public mind to scrutinize into the pretences by which here and there a victim is preserved from it'.[34]

Capital punishment sustained these absurd pretences, and they in turn made capital punishment acceptable. The pretences saved lives, and mercy, by regulating bloodshed, reconciled the country to harsh laws. The pretences freed criminals, and the prevalence of crime justified harsh laws. The pretences and the death penalty were 'consanguineous vices—vices that act in partnership, and play into one another's hands'.[35] The amelioration of capital punishment would expose the pretences, and the felony counsel restriction, which was closely associated with the maxim that the judge was 'counsel for the prisoner' and apparently arbitrary in its application to some crimes and not to others, would inevitably attract suspicion at this time.

Secondly, the felony counsel restriction was not in harmony with public feeling and certainty of punishment, and so was condemned by the new penal logic. The restriction on counsel in felony trials appeared unfair because it denied counsel where life was imperilled, while in civil actions and misdemeanor trials the entire defence could be conducted by a professional representative. The increasing role of counsel in the felony trial as the eighteenth and nineteenth centuries progressed aggravated this appearance of unfairness. Prosecution counsel had advantages of

[32] 4 Blackstone (1765–69) 239, 343–4. The oxymoron 'pious perjury' was a perversion of logic and constitutional theory.

[33] *The Rationale of Judicial Evidence* in 6 Bentham (1843) 349–51.

[34] *Ibid*, 349–51.

[35] *Ibid*, 351.

expertise and experience over an unrepresented prisoner, and a greater scope for their expertise and experience, through their address to the jury, over the prisoner with counsel. Severity of procedure, like severity of punishment, created sympathy for the prisoner, so that the felony counsel restriction led to undue restraint by counsel in the conduct of prosecutions, a leaning by the judge towards prisoners, and a reluctance of juries to convict for fear that something important had been left unsaid. It introduced uncertainty into the criminal trial which might enable prisoners to escape. It was an obstacle to the certainty of conviction required by the new penal logic.

After 1823 the initiative in the reform of the criminal law passed to Sir Robert Peel at the Home Office. Peel was a thorough though moderate reformer who accepted the new truths of the psychology of the criminal and the need for certainty.[36] He established a modern police force, increased the provision for the payment of prosecution expenses, simplified the definition of offences and the construction of indictments, abolished benefit of clergy and allowed judges to abstain from passing the death sentence when they intended to recommend mercy. He proceeded cautiously on capital punishment. His consolidation of criminal statutes abolished many obsolete and overlapping capital offences, and he repealed the death penalty for minor offences, including some capital larcenies.[37] These improvements placed a new emphasis on efficiency and functional integrity in the administration of the criminal law.

Efficiency and functional integrity would mean supplanting the amateur with the professional in the criminal process. In this respect it complemented the longer term expansion of the role of counsel in the criminal trial, discussed in Chapter 2. The transformation of the prisoner's speech from a personal statement into a professionally prepared argument, for example, and the discomfort with the judicial interrogation of prosecution witnesses signify an awareness of a proper field of expertise for counsel. The felony counsel restriction was an obstacle to the realisation of the professional trial, and was discredited by its association with the capital felony process. Only a rational justification, acceptable to the spirit of the times, could save it from repeal. The 16 years of debate over the felony counsel restriction are considered in the next chapter.

[36] See, for example, (1826) 14 P. D. 1233: 'the numerous class that speculates keenly on the advantages to be derived from crime, compared with the risk of its punishment, sees in every instance of undeserved impunity, a fresh encouragement to the adventure. They may, and probably they do, grossly miscalculate—but what is that very circumstance, but a great additional evil to society?...That law I apprehend to be most perfect, which most certainly ensures the conviction of the guilty man, and the acquittal of him who has been unjustly accused. But the acquittal of the innocent ought, in justice to innocence, to be upon the merits of the case'.

[37] On Peel's reforms see 1 Radzinowicz (1948–86) ch. 18.

4

Full Defence by Counsel

The years 1821 to 1837 saw a debate over the role of defence counsel in the criminal trial, culminating in the Trials for Felonies Act of 1836, usually called the Prisoners' Counsel Act, and a judicial Practice Memorandum of 1837.[1] These measures together implemented two changes in procedure. First, the felony counsel restriction was abolished, so that all prisoners became entitled to make a full defence by counsel; and secondly, prisoners acquired the right to inspect and demand copies of the depositions made by witnesses for the prosecution. There was no essential relationship between these two amendments which necessitated their simultaneous enactment. The principle of full defence by counsel had been often debated and twice accepted in the House of Commons when in 1836, as it again passed through the House, a select committee engrafted on to the bill clauses granting the prisoner access to the depositions.

Chapters 4 and 5 consider the enactment and the implementation of the Prisoners' Counsel Act. The first two sections of this chapter outline the course of the debate and introduce the Criminal Law Commissioners, who produced an important report on full defence by counsel in 1836. The third section considers the main argument of the reformers, which was that full defence by counsel was more conducive to the discovery of the truth than the existing procedure. The final section examines the contribution of the campaign for the amelioration of capital punishment to the success of the Prisoners' Counsel Act and, more generally, the Act's place in the transformation of the criminal law which occurred at this time.

Chapter 5 considers the effect on the form and implementation of the Act of fears of the abuse of advocacy which, it was argued, might impede the investigation of truth and undermine the authority of judge and jury. Defence access to the depositions was likely to aggravate these

[1] The Prisoners' Counsel Act (6 & 7 Will. 4, c. 114) and the Practice Memorandum are reproduced in Appendix 1.1 and 1.3 respectively.

dangers by arming counsel with foreknowledge of the prosecution case and a documentary basis for the cross-examination of prosecution witnesses. The initially distinct proposals relating to defence by counsel and the depositions thus became linked by a fear of the power of advocacy. This fear did not defeat either proposal, but explains the deletion by the House of Lords of a clause in the Act guaranteeing the prisoner's counsel the last word to the jury, and important restrictions in the 1837 Memorandum on the use of the depositions by defence counsel.[2]

The Prisoners' Counsel Act Debate

The Prisoners' Counsel Act debate occurred in two phases; the first from 1821 to 1828, and the second from 1833 to 1837.[3] The first phase began with the introduction of the Capital Crimes' Defence Bill of 1821. This bill seems to have been a personal initiative of its proposer, Richard Martin, whose short reported speech suggests specific instances of injustices to prisoners for want of counsel inspired the measure. Sir James Mackintosh spoke in favour of the bill, and over the next five years many other leading lawyers in the House of Commons added their voices to the call for change.[4] Thomas Denman helped to prepare and bring in Martin's 1823 bill and supported the proposals of subsequent years,[5] Stephen Lushington appeared in the ranks of reformers in 1824, and during the 1826 debate James Scarlett and Henry Brougham announced their conversions to the principle of full defence by counsel. Nevertheless, full defence by counsel could not gather sufficient votes to pass the House of Commons, and was decisively defeated in major debates in 1824 and 1826.

The opposition to full defence by counsel in the first phase was led by

[2] The enactment of the Prisoners' Counsel Act has received little scholarly attention and its implementation no more than the occasional passing reference, so that Chapters 4 and 5 rely almost exclusively on primary sources. Three recent articles which give some consideration to the Prisoners' Counsel Act debate are McGowen (1983); Beattie (1991); and the rudimentary Hostettler (1982) (reproduced with some amendments as chapter 4 of Hostettler (1992)).

[3] Cf. Beattie (1991) 250.

[4] (1821) 4 P. D. 1512 (Martin) and 1513–14 (Mackintosh). In the first phase of the debate full defence by counsel was raised in the House of Commons seven times in eight years without success. There are three reported debates in the *Parliamentary Debates* during this phase, in (1821) 4 P. D. 1512, (1824) 11 P. D. 180 and (1826) 15 P. D. 589.

[5] Thomas Denman (1779–1854) was called to the Bar in 1806 and first entered Parliament in 1818. He was Common Sergeant (a City of London judge at the Old Bailey) from 1822 to 1830, when he became Attorney-General in the new Whig administration. He was Lord Chief Justice from 1832 until his retirement due to ill health in 1850. He was a close associate of Lord Brougham's in legal matters from the time they appeared together as counsel for Queen Caroline at her 'trial' in 1820.

Sir John Copley.[6] His cogent speeches in 1824 and 1826 reasoned from the premise that a trial was an 'investigation of truth'. He argued that the existing trial procedure was conducive to the discovery of the truth by ensuring a calm and dispassionate inquiry. 'Nothing could be conceived', he said, 'more impartial, cool, and considerate than proceedings in courts of criminal justice. There could be no course more entirely favourable to the development of the truth. The greatest order, no extraordinary excitement, temperate, candid inquiry, by parties almost wholly disinterested—these were the aspects which were presented in a criminal trial'.[7] He then contended full defence by counsel would change the character of the inquiry, and so impede the discovery of the truth. Defence counsel would make speeches 'full of inflammation and exaggeration', prosecution counsel would reply in kind, and 'the trial of truth would be converted into a war of wit, ingenuity and eloquence'.[8] Truth and the ingenuity and eloquence of counsel were, in Copley's view, incompatible in the criminal trial.

Supporters of full defence by counsel readily accepted that the trial was an investigation of the truth. They joined issue with Copley on the ingenuity and eloquence of counsel, which they saw as conducive to the discovery of the truth by ensuring a thorough discussion of all the facts of the case. The relationship between truth and advocacy thus emerged as the major issue in the Prisoners' Counsel Act debate.

Copley's speeches raised two subsidiary questions which were to trouble the supporters of full defence by counsel throughout the debate. Firstly there was the question of which counsel would be entitled to the last word to the jury. Copley drew attention to 'the extreme value of having the last word, and of avoiding an able reply from the opposite side'. He referred to the tactical struggle for the last word in civil actions, which often interfered with the presentation of defence evidence, and so was 'a strong barrier to the discovery of truth'.[9] Secondly, there was the problem of the summing-up. The judge's summing-up would need to correct any incomplete, inaccurate or unbalanced statements in the speech of the prisoner's counsel, but such a summing-up might 'create, however unintentionally, an impression unfavourable to the prisoner in the minds of the jury'. This appearance of acting against the prisoner, in

[6] John Singleton Copley entered Parliament in 1818 after distinguishing himself as a defence counsel in the treason trial of Watson and Thistlewood in 1817. He rose rapidly, becoming Solicitor-General in 1819, and Attorney-General in 1824. He was raised to the peerage as Lord Lyndhurst in 1827, and served as Lord Chancellor in the Canning, Goderich and Wellington administrations from 1827 to 1830. He sat as Chief Baron of the Exchequer from 1831–34, and was again Lord Chancellor in Peel's 1834–35 and 1841–46 administrations. He spoke against full defence by counsel in the House of Commons in 1821, 1824 and 1826.

[7] (1824) 11 P. D. 206. See also (1826) 15 P. D. 598–9.

[8] (1824) 11 P. D. 207 and 208.

[9] (1824) 11 P. D. 207–8. See also (1826) 15 P. D. 600–1.

the summing up as in the judicial interrogation of prosecution witnesses discussed in Chapter 2, was of considerable concern to judges, most of whom opposed the Prisoners' Counsel Act.[10]

Full defence by counsel was much more favourably received in the second phase of the debate, passing the House of Commons in 1834, 1835 and 1836. It passed the House of Lords and became law in 1836, and then received an important judicial gloss in the Practice Memorandum of 1837. The passage of years—15 between the first Capital Crimes' Defence Bill and the enactment of the Prisoners' Counsel Act, eight between the rejection of full defence by counsel in the Commons in 1826 and its acceptance there in 1834—was kind to the cause of counsel. It saw a season of legislative stagnation—the long Tory winter of Liverpool and Eldon—give way firstly to the temperate improvements of Peel, and then after the 1830 General Election to the hospitable environment of a Whig administration committed to reform. These were the years that Dicey believed saw a shift in the predominant current of legislative opinion from the quiescence of reactionary Toryism to the new age of Benthamite individualism.[11]

The shifts in power and opinion in this period were reflected in the development of the Prisoners' Counsel Act debate. During the debate there was a visible loss of confidence in the immutable wisdom of the common law, in 'the paradoxical commonplace that English law was the perfection of human reason'.[12] Reformers respected this commonplace at the beginning of the debate, and felt obliged to praise the criminal law even as they tried to change it.[13] However, Peel's steps to rationalise the criminal law exposed the law's fallibility and gave credibility to change. George Lamb anticipated the brighter future of criminal law reform when opening the 1826 debate on full defence by counsel:[14]

> The time was gone by, however, when they were in the habit of looking upon the wisdom of their ancestors as something infallible: it had ceased to carry with it that cabalistic name which it formerly possessed...He [Lamb] was relieved, in this second time of bringing forward the present question, from being met by those panegyrics which they had heard so often upon their criminal proceedings, and by declarations of their being the very perfection of human wisdom; for they had at that moment before them a bill [the Criminal Justice Bill of 1826], which intimated, in pretty strong terms, that all the criminal laws were not thought

[10] For Copley's comments on the position of the judge see (1821) 4 P. D. 1513; (1824) 11 P. D. 206–7; (1826) 15 P. D. 601 (quotation in text). The attitude of the judges during the Prisoners' Counsel Act debate is discussed in Chapter 5.

[11] Dicey (1905) Lecture IV.

[12] The quotation is from Maine (1861) 78, cited in Dicey (1905) 167n.

[13] For example, see (1821) 4 P. D. 1513 (Mackintosh); (1824) 11 P. D. 198 and 200–1 (Mackintosh); and (1826) 15 P. D. 624 (Scarlett).

[14] (1826) 15 P. D. 591–2. The Criminal Justice Bill became the Criminal Laws Act 1826 (7 Geo. 4, c. 64).

entirely perfect. He looked at that bill with still greater satisfaction, because he considered it a precursor of still more extensive alterations.

As faith in the immutable wisdom of the law faded the assertiveness of supporters of full defence by counsel grew. By the beginning of the second phase of the debate the Commons was thoroughly acclimatised to the idea of reform, and the reformers sufficiently confident to explore the implications of full defence by counsel and to experiment with subsidiary amendments. There were, for example, proposals relating to the number and order of counsel's speeches—invariably structured to give the prisoner's counsel the last word—and the assignment of counsel without fee to undefended prisoners, the defence of prisoners in inferior courts, and finally, in 1836, defence access to the depositions. The opposition in the Commons during the second phase was further weakened by the absence of any leader of the stature of Copley in the earlier debates.

The passage of time also favoured full defence by counsel by introducing new blood into the Commons committed to this principle, and by pushing its established supporters into positions of judicial and political influence. The most important new members were William Ewart, the promoter of the Prisoners' Counsel Bill in the debate's second phase, and John Campbell and Frederick Pollock, both of whom quickly rose to the Attorney-Generalship.[15] The election of the Grey administration made Brougham Lord Chancellor, in 1832 Denman became Chief Justice of King's Bench, and in 1834 Scarlett, *facile princeps* of the Bar, was made Chief Baron of the Exchequer and received a peerage in the title of Lord Abinger. Finally, the passage of time won over to full defence by counsel its most articulate opponent. Sir John Copley, now Lord Lyndhurst and a commanding figure in the House of Lords, piloted the Prisoners' Counsel Bill through the Lords in 1836. He explained that further reflection, his experiences at the Bar and as a common law judge, and 'the progress of opinion upon this subject' had led him to reappraise full defence by counsel and support the measure.[16] Some contemporaries accused him of a cynical lack of principle, but there seems little reason to doubt the sincerity of his change of opinion.[17] He had previously expressed a

[15] Campbell was Solicitor-General 1832–34, and Attorney-General from April 1835, and Pollock was Attorney-General in Peel's short-lived administration of November 1834 to April 1835.

[16] (1836) 34 P. D. 764–5 (quotation at 764), 770–1; (1836) 35 P. D. 180. Lord Lyndhurst acquired experience as a judge in criminal cases as Chief Baron of the Exchequer from 1831 to 1834.

[17] For condemnation of Lord Lyndhurst's change of opinion see (1836) 35 P. D. 179 and 180–1 (Lord Radnor) and Charles Phillips to Lord Brougham, July 1836, *Brougham Papers* No 28, 446. Phillips wrote that Lord Lyndhurst 'intended from the beginning to burke the bill' by stripping the last word and depositions clauses—in Phillips' opinion the most useful clauses to prisoners—from full defence by counsel.

willingness to reconsider full defence by counsel,[18] and his speeches in its favour are as well-reasoned, and in some significant respects consistent with, his earlier statements. In particular, he adhered to his earlier views that the trial was an investigation of the truth, and that the best mode of discovering the truth was the principal issue in the debate, but now saw advocacy as conducive rather than inhibitive to the emergence of the truth.[19]

Notwithstanding its powerful advocates in both Houses of Parliament and the authority of a report of the Criminal Law Commissioners, the Prisoners' Counsel Bill almost failed to pass in 1836 when a bitter division appeared amongst its supporters over the subsidiary question of the last word. The promoters of the bill in the House of Commons considered that the full investigation of the truth, and fairness to the prisoner, required a clause in the Bill which guaranteed the prisoner's counsel the last word. This meant a departure from the established rules of speech order in civil trials, and also aggravated the other subsidiary problem of the summing-up by requiring the judge to sum up in every case immediately after the speech of the prisoner's counsel. Lords Lyndhurst and Abinger opposed the last word clause, and ensured the House of Lords deleted it from the Bill.[20] The Bill then returned to the House of Commons where its strongest supporters—including Ewart, Pollock and O'Connell—declared it preferable to retain the felony counsel restriction rather than implement full defence by counsel without a last word clause. They convinced the Commons to reject the Lords' amendment, and as the end of the session approached the deadlock over this clause threatened the entire Bill. It was only on the penultimate day of the session that the House of Commons relented, the view of the Lords prevailed, and the Prisoners' Counsel Act passed into law without a last word clause.

Another question which troubled the final stages of the Prisoners' Counsel Bill was the prisoner's right to the depositions. The rights to inspect and take copies of the depositions were added to the Prisoners' Counsel Bill by a select committee of the House of Commons in 1836, and passed the House of Lords in the face of strong opposition from Lord Abinger. The matter did not, however, end there for the following year the judges issued their Practice Memorandum on the Prisoners' Counsel Act which linked the use of the depositions to the last word to the jury in a manner highly prejudicial to the prisoner. The debate over the depositions and last word clauses and the Practice Memorandum of 1837 are considered in Chapter 5.

[18] (1824) 11 P. D. 208.

[19] (1836) 34 P. D. 763, 769 and 770. He also maintained his view, discussed *infra* p. 78–9, on the simplicity of most criminal cases.

[20] The last word clause passed by the House of Commons in 1836 and deleted by the House of Lords is set out in Appendix 1.2.

The Prisoners' Counsel Act came into force on 1 October 1836. Section 1 provided that 'all Persons tried for Felonies shall be admitted, after the Close of the Case for the Prosecution, to make full Answer and Defence thereto, by Counsel learned in the Law, or by Attorney in Courts where Attornies practise as Counsel'. Section 2 declared the right to counsel extended to all summary prosecutions before justices of the peace. Section 3 enacted that all persons 'held to bail or committed to Prison for any Offence against the Law shall be entitled to require and have, on Demand...Copies of the Examinations of the Witnesses respectively upon whose Depositions they have been so held to bail or committed to Prison, on Payment of a reasonable Sum'. Section 4 entitled all accused persons 'at the Time of their Trial' to inspect all depositions taken against them.[21]

The Criminal Law Commissioners

The most important single statement in the Prisoners' Counsel Act debate was the *Second Report* of the Criminal Law Commissioners.[22] It firmly endorsed full defence by counsel, first emphasising the necessity of counsel to ensure a thorough investigation of the truth, and then proceeding to reject the arguments against counsel. The use of royal commissions to facilitate legislation was a characteristic of nineteenth century law reform, and the *Second Report* is an excellent example of this process in action.

Lord Brougham established the Criminal Law Commission in 1833. It had the grand objective of driving the rationalisation of the criminal law beyond Peel's consolidating legislation to its ultimate conclusion of complete code. The five original Commissioners were instructed to digest 'into one Statute all the Statutes and Enactments touching Crimes, and the trial and punishment thereof, and...all the provisions of the common or unwritten law touching the same'. The Commissioners included only two recognised specialists in the criminal law, Thomas Starkie and William Wightman, with its other three members, Henry Bellenden Ker, Andrew Amos and John Austin, sharing an intellectual commitment to codification and involvement with Lord Brougham in other projects.[23]

The Commission was almost immediately imperilled by the political self destruction of Lord Brougham, which exposed the project to threats of a failure of political will and judicial hostility to codification. There

[21] The Prisoners' Counsel Act is reproduced in Appendix 1.1.

[22] *Second Report of His Majesty's Commissioners on Criminal Law* (1836) Parl. Papers XXXVI 183. A select committee of the House of Lords also heard evidence on full defence by counsel, but never prepared a report. The evidence heard before this committee was published as *Prisoners Defence Bill. Minutes of Evidence taken before the Select Committee of the House of Lords etc* (1836) Lords' Papers 119.

[23] **Thomas Starkie**: Starkie (1782–1849) was called to the bar in 1810 and joined the

were also internal pressures, with Austin doubting the Commission's capacity to achieve anything constructive and Wightman showing little interest in its work.[24] Only the extraordinary perseverance of Starkie and Ker enabled the Commission to survive until 1845. Their work, 'the most thorough theoretical examination the subject [of criminal law] has received at an official level before or since',[25] eventually amounted to nine reports and included draft codes of substantive criminal law and criminal procedure.[26] On Lord Brougham's fall from grace the Home Office quickly diverted the Commission from its original purpose to the compact topics of full defence by counsel, capital punishment and juve-

Northern Circuit. He was appointed Downing Professor of Law at the University of Cambridge in 1823, and became a County Court Judge in 1847. He was the author of a number of text books, most importantly the *Practical Treatise on the Law of Evidence* which appeared in 1824. His name appeared first in the Commission and his correspondence shows that he considered himself its chairman: see, for example, Starkie to Brougham, 21 July 1833 and 14 August 1842, and Starkie to the Lord Chancellor (Lord Lyndhurst) 8 May 1842, *Brougham Papers Nos. 46,010, 10,877* and *14,215*. **William Wightman**: William Wightman (1784–1863) was Junior Counsel to the Treasury and left the Commission on becoming a judge of the Court of Queen's Bench in 1841. **Henry Bellenden Ker**: Ker (1785–1871) was a leading conveyancer and an indefatigable servant of law reform. He produced an important report on partnership law in 1837, was involved with real property reform, and headed the Statute Law Commission from 1854 to 1859. His correspondence late in life with Lords Brougham, Lyndhurst and Cranworth was the subject of the Selden Society annual lecture in 1955: see Carr (1955). A substantial collection of his letters, many discussing the affairs of the Criminal Law Commission, are preserved amongst the *Brougham Papers*. **Andrew Amos**: Amos (1791–1860) was Professor of English Law at University College London. He left the Commission in 1837 on his appointment to the Council of India, but served as a member of the second Criminal Law Commission from 1845 to 1849. **John Austin**: Austin (1790–1859) was admitted to the bar in 1818 and practised as an equity draftsman and member of the Norfolk Circuit before taking up an appointment as Professor of Jurisprudence at University College London. He delivered his *Lectures on Jurisprudence* between 1829 and 1832, although they were not published, and Austin's fame as a jurist established, until after his death. On the work of the Criminal Law Commission see also Cornish and Clark (1989) 598–601; Cross (1978); Lobban (1991) ch. 7; and 4 Radzinowicz (1948–86) 310–11.

[24] Ker later recalled that Wightman 'did little or nothing' and that he eventually complained to the Home Office about Wightman's lack of assistance: Ker to Brougham 'Monday', *Brougham Papers, No. 11,681* (filed under 1850). On Austin's unhappiness with the Commission see 1 Austin (1879) 11 (preface by Sarah Austin), and 'John Austin' (1860) *Law Magazine & Review*. Austin resigned from the Commission in 1836 and was replaced by another barrister, David Jardine.

[25] Cross (1978) 8.

[26] The Commission produced eight sequentially numbered reports on the criminal law and one report on statute law generally. The *Report of the Commissioners Appointed to Inquire into the Consolidation of the Statute Law* (1835) Parl. Papers XXXV 365, often overlooked by historians discussing the work of the Commission, appeared in 1835 between the *First* and *Second Reports*. **Ker and Starkie**: Ker had a sharp and irascible nature and considered Starkie obstinate, tiresome and disorganised. He was also generous in his praise of Starkie's hard work and ability; for example: 'I look forward to an awful year with Starkie...Desultory & wayward & never finishing anything. Writing the middle, the end & the beginning on scraps of paper and then muddling this M.S.S. into a crumpled heap in his breeches pocket, at the end of the month he brings out this mass to be digested. Patience. He is very learned, and very acute': Ker to Brougham, 'Sunday', 1843, and see also 'Wednesday 5th' 1843 and 'Monday' (filed under 1850), *Brougham Papers, Nos. 11,617, 11,613* and *11,681* respectively.

nile offenders, and directed that it confine its work on codification to statute law and leave the common law untouched. Ker responded to this belittling of the Commission by seeking to publicise its work and searching for new political allies. In November 1835 he told Lord Brougham that he hoped by the next meeting of Parliament the Commission could produce 'a good *General* report' that 'will get us friends amongst the Criminal law reformers'.[27] The next report was the *Second Report* that separately considered the topics of full defence by counsel and capital punishment. It was a more comprehensive and in some ways more theoretical statement than the parliamentary speeches in favour of full defence by counsel, revealing more clearly the ideological kinship of full defence by counsel with the new penal logic of the campaign against capital punishment.

It was also a partisan statement, from start to finish an argument for full defence by counsel, extolling the advantages of advocacy in the investigation of the truth and making no attempt to state or evaluate the merits of the felony counsel restriction.[28] The indications that the Criminal Law Commissioners set out to confirm a predetermined opinion include the identity of the witnesses they chose to hear, the questions they asked, their use of the evidence, and the timing of the release of the *Second Report*. The majority of the evidence came from committed advocates of full defence by counsel, and included lengthy examinations of Ewart and Pollock. The judges, most of whom were known to oppose full defence by counsel, were not consulted. The Commissioners' questioning often led the witnesses, who for their part were usually willing to be led, to conclusions supporting full defence by counsel.[29] The report often made direct reference to the evidence, but only to evidence in favour of full defence by counsel. Finally, the report conveniently appeared in June 1836 immediately before the debate on the Prisoners' Counsel Bill in the House of Lords. In fact Lords Lyndhurst and Denman ensured the postponement of the second reading of the Bill in the Lords to enable the report to be printed and read. Lord Lyndhurst called it

[27] Ker to Brougham, 25 November 1835, *Brougham Papers No. 10,190* (emphasis original).

[28] The *Second Report* can properly be considered an attempt to influence legislative opinion through *suscitation*. Suscitation is a term coined by S. E. Finer to describe the manipulation of the reports of select committees and royal commissions by Benthamite reformers by means such as controlling the membership of the inquiry, carefully preselecting the witnesses, and suppressing in their reports evidence unfavourable to the recommendations they wish to make. The advantages of suscitation were that the reformers' view 'received an *official* status' and their supporters were able to put their views publicly as part of the evidence: see Finer (1972) 19–27 (quotation at 19, emphasis original).

[29] See, for example, the evidence referred to on p. 9 of the *Second Report*. The evidence is reproduced in full in the appendices of the report.

'most elaborate and learned' and he and Lord Denman made a number of references to it in subsequent debate.[30]

Truth and Adversarialism

'[I]t will hardly, we think, be disputed', wrote the Criminal Law Commissioners, 'that the permitting the advocate to speak for the client tends, generally, to the discovery of truth and the consequent advancement of justice, since the practice has obtained in every civilized age and country'. This appeal to the practice of every civilised society was followed by an appeal to every individual's experience. 'The principles of legal investigation ought not to differ from those suggested by every man's experience in the ordinary transactions of life...Such experience would seem to require that some statement and explanation should accompany the proof of the facts in dispute'. Without such a statement or explanation 'the truth may not suggest itself to the inquirer'. The statement or explanation must be heard in an effective and not illusory manner, which in most cases required a professional advocate. 'That an accused but innocent person should, generally speaking, be as well able to state his case...as a skillful advocate, is a position which it would be difficult to support *a priori*, and which is, we believe, at variance with experience'. In this pragmatic fashion the Criminal Law Commissioners began their justification of full defence by counsel in their *Second Report*. The bonds uniting truth and the advocate were civilisation and experience.[31]

The Commissioners also used civilisation as a moral standard to pass judgement on the history of the felony counsel restriction. The felony counsel restriction was 'a relic' of 'the numerous and oppressive disabilities' to which prisoners were subjected in former times, and was not 'a regulation advisedly contrived in a free and enlightened age'. It was a distinction derived from 'a remote and illiterate age'.[32] Similar thinking appears in many of the speeches in Parliament in support of full defence by counsel. Sir James Mackintosh, for example, endorsed the praise of other speakers for the criminal law, but, he said, 'it had not always been what it was at present. It had stains resulting from the practices of barbarous times, which, one by one, had been gradually washed away'. The felony counsel restriction was

[30] See (1836) 34 P. D. 762, 763, and 775–6 and (1836) 35 P. D. 180–1. There are errors in the *Parliamentary Debates* accounts of the latter two references. The reference to 'Lords' Committee' at (1836) 34 P. D. 775 should be to the Criminal Law Commissioners, before whom Pollock, Harmer and Wilde gave evidence, and stand in contra-distinction to 'Lordships' Committee' on 776. The reference to 'Committee' at (1836) 35 P. D. 181 is clearly an error for 'Commission'.

[31] *Second Report* (*supra* n. 22) at 2.

[32] *Ibid*, 6n., 11n. and 11–12.

'now the only great remaining blot'.[33] The progress of the criminal law from barbarity to civilisation demanded the abolition of the felony counsel restriction.

The Commissioners used this view of the historical development of the criminal trial to condemn the argument that the prisoner did not require counsel because the proof of the crime should be so clear and manifest as to exclude the possibility of a defence. The Commissioners ridiculed this 'strange and unreasonable' argument, 'obviously false with reference to modern times, and would in any age appear absurd if it were not explicable by the ancient history of the Law of England'.[34] In fact, the 'clear and manifest proof' argument was not ancient history, but a post-medieval rationalisation of the felony counsel restriction which first appeared in Coke's *Third Institute*.[35] The Commissioners misdescribed and dismissed this rationalisation of the felony counsel restriction as an absurdity, but it deserved closer attention. It was based upon a perception of facts which left no place for advocacy in the criminal trial, and which the Commissioners and other supporters of full defence by counsel significantly did not share.

The 'clear and manifest proof' argument assumed that evidence was readily comprehensible by the jury. The witnesses needed only to state the facts within their knowledge and the jury would understand the truth of the events. 'It is called...evidence', said a seventeenth century lawyer, '*because it is evident;* it is one reason why prisoners for their lives are not allowed counsel for matters of fact, because the evidence is, and ought to be, so clear and plain that every one should be satisfied, both jury and standers-by'.[36] The jury at this time was likely to contain experienced jurors, would be firmly guided by the judge, and its verdicts, of course, had to be unanimous. Facts were a simple phenomenon, entrustable to such a jury, and there was no need either for counsel or a developed law of evidence.[37]

The prisoner's defence was also treated as a simple factual explanation. The prisoner was as capable of speaking to facts as a witness, and his defence was as readily intelligible to the jury as the testimony of a witness. This view of the prisoner's defence as a factual statement, which required professional expertise neither to be made nor to be understood, appears in the often quoted justification of the felony counsel restriction of Serjeant Hawkins:[38]

[33] (1824) 11 P. D. 200–1. [34] *Second Report* (*supra* n. 22) at 11.

[35] See *supra* p. 28 for Coke's statement, from which the expression 'clear and manifest' is taken.

[36] per John Cook (Solicitor-General and a judge in Ireland during the Commonwealth), *The Trial of John Cook* (1660) 5 State Trials (1809–26) 1093–4 (emphasis added).

[37] On jury composition and control see Langbein (1978) 273–7 and 284–300 and Beattie (1986) 378–95, and on the law of evidence in seventeenth century trials Langbein (1978) 300–6.

[38] Hawkins (1724) book 2, ch. 39, s. 2.

generally every one of common understanding may as properly speak to a matter of fact as if he were the best lawyer, and that it requires no manner of skill to make a plain and honest defence, which in cases of this kind is always the best; the simplicity, the innocence, the artless and ingenuous behaviour of one whose conscience acquits him, having something in it more moving and convincing than the highest eloquence of persons speaking in a cause not their own...Whereas, on the other side, the very speech, gesture, countenance and manners of defence of those who are guilty, when they speak for themselves, may often help to disclose the truth, which probably would not so well be discovered from the artificial defence of others speaking for them.

The jury only needed to hear the witnesses' evidence and the prisoner's explanation, observe their behaviour in court, and listen to the judge's guidance in order to discover the truth. Counsel could not add any new facts to this process of discovery; indeed their speeches, questions and objections might conceal or confuse the truth.[39]

This equation between the 'plain facts' and the emergence of the truth continued into the era of the Prisoners' Counsel Act debate. It animates the duty of prosecution counsel restraint, discussed in Chapter 2, which restricted prosecution counsel in his opening address to a bare narrative of the facts. It appears in Copley's important speeches in 1824 and 1826 in opposition to full defence by counsel. Facts to Copley radiated truth, and one purpose of trial procedure was to ensure that there were no obstacles between the jury and the light. He praised the existing procedure for its order, absence of extraordinary excitement, its coolness, collectedness, and its spirit of temperate candid inquiry, which protected the jury from obstruction in their contemplation of the facts.[40] The existing procedure enabled the evidence to 'be fairly taken down on both sides', ensured 'no obstruction be offered on the part of either counsel' and left 'the jury, upon a calm consideration of the facts of the case, to deliver their verdict'.[41] The relationship between the facts and the truth was so straightforward that defence counsel, if allowed to speak, would have nothing to say. The speech by prosecution counsel, which 'addressed itself merely to facts', meant that any subsequent speech 'for the defence would be a mere repetition of that which was already known'.[42]

[39] The 'plain facts' view was a premise of the aphorism that the judge was counsel for the prisoner. If facts were plain then the judge could discover any possible defence from the evidence, the prisoner's statement, and his own questioning during the trial, and did not require any greater or private communication with his 'client'. The aphorism assumed, Horace Twiss pointed out, that 'the evidence would come out passage by passage, and the Judge would have nothing to do but decide on its application, and then, without any contest, there would be an end of the matter': (1835) 28 P. D. 629.

[40] (1824) 11 P. D. 206; (1826) 15 P. D. 598 and also 599 (where Copley relates 'the truth' to the 'plain facts').

[41] (1826) 15 P. D. 601.

[42] (1826) 15 P. D. 599. 'Those who opposed the prisoner's [sic] counsel bills argued that facts were facts and did not need much elucidation': Beattie (1991) 254.

The Criminal Law Commissioners in the extract quoted at the beginning of this section used the figure of *everyman* to introduce and lend authority to a very different perception of facts. They thought that every man's experience required some statement or explanation to accompany the proof of the facts in dispute and that the prisoner could not make this statement as well as a skillful advocate. The Commissioners saw facts as a complex and sometimes misleading phenomenon, which required the explanation or interpretation of counsel to yield up their meaning. The jury, they believed, had to gaze through a filter of professional expertise to see the truth in the facts.

The possibility that in *some* cases the facts might be too complex for the jury to comprehend without the assistance of counsel was sufficient justification for full defence by counsel for some of its supporters. Lord Lyndhurst, for example, supporting full defence by counsel during the second phase of the debate, maintained his earlier view that the facts of criminal cases were usually plain and simple. 'In nine cases out of ten', he said, 'it was of no consequence whether counsel had the privilege or not [to address the jury]. The facts would be so clear that it would be quite unnecessary to make any observations on one side or the other'. But, he continued, there were some cases of the utmost importance where counsel should have the opportunity of making observations on the evidence[43] A similar view was expressed by James Scarlett in 1826:[44]

> The circumstance of a man being brought to trial, almost always amounted to a certainty of his guilt, and where the case against him was clearly proved, the counsel would have little more to do than to point out the circumstances which made for him...He [Scarlett] thought the cases were few, in which counsel could be of important benefit to the prisoner; but in such cases they were of great importance.

The *Second Report* and the parliamentary speeches in favour of full defence by counsel identify four complex fact situations where prisoner, judge and jury required the assistance of counsel. First, and most importantly, there were cases of circumstantial evidence. Prosecution counsel were more likely to make an opening speech in cases of circumstantial evidence, to enable the jury to understand the evidence to follow, and reformers argued a speech by counsel was equally necessary to make the defence intelligible. The unskilled prisoner was not competent to respond to a prosecution based on circumstantial evidence, 'to point out its inconsistencies, to unravel the web, to avail himself of doubts, and to convince the jury of his innocence'.[45] Circumstantial evidence, Lord Lyndhurst

[43] (1836) 34 P. D. 769 (cf. (1821) 4 P. D. 1513). He referred to cases of circumstantial evidence, discussed *infra*, as an instance of the class of cases requiring counsel.
[44] (1826) 15 P. D. 623. See also *Second Report* (*supra* n. 22) at 14.
[45] (1824) 11 P. D. 210 (Dr. Lushington, discussing the trial of *Patch*).

said, was 'a labyrinth to a person who had not known anything of the case before' and so the guidance of counsel, who knew the case through previous communication with the prisoner's attorney, was of infinite importance to the judge and jury.[46] 'It was in cases founded on circumstantial evidence', said James Scarlett, 'that he thought counsel for the prisoners were most required. He had himself often seen persons whom he thought innocent, convicted, and the guilty escape, for want of some acute and intelligent counsel to shew the bearings of the different circumstances on the conduct and situation of the prisoner'.[47]

If circumstantial evidence could not be understood without the assistance of counsel, it followed that prosecution counsel, as well as the prisoner's counsel, must be free to comment on the evidence. Such comment was, however, at this time prohibited by the duty of prosecution counsel restraint. The Criminal Law Commissioners had no doubt that the duty of prosecution counsel restraint impeded the investigation of the truth:[48]

> We think that even the present restrictions on the speeches of Counsel for the prosecution are very injurious to the interests of justice; inasmuch as they frequently occasion the acquittal of guilty persons, in consequence of the evidence for the prosecution not being thoroughly understood by Juries, and the legitimate inferences to be drawn from that evidence not being presented to the minds of the Jury, or, at least, not being adequately impressed upon them.

The problem of the escape of the guilty in cases of circumstantial evidence was raised in Parliament following the trial of James Evans. Evans was tried at the Lancaster Spring Assizes of 1826 for the murder of his employer, who had been found dead with serious head wounds in his burning warehouse. There was no direct evidence against Evans, and the prosecution primarily relied upon circumstances of opportunity, suspicious behaviour and some spots of blood on his clothing. James Scarlett, the leader of the Northern Circuit, was prosecution counsel, and his opening clearly exceeded the limits of the duty of restraint in commenting on the evidence and anticipating defences of accidental death and murder by persons unknown. He was interrupted at one point by the judge and told to confine himself to the facts. Subsequently, Evans and his counsel made a vigorous defence, Mr. Justice Bayley summed up in his favour, and the jury acquitted him without retiring from the courtroom.[49]

[46] (1836) 34 P. D. 770. See also at 770 (Denman).
[47] (1826) 15 P. D. 623. On circumstantial evidence see also Beattie (1991) 254–5.
[48] *Second Report* (*supra* n. 22) at 16.
[49] The best newspaper report of the prosecution case in *Evans* is *The Manchester Guardian and British Volunteer*, Saturday 18 March 1826. For other accounts of the trial see *The Times*, Monday 20 March 1826, and *The Leeds Mercury*, Saturday 25 March 1826.

Evans was raised in the House of Commons debate on full defence by counsel the following month by John Williams, another member of the Northern Circuit, to illustrate the threat to the prisoner from prosecution eloquence. Sir Robert Peel turned the example to vindicate the status quo. He pointed to the intervention of the judge on the prisoner's behalf, and also asked rhetorically whether, if defence counsel had been permitted a speech to the jury, Evans would have survived Scarlett's reply to this speech. Scarlett himself answered this question, by intimating that the felony counsel restriction had saved Evans' life:[50]

> The inhabitants [of Manchester, where the murder occurred] came to him [Scarlett] with a very modest request to present a statement of the facts to the judge, and to determine in what order the witnesses should be called. His intention was, to have stated the facts on both sides, and to have compared them together, so as to shew on which side the balance inclined, but he was prevented by the judge. The consequence was, that the prisoner was acquitted, whether right or wrong he [Scarlett] would not say; but if he had been tried in the ordinary way, he would not have escaped.

The skills of counsel were essential to unravel the thread of truth from circumstantial evidence. The felony counsel restriction and the duty of prosecution counsel restraint impeded the exercise of forensic skill, so in the interests of truth had to be abolished.

There were three other causes of factual complexity referred to in the debate. First there was the credibility of witnesses. The 'plain facts' view of truth assumed honest witnesses of accurate memory, or at least that witnesses could be brought to the truth by the questioning of the judge or counsel. The 'complex facts' view emphasised that truth sometimes had to be found amongst conflicting, misleading and incomplete accounts of events, and from corrupt, foolish, confused or reluctant witnesses. Cross-examination tested the credibility of evidence, but a speech from counsel was necessary to bring its significance home to the jury. Examples of the conviction of innocent prisoners on perjured evidence added weight to this argument.[51] Secondly cases involving the 'haze and shadow' of mixed questions of fact and law, such as the state of mind separating murder from manslaughter, required counsel to explain the prisoner's defence to the jury.[52] The final example of factual

[50] (1826) 15 P. D. 604 (Williams), 607 (Peel) and 623 (Scarlett). The practice of the Northern Circuit in respect of opening speeches is referred to by Brougham in the same debate at 627–8. The sense of the quotation from Scarlett's speech has been somewhat muddled by the convention of the *Parliamentary Debates* of transferring speeches from the first to the third person.

[51] *Second Report* (*supra* n. 22) at 4; (1824) 11 P. D. 217–18 (Denman); (1834) 24 P. D. 165–66 (O'Connell) and 169 (Pollock). On the difficulties of extracting the truth by cross-examination alone see (1835) 28 P. D. 870 (Lushington) and 871–2 (Sjt. Talfourd).

[52] (1826) 15 P. D. 611–12 (Twiss); (1824) 11 P. D. 218 (Denman); (1835) 28 P. D. 868 (Buller).

complexity requiring the skills of counsel was trials of multiple accused, where to reach true verdicts the jury had to keep separate the proofs against each accused, and perhaps disentangle wholly inconsistent defences. The judge in these cases, Horace Twiss argued, could not adequately explain to the jury the proof and defence relating to each prisoner 'although the Counsel for each might do it'.[53]

After declaring that the practice of 'every civilised age and country' showed full defence by counsel was conducive to the discovery of the truth the Criminal Law Commissioners added that the practice was 'adopted by our own law in all judicial proceedings excepting trials for Felonies'.[54] The felony counsel restriction was not only barbarous, but was an anomaly within the common law. This argument was pressed by supporters of full defence by counsel throughout the debate, drawing upon a long history of criticism of the felony counsel restriction by rhetorical comparison with the practice in civil trials. As early as the seventeenth century Judge Jeffries had asked why a man should have counsel for a twopenny trespass but not 'if he steal, commit murder, or felony, nay, high treason, where life, estate, honour and all are concerned', and Sir Bartholomew Shower had asked what rule of justice could warrant the denial of counsel 'when in a civil case of a halfpenny cake' a man may plead by counsel.[55] In the Prisoners' Counsel Act debate James Scarlett saw the civil analogy as an unanswerable argument in favour of counsel. The investigation of truth was the objective of civil and criminal trials, he reasoned in 1826, 'and, if the practice and the results were good in the one, they must also be good in the other. There could be no distinction made between the two'.[56]

The reverence of defenders of the felony counsel restriction for the perfection of the common law created some difficulties for them in responding to this argument. They could not, without embarrassment, condemn the role of counsel in civil trials, or suggest that fact finding was flawed in civil cases, and so had to argue that civil and criminal trials were not comparable. Counsel might be conducive to the discovery of the truth in civil cases, but in criminal cases the different nature of the facts, the prosecutor's character as 'a minister of public justice', and the absence of appeals meant a limited role for counsel was most conducive to the truth.[57]

[53] (1835) 28 P. D. 631–2 (Twiss); (1836) 34 P. D. 769 (Lyndhurst).

[54] *Second Report* (*supra* n. 22) at 2.

[55] *The Trial of Thomas Rosewell* (1684) 10 State Trials (1809–26) 267 (Jeffries); *Second Report* (*supra* n. 22) at 8 (Shower).

[56] (1826) 15 P. D. 622–3 (Tindal); and see also (1836) 35 P. D. 182–3.

[57] (1826) 15 P. D. 620. Tindal had a 'plain facts' view of the criminal trial. 'A question of civil right', he said, 'might be surrounded with the most intricate and difficult points of law; while the simple issue, whether a man did or did not break into a house, was a plain matter of fact, and could be best elucidated and determined by the production of evidence'.

Some supporters of the principle of full defence by counsel also developed misgivings about the civil analogy when discussion moved to the practicalities of the principle's introduction. If civil litigation were the model for the discovery of the truth then prosecution counsel, like the plaintiff's counsel, should be free from any duty of restraint and must have a right of reply, and both counsel must struggle to the best of their abilities for the verdict. The right of reply was of grave concern to some defenders of full defence by counsel for the last word was highly valued in civil actions, and defence counsel often chose to call no evidence to deprive the plaintiff of the reply. A procedure that might compel the defence to withhold evidence, they thought, was not conducive to the discovery of the truth. The civil litigation analogy now divided supporters of full defence by counsel into those who insisted on the introduction of civil practice into criminal trials, and those who wished to legislate a last word clause which would guarantee the prisoner's counsel the final speech.

Advocates of the last word clause sought to escape the civil litigation analogy, but could not condemn the role of counsel in civil trials or suggest civil procedure was flawed without endangering the principle of full defence by counsel. They were driven, not without irony, to adopt the same arguments as opponents of full defence by counsel and point to the differences between a plaintiff and a prosecutor:[58]

> There was a very great difference between allowing Counsel for a plaintiff in a civil case to reply, and allowing a prosecutor's Counsel to reply. The plaintiff had an interest at stake; and if the defendant called witnesses, the plaintiff must be allowed to reply upon this evidence; but the King had no interest in making out the guilt of his subjects; and therefore he said, give the accused the last word.

The House of Lords, however, refused to accept a last word clause. The opposition was led by James Scarlett, now Lord Abinger, who insisted 'that criminal charges should be put on the same footing as civil charges'. Abinger elevated the civil analogy from one argument in the ranks of many in favour of counsel to an authority which decreed the shape of criminal trials. The enactment of the Prisoners' Counsel Act without the last word clause confirmed the authority of the analogy.[59]

The civil analogy encouraged a conceptualisation of the criminal trial as a private contest between prosecutor and prisoner. Resistance to the civil analogy, on the other hand, drew upon the royal or public element of the prosecution by indictment. The prosecution on this view was motivated by public responsibility and not individual feeling, and neither Crown nor accused sought a victory or suffered a defeat in the

[58] (1834) 24 P. D. 169 (Pollock).

[59] (1836) 35 P. D. 182 and 183. The civil analogy was not, of course, the only argument against the last word clause, but was used to powerful effect by Lord Abinger. The struggle over the last word clause is further discussed in Chapter 5.

verdict. The public and private elements in the prosecution of crimes in this way sustained conflicting visions of the trial.

Civilisation, experience, the civil analogy and complex facts established for reformers that full defence by counsel was conducive to the discovery of the truth. A speech would enable defence counsel to point out the improbabilities and inconsistencies of the prosecution case, to simplify their cross-examinations, to ensure the prisoner's case was fully argued, and to guide the judge and jury through labyrinthine evidence, and by such advocacy to ensure that criminal trials satisfied the norms of civil trials, civilisation and everyman's experience, and that complex facts were understood; all of which would contribute to the discovery of the truth. By such reasoning the many advantages claimed for counsel could all ultimately be justified by an improvement in the investigation of the truth. In similar fashion arguments against full defence by counsel were measured and dismissed by the standard of truth. The second half of the Criminal Law Commissioners' analysis, for example, considered and rejected 'certain evils...which, it has been contended, would render the speeches of Counsel positively mischievous'. The possibility that the speeches of defence counsel might deter victims from prosecuting was rejected as 'too remote and indefinite to be weighed against the sacrifice of any means conducive to the attainment of truth'; full defence by counsel could not be excluded from inferior courts because 'the power to be heard by Counsel is essential to the attainment of truth'; and the increased time and expense of trials with speeches could not 'be fairly placed in comparison with the mischief which would result from rejecting means essential to the discovery of truth'.[60] Truth was the supreme norm, which overpowered any defence of the felony counsel restriction.

Truth was initially claimed by the defenders of the felony counsel restriction. Sir John Copley argued effectively in the 1824 and 1826 debates that the felony counsel restriction favoured the development of the truth by ensuring a calm and dispassionate inquiry. The 'wit, ingenuity and eloquence' of counsel would distemper the inquiry and obstruct the investigation of the truth.[61] Reformers managed to belittle this argument as an over-fastidious concern with decorum, and to brush it aside with their own conception of the investigation of the truth. Sydney Smith in the *Edinburgh Review*, for example, replied to Copley in these terms:[62]

[60] *Second Report* (*supra* n. 22) at 12–17, quotations at 12, 13, 14 and 15 respectively.

[61] (1824) 11 P. D. 205 (quotation at 208); (1826) 15 P. D. 596.

[62] Smith (1826–27) 86–7. See also *Second Report* (*supra* n. 22) at 12–13. Alternatively reformers argued that Copley presented a 'utopian picture' of the decorum achieved by the felony counsel restriction. In reality, they said, it encouraged stratagems by defence counsel, such as insinuations in cross-examination and contrived legal objections to parade a point before the jury, which were detrimental to the investigation of the truth: see (1826) 15 P. D. 527 (Brougham) and 631–2 (Denman).

Whence comes it (we should like to ask Sir John Singleton Copley, who seems to dread so much the conflicts of talent in criminal cases) that a method of getting at truth which is found so serviceable in civil cases, should be so much objected to in criminal cases? Would you have all this wrangling and bickering, it is asked, and contentious eloquence, when the life of a man is concerned? Why not...Of what importance is a little disgust at professional tricks, if the solid advantage gained is a near approximation to truth? Can anything be more preposterous than this preference of taste to justice, and of solemnity to truth? What a eulogium of a trial to say 'I am by no means satisfied that the Jury were right in finding the prisoner guilty; but every thing was carried on with the utmost decorum. The verdict was wrong, but there was the most perfect propriety and order in the proceedings. The man will be unfairly hanged; but all was genteel!'

Reformers came to see the ingenuity and eloquence of counsel as essential to the discovery of the truth, and not as a matter requiring apology or justification. They admitted their opponents' claims that full defence by counsel would introduce forensic zeal, contentiousness and eloquence into the criminal trial, and the trial might take on some of the characteristics of a contest between counsel.[63] Zeal and eloquence were the exercise of the professional skill of counsel and so were to be encouraged. The clash of talent was the catalyst of truth, and so should be applauded:[64]

As to the excitement of passion and contention of Counsel for victory, which had been dwelt upon, it was from the contention of Counsel that truth was elicited for the judgment of the Judge and Jury in civil causes, and he thought that truth would equally result from the contention in criminal cases.

'It is the duty of the Advocate', said the Criminal Law Commissioners at the close of the debate, 'by the most strenuous exertion of his powers, to urge his own view of the case, and by force of argument to compel the Jury to adopt it'.[65] The zeal and eloquence of counsel was defensible, commendable and finally ethically responsible in criminal cases. The arguments for full defence by counsel thus came to sanction an aggressive adversarialism.

The long-term trend in the criminal trial was towards adversarialism and, as reformers were quick to point out, there was by the 1830s considerable contention in the felony trial. Counsel often vigorously contested points of law and procedure and, as discussed in Chapter 2, their aggression in cross-examination at the Old Bailey was a matter of concern.[66] The Prisoners' Counsel Act debate consummated this long-term

[63] (1824) 11 P. D. 203 (Mackintosh) and 215–16 (Denman); (1836) 35 P. D. 175 (Lyndhurst).

[64] (1834) 24 P. D. 168 (Grant).

[65] *Second Report* (*supra* n. 22) at 8.

[66] Thomas Denman, who was Common Serjeant (i.e. a City of London judge) in the 1820s, stressed the 'very considerable degree of warmth' from counsel in criminal trials at this time: see (1824) 11 P. D. 215 and (1826) 15 P. D. 631–2. On Old Bailey cross-examinations see Chapter 2.

trend towards adversarialism in two distinct ways. First, the Act expanded the scope for contention by introducing the speech of defence counsel and, where the prisoner called evidence, the prosecution reply. A third arena for forensic struggle, the jury address, had been added to the examination of witnesses and legal argument. Secondly, the debate rationalised courtroom contention as a means to discover the truth. The Criminal Law Commissioners did not use the expressions 'adversarialism' or 'adversary system' but they understood and advocated the idea of truth through forensic contention. This idea had enormous significance for the place and power of the barrister in the criminal process. The work of counsel has always had its detractors, and has often been derided, despised and made synonymous with the prostitution of truth to sophistry and chicane, and was denounced in this fashion, even by lawyers, during the Prisoners' Counsel Act debate. The wranglings of counsel could be freed from this disgrace, admired, and made a light of truth; seated, as it were, upon a rock—the gordian knot of paid advocacy not cut, but untied—all by a simple idea of adversarialism.

This enthusiasm for adversarialism had important implications for the judge. A corollary of the idea that the contention of counsel was the best means to uncover the truth was that a judge without the assistance of counsel was likely to fall into error, especially in complex cases. The judge had not communicated before the trial with the parties or had an opportunity to reflect on possible lines of defence, and so lacked the background knowledge necessary to examine witnesses or instruct the jury effectively. It 'is next to impossible', said the Criminal Law Commissioners, 'that the acutest mind should, on the mere hearing of a long detail of conflicting circumstances, and without the aid of comments from professional advocates intimately acquainted with all the facts, be able to state its various bearings with the requisite fullness and accuracy'.[67] Secondly, adversarialism demanded a sharp distinction between the duties of judge and counsel, which could not be mingled in any way. The judge could not adequately perform the functions of an advocate, and would betray his character as a judge if he attempted to do so. For this reason reformers savagely attacked the aphorism that the judge was counsel for the prisoner, with its implications of role-bending and indulgence to one party.[68] He had to be impartial between the parties, as in

[67] *Second Report* (*supra* n. 22) at 7. See also (1836) 34 P. D. 767 (Lyndhurst); (1836) 35 P. D. 186 (Cottenham L.C.). The Commissioners anticipated a degree of preparation by counsel ('intimately acquainted with all the facts') considerably in advance of normal assize practice at this time: see Chapter 2.

[68] The most sustained criticism is in the *Second Report* (*supra* n. 22) at 7–10. See also (1824) 11 P. D. 216 (Denman); (1826) 15 P. D. 610–11 and (1835) 28 P. D. 629–30 (both Twiss) and the references in the preceding note.

civil trials. Adversarialism envisaged a specialised role for the judge, controlling the contest between counsel and summing up its results for the jury. There was no longer any place for the activism and paternalism of the judge of the capital felony process.

The Transformation of the Criminal Process

Penal Reform and the Prisoners' Counsel Act

The campaign for the amelioration of capital punishment made a considerable contribution to the success of full defence by counsel. It created a climate of discussion and legislative activity which facilitated the acceptance of full defence by counsel. It gave full defence by counsel some influential supporters, notably Mackintosh, Ewart and Lushington, who were prominent in their advocacy of both causes. It also provided a powerful set of ideas which encouraged an expanded role for counsel. The nature of this ideological contribution to the Prisoners' Counsel Act debate is considered in the remainder of this chapter.

The first challenge to the felony counsel restriction was the Capital Crimes' Defence Bill of 1821, which proposed to allow counsel to prisoners accused of capital crimes while leaving the practice unchanged in respect of non-capital felonies. This linkage of the privilege of counsel to capital punishment reappeared from time to time during the debate, although after 1824 the issue was the retention or the complete repeal of the felony counsel restriction.[69] It gave the novel procedural reform of defence by counsel, a personal initiative of Richard Martin, a claim to the attention and perhaps the backing of opponents of the death penalty. The 1821 bill attracted the support of Mackintosh, who immediately introduced resonances of the concern of penal reformers with the prevention of crime by referring to the need to ensure the conviction of the guilty:[70]

> He did not seek this privilege [of counsel] to enable criminals to have a better chance of escaping; for their escape he thought the greatest slur upon the practice of the law. His object was, not that these should escape, but that the innocent should have a better protection. The utmost that could result from agreeing to this measure would be a greater number of guilty persons would be convicted, which must be regarded as a good and not as an evil.

[69] The 1822, 1823, and 1825 bills, which disappeared without reported debates were also limited to capital crimes. For later suggestions to restrict counsel to capital cases see (1835) 28 P. D. 870 and (1835) 29 P. D. 356 (both Eardley Wilmot) and *Second Report* (*supra* n. 22) at 18.

[70] (1821) 4 P. D. 1513–14.

This objective of the conviction of the guilty and the acquittal of the innocent was repeated throughout the debate. It was devoid of any sentimentality for the vulnerability of the prisoner. Like Romilly in the capital punishment debate, advocates of full defence by counsel did not expect concern for the prisoner to change the law, so built their case on the solid grounds of a closer approximation to truth and a promise of better results. There was a practical problem of categorisation, of the separation of wheat and chaff—the innocent had to be acquitted and the guilty must be convicted. Full defence by counsel, they argued, meant more efficient justice, and some, like Mackintosh in the above quotation, anticipated that it would increase the conviction rate. The objective was right verdicts, not prisoners' rights.[71]

The attainment of right verdicts required harmony between the criminal law and public feeling. Chapter 3 discussed the importance of this harmony in Romilly's penal thought, and a similar concern at the consequences of a lack of public confidence in the law appears in the Prisoners' Counsel Act debate. Spectators at felony trials, reformers argued, considered unfair a procedure which entitled the representative of only one party, and that the prosecutor, to address the jury, and they left the court not satisfied that justice had been done.[72] This impression, Brougham warned, might create a disturbing sympathy between public and prisoner, with the public always satisfied by an acquittal, even though the prisoner was guilty.[73] It might also create doubt. 'Did not', Dr Lushington said, 'impartial people, in such cases, always exclaim, "We have heard the speech on one side of the question; but who can tell what a counsel in his favour could have made out, if he had been permitted to speak?"'[74] If this sympathy and doubt affected the jury the result was likely to be too many acquittals.

In the campaign against capital punishment the presentation of petitions to Parliament was used, with great effect, to demonstrate public dissatisfaction with the law.[75] The same tactic was used in the 1824 debate on full defence by counsel to establish that jurors found the felony counsel restriction harsh and unreasonable. A petition presented

[71] See especially (1826) 15 P. D. 609 (Twiss, who uses the expression 'right verdicts'), 624 (Scarlett), 627 (Brougham), 632 (Denman); (1836) 35 P. D. 183 (Abinger, who refers to the efficiency of justice).

[72] (1826) 15 P. D. 595 (Lamb) and 626 (Brougham); (1824) 11 P. D. 209 (Lushington). The importance of the image of justice in the Prisoners' Counsel Act debate and the campaign against capital punishment are examined by McGowen, who argues that the 'central feature of early nineteenth-century reforms of law and practice was the attempt to create an image of impersonal justice'. Punitive severity and the denial of counsel, which appeared unfair, stood in the way of this objective: see McGowen (1983), quotation at 124.

[73] *Ibid*. Cf. (1824) 11 P. D. 187–8 and 202, where Lamb and Mackintosh discuss the 'ill-founded sympathy' of the public for the 'guilty ruffian' Thurtell at his trial in 1824.

[74] (1824) 11 P. D. 209.

[75] See 1 Radzinowicz (1948–86) 512–13, 526–8, 591–3.

at the beginning of the debate from 'certain Jurymen' at the Old Bailey said:[76]

> the petitioners have found by experience, in the course of their attendances as Jurymen at the Old Bailey, that the opening statement for the prosecution too frequently leaves an impression more unfavourable to the prisoner at the bar than the evidence of itself could have produced; and it has always sounded harsh to the petitioners to hear it announced from the bench, that the counsel, to whom the prisoner has committed his defence, cannot be permitted to address the jury on his behalf, nor reply to the charges which have, or have not, been substantiated by the witnesses; the petitioners have felt their situation peculiarly painful and embarrassing when the prisoner's faculties, perhaps surprised by such an intimidation, are too much absorbed in the difficulties of his unhappy circumstances to admit of an effort towards his own justification against the statements of the prosecutor's counsel, often unintentionally aggravated through zeal or misconception.

The petitioners did not state whether their pain and embarrassment had induced them to disregard their oaths and deliver an untrue verdict. Nevertheless, the implication that this might occur was clear, and Dr. Lushington in the debate which followed referred to compassionate jurymen who delivered verdicts of acquittal 'well persuaded of the guilt of the prisoner'.[77]

Public dissatisfaction with the law and the escape of the guilty were prime concerns of the new penal logic of the campaign against capital punishment.[78] The prominence of the same concerns in the Prisoners' Counsel Act debate suggests reformers brought the same logic to their analysis of the proper role of counsel in the defence of prisoners. The shared logic is most obvious in the *Second Report* where the Commissioners examined, in separate sections, both full defence by counsel and the death penalty.[79] The second section, entitled *Punishments and Particularly that of Death*, accepts the truths of the new penal logic and resembles in its reasoning Romilly's 1810 speech discussed in Chapter 3. Like Romilly the Commissioners argued that mild and certain punishment was the key to the prevention of crime and supported this conclusion, as Romilly had done, with reference to the risk-taking psychology of criminals, to statistics showing the reluctance of juries to convict of

[76] (1824) 11 P. D. 180–1. [77] (1824) 11 P. D. 210–11. [78] See Chapter 3.

[79] The felony counsel restriction and severity of punishment sometimes appear as analogous evils in parliamentary debate; for example, by Henry Brougham in this passage: 'Then again, by this peculiarity [the felony counsel restriction], were they not adding to the undue chances of escape by the criminal? The laws against criminals were already too severe; and, from that circumstance, many criminals escaped altogether, who certainly deserved some punishment. In the same manner as the prisoner was placed on trial under great and evident disadvantage, there was often an undue leaning in his favour': (1826) 15 P. D. 627. See also 624 (Scarlett).

capital crimes, and by refuting Paley's defence of selective terror.[80] They also emphasised that the popular character of the criminal process made certainty dependent on a harmony between the law and public feeling. The Commissioners stated, in language which would be equally appropriate in their analysis of the felony counsel restriction, that the 'administration of a Law not in accordance with the opinions of society, and shocking their moral or religious sentiments, cannot but be precarious; and without supposing that they break deliberately the sacred obligation of their oath, we may presume that slight grounds will satisfy the conscience of Jurors in acquitting a party accused of infringing it'.[81]

The first section of the *Report*, on full defence by counsel, also drew attention to the popular character of the criminal process, and condemned the felony counsel restriction and capital punishment by the same test of public dissatisfaction with the law:[82]

> When it is considered that Criminal Justice in this country is administered principally through the medium of a popular tribunal, it will be at once perceived how exceedingly important it is, not merely that the administration of Criminal Justice should be moderate and just, but that it should appear to be such to those to whom, as Jurors, duties so important are confided. Experience fully proves, as might be easily anticipated, that the very apprehension lest a punishment disproportionate to the crime should be inflicted, frequently deters the injured from prosecuting and Jurors from convicting; and we may venture to assert, that the law which closes the lips of the Prisoner's Advocate in every case of Felony...appears to the generality of people to be harsh and unreasonable. Such a feeling is necessarily prejudicial to an inquiry which has truth only for its object; an additional temptation is thrown out to show undue favour to the Prisoner; and...this unjustly tends to the escape of the guilty.

The *Second Report* integrated the abolition of the felony counsel restriction and the amelioration of capital punishment within the same logic of reform. The second section of the *Report* accepted the need for certain punishment and its dependence on harmony between the measure of punishment and public feeling. The first section discussed the investigation of the truth in the trial phase and, in the above quotation, recognised that truth ultimately depended on a similar harmony. In a popular system of criminal justice the discovery of the truth, like certain punishment, required the cooperation of the public, especially jurors, and the denial of counsel, like severe punishment, jeopardised this cooperation.

80 *Second Report* (*supra* n. 22) at 19–36.

81 *Ibid*, 32. See also 27.

82 *Ibid*, 17. Note that the opening clause of this quotation ('When it is considered that Criminal Justice in this country is administered principally through the medium of a popular tribunal') is repeated verbatim to introduce the discussion of the need for harmony between public feeling and the measure of punishment in the second section of the *Report* (*ibid*, 27).

The promise of penal reformers of the better prevention of crime through mild and certain punishment could not be realised if public dissatisfaction with the earlier phases of the criminal process allowed felons to escape. For this reason the new penal logic of the capital punishment debate supported, indeed required, the abolition of the felony counsel restriction.

As a matter of logic, of course, the procedure which replaced the felony counsel restriction had to enjoy public approval. Public confidence in adversarialism was assumed rather than discussed by reformers. A practice which 'has obtained in every civilised age and country', and satisfies the principles of legal investigation 'suggested by every man's experience in the ordinary transactions of life' must have public approval.[83] The close connection between adversarialism, sanctioned by civilisation and individual experience, and the new penal logic is considered in the next section.

Penal Reform and Adversarialism

In the third chapter of his *Discipline and Punish* Foucault notices a lyrical insistence amongst penal reformers of the eighteenth century that punishment be humane 'without any definite meaning being given to this principle, which nevertheless is regarded as insuperable'. He describes in this chapter the birth and characteristics of this 'enigmatic "leniency"'.[84] The principle of moderation in punishment, Foucault argues, originated in social and political struggles,[85] but was first articulated as a discourse of the heart, leaping 'forth like a cry from the body, which is revolted at the sight or at the imagination of too much cruelty'. It appears as a sensibility of the reasonable men of the social body—those who make laws, sit in judgement, watch executions and do not commit crime—to whom excessive punishment causes pain 'with all the hardness of heart that it may bring with it, all the ferocity induced by familiarity, or on the contrary ill-founded feelings of pity and indulgence'. It is the sensibility of the spectator and not the victim of the law. 'Thank God', wrote an eighteenth century French writer quoted by Foucault, 'for those gentle, sensitive souls on whom those horrible executions exert a kind of torture'. This sensibility carried within it a principle for the regulation of the punitive power, an 'economic' calculation of the effect of punishment to ensure it was exactly enough to prevent the

[83] *Second Report* (*supra* n. 22) at 2. [84] Foucault (1977) ch. 3 (quotations at 74 and 75).
[85] Foucault sees reform originating in the struggle of the bourgeoisie against the monarchical super-power above, and intolerable economic predations from below: *ibid*, 75–89. The social and political origins of penal reform are outside the scope of this book, but I would not accept without qualification that Foucault's analysis can be applied to England.

repetition of the crime and no more. '"Humanity" is the respectable name given to this economy and to its meticulous calculations'.[86]

This 'humanity', Foucault argues, transformed punishment into a technique of punitive signs, which reformers believed capable of controlling behaviour, and so capable of reducing economic predations on the property of the bourgeoisie. Foucault identifies six major rules of this technique of penal semiotics. The first rule is *the rule of minimum quantity,* which sets punishment at the level where the criminal's interest in avoiding the penalty marginally exceeds the possible advantage of the crime. Secondly, there is *the rule of lateral effects,* which recognises that the object of punishment, and so the place it must have its most intense effects, is the public mind and not the body of the prisoner. Thirdly, there is *the rule of sufficient ideality,* which acknowledges that punishment affects the public mind by the representation of pain—by the 'pain' of the idea of 'pain'—and so it must maximise this representation rather than the actual physical sensation of pain. The rules of lateral effects and sufficient ideality can be illustrated by Beccaria's suggestion to replace the death penalty with perpetual slavery. If the pains of slavery were added up, Beccaria argued, it may be more cruel than capital punishment, but this pain is 'drawn out over an entire lifetime, while the pain of death exerts its whole force in a moment. And precisely this', continued Beccaria, 'is the advantage of penal servitude, that it inspires terror in the spectator more than in the sufferer, for the former considers the entire sum of unhappy moments, while the latter is distracted from the thought of future misery by that of the present moment'.[87] In this example the rule of lateral effects is illustrated by the effect of punishment on the spectator, and the rule of sufficient ideality by the maximisation of the representation of terror to the spectator with minimal pain to the sufferer.[88]

Fourthly, there is *the rule of perfect certainty,* essential to the effectiveness of this system of penal semiotics. 'With the idea of each crime and the advantages to be expected of it', explains Foucault, 'must be associated the idea of a particular punishment...the link from one to the other must be regarded as necessary and unbreakable'. The law must be clearly defined and published to ensure crimes and punishments are known to all; there must be a vigilant police to ensure no crime escapes the gaze of justice; criminal justice must be public, so all may recognise the reasons for a penalty; and the monarch must renounce the prerogative of pardon, so that the force of the idea of punishment is not weak-

[86] Foucault (1977) 89–94 (quotations at 91 and 92).
[87] Beccaria (1963) ch. VI
[88] Foucault (1977) 94–5.

ened by the hope of mercy. Procedural certainty, however, also depends upon public acceptance of the forms of legal proof of the crime, which is the concern of Foucault's fifth rule. *The rule of common truth* requires the verification of the crime during the trial to 'obey the general criteria for all truth. In the arguments it employs, in the proofs it provides, legal judgement must be homogeneous with judgement in general'. This rule rejects ritual forms, torture and semi-proofs in the investigation of truth, and demands respect for the presumption of innocence, empirical research and ultimately for expert evidence. Finally, there is *the rule of optimal specification* which recognises that the more complete the classification of offences the more effective penal semiotics will be. 'An exhaustive, explicit code is required, defining crimes and fixing penalties.'[89]

This technique of penal semiotics involved 'a shift in the mechanics of example' of major dimensions for the criminal process, a new philosophy for the suppression of crime which discarded excessive violence and relied instead on 'a play of representations and signs circulating discreetly but necessarily and evidently in the minds of all'.[90] The great strength of Foucault's analysis is the rigour and comprehensiveness with which it elaborates the implications of this shift, in the form of the six 'rules', to show a systematic reorientation of the criminal process. His analysis is a powerful demonstration of the interdependence of criminal law reform. There are, of course, problems in attempting to use this analysis to explain English legal developments. Foucault's abstract, sometimes speculative, style, his lack of attention to details of chronology, legal practice or political change, and his reliance primarily on French sources mean his conclusions must be used with care. There is, however, a close correlation between many features of Foucault's description of the technique of penal semiotics and the ideas of English penal reformers such as Romilly and the Criminal Law Commissioners. These features can be developed to illustrate the relationship between the adoption of adversarialism in the criminal trial and the amelioration of capital punishment.

At the heart of English penal reform of the 1820s and 1830s was a shift in the mechanics of example as the new penal logic superseded the selective terror of the capital felony process. The ideals of the new penal logic were rules of minimum quantity and perfect certainty, which reformers believed had tantalising potential. This potential was admired by Sir Samuel Romilly in his famous speech on capital punishment in 1810:[91]

[89] *Ibid*, 95–101. [90] *Ibid*, ch. 3 *passim* (quotations at 93 and 101).
[91] (1811) 19 P. D. App. 12. For a discussion of this speech see Chapter 3.

if it were possible that punishment, as the consequence of guilt, could be reduced to an absolute certainty, a very slight penalty would be sufficient to prevent almost every species of crime...If the restoration of the property stolen, and only a few weeks, or even a few days imprisonment, were the unavoidable consequence of theft, no theft would ever be committed. No man would steal what he was sure he could not keep; no man would, by a voluntary act, deprive himself of his liberty, though but for a few days.

Perfect certainty, Romilly and Foucault agree, meant certainty at all phases of the criminal process. Certainty depended on harmony of the law with public feeling and in the trial phase, as we have seen, the felony counsel restriction did not enjoy this harmony. In this straightforward way the new penal logic rejected the felony counsel restriction. The acceptance of counsel was an inevitable corollary of this rejection, but the nature and degree of this acceptance requires explanation. The enthusiasm of some reformers for counsel went well beyond a belief in an increased role for defence counsel to embrace the release of prosecution counsel from the duty of restraint, the replication of civil procedure in the criminal trial, and the welcome reception of the contentiousness of lawyers. The enthusiasm was, in short, for the 'lawyerisation' of the trial—for prosecution and defence counsel and especially for the benefits of their interaction. There was a faith that the free pursuit by counsel of the individual interests of prosecution and prisoner would reveal the truth, as if pointed to by some invisible hand. Foucault's analysis of penal semiotics shows how this acceptance of adversarialism might be a consequence of the philosophy of mild and certain punishment.

Foucault's rule of common truth describes a specific instance of the need for harmony of the law and public feeling recognised by early nineteenth century reformers. It postulates a dependency of certainty on public confidence in the demonstration of the proof of a crime. The spectator must leave the court in no possible doubt of the correctness of the verdict. The presumption of innocence and proof beyond reasonable doubt conform to this expectation. However, the consideration of the evidence had to match the standard of proof—all the facts had to be disclosed, all their complexities discussed and all possible defences raised by them considered before the jury retired to consider its verdict. This improvement in the quality of proof might be achieved if counsel, as in the civil trial, were given maximum freedom. The attractions of adversarialism were a greater thoroughness of inquiry as well as the elimination of an apparently arbitrary anomaly, altogether an impression that nothing more could have been said or done for the prisoner. It offered a comprehensive investigation of the truth within a procedure sufficiently fair to deprive the prisoner of any sympathy from judge, jury or spectators. The exemplification of the rule of common truth was the verdict beyond reproach, which seemed to be the potential of adversarialism.

The New Order

Any examination of the criminal law during the 1820s and 1830s must recognise that its overriding objective was the prevention of crime, and at the heart of reform was a new approach to this objective. Other ideas and values of course entered the debate and influenced particular reforms, but the prevention of crime through mild and certain punishment was the pervasive inspiration. The attainment of this objective required the maximum efficiency in the detection, prosecution, and trial of offenders, and the elimination of all anomalies, discretions and uncertainties which might encourage hopes of escape. The imperative of certainty is seen in the amelioration of capital punishment and the Prisoners' Counsel Act. It underlay many of Peel's reforms; for example, his new police, the abolition of benefit of clergy, and in the increased provision for the funding of prosecutions from the county rate. Certainty also required the law to be comprehensible and accessible. Peel's consolidating legislation gave order to the chaotic statute law inherited from the eighteenth century and the project of the Criminal Law Commissioners promised to build on his work. Codification added to certainty the advantage of optimal specification. Finally the development of secondary punishments has an obvious connection with the amelioration of capital punishment. The new penal logic was the spirit infusing reforms of the criminal process, creating a system adapted throughout to milder punishments.

Reformers attempted to prove that the philosophy of selective terror and the capital felony process did not prevent crime. They produced petitions from victims of crime and from jurors, compiled statistics from government returns, and gave evidence before official committees and commissions to show the escape of criminals from punishment. They asserted that mild and certain punishment would increase the number of prosecutions and convictions. The Criminal Law Commissioners tried to demonstrate the first fruits of reform by reproducing in their *Second Report* evidence of the comparative conviction rates—the proportion of convictions to committals—for a group of capital and non-capital currency and property offences (including offences from which the death penalty had recently been removed). They found a proportion of 47 convictions to every 100 commitments amongst the capital offences, and 72–73 convictions per 100 commitments amongst the non-capital offences. These ratios enabled the escape of criminals over a three-year period by reason of the death penalty to be quantified: 'if we had obtained the same ratio of convictions [for capital offences] as in non-capital cases, there would have been perhaps 500 or 600 additional persons subjected to punishment who have now escaped with impunity by verdicts of acquittal'.[92]

The total conviction rates for indictable offences in England and Wales for the period from immediately prior to the beginning of Romilly's campaign until after the Prisoners' Counsel Act can be extracted from official returns. These figures include capital and non-capital offences. They show a steady increase in the conviction rate from around sixty percent in the first decade of the century to over seventy-three percent by 1840. These figures must be treated with care, but do indicate that during the period reformers struggled to establish a more efficient criminal process, a significant increase in efficiency seems to have occurred.[93]

The most difficult quality to decipher in this period of reform, and probably the least useful analytically, is humanity. Dicey saw the promotion of humanity—'that is, the protection of human beings from unnecessary pain and suffering'—as one of the objects of the reformation of punishments. Foucault takes an opposite view and disparages humanity as the 'respectable name' given to the meticulous calculations of the technique of penal semiotics. Romilly, however, conforms to neither of these simple views. He expounded the cold logic of improved crime prevention through certain punishment and tried to avoid discussion of humanitarianism which he saw as a political liability. If humanity is equated with less executions then this period of reform saw an advance in humanity, but beyond this simple proposition any statement about humanity is suspect. The terror of death was removed from many offences, but fewer prisoners than before escaped the harsh realities of transportation and imprisonment. The rule of law replaced the capricious and anomalous procedure of the capital felony process, but each anomaly removed closed a door marked 'mercy' to prisoners. The law learnt to send a signal of humanity, in order to force out the humanity of prosecutors, jurors, judges and the Crown.

This ambiguity in the demise of the capital felony process was manifested in the new role for defence counsel in the criminal trial. The Prisoners' Counsel Act enabled counsel to conduct a prisoner's entire defence, and the philosophy of adversarialism encouraged counsel to

[92] *Second Report* (*supra* n. 22) at 22.

[93] See Appendix No. 2, 'Conviction Rates for England and Wales 1805–1840'. The difficulties posed by these figures include: (1) establishing causal links between the legislation or other activities of reformers and increases in the conviction rate; (2) interpreting the timing of increases; (3) the different 'weight' of particular offences within the figures; for example, privately stealing from the person, a very common offence (capital punishment removed 1808) would have a much greater influence over the total figures than changes to offences rarely prosecuted.

present the prisoner's case in the best possible light, and struggle to the best of his ability for an acquittal. The best professional defence, however, was confidently expected to ensure more guilty verdicts—the more complete the defence, the greater the probability of conviction—a result which may be called the Paradox of Legal Representation. The explanation of the paradox is that the increased conviction rate is not a simple consequence of proper legal representation, but rather of the contribution of counsel to the investigation of truth, the elimination of doubt, and the greater confidence of juries in reaching their verdicts. For the same reasons counsel would also contribute to the better protection of the innocent. In short, the professional defence of prisoners would mean more right verdicts, but because so many criminals had previously escaped the law the net effect would be an increased conviction rate. Counsel were to be a blessing to the innocent, and a curse to the guilty—a fine idea but, as Chapters 5 and 6 show, one fraught with difficulties for defence counsel.

5

The Complexities of Defence Inequality

Amidst the conflicting arguments and assumptions of the Prisoners' Counsel Act debate Frederick Calvert, a barrister and miscellaneous writer, sought to identify the matters on which all appeared to agree. 'I find two principles accepted with universal consent', he wrote in an 1836 pamphlet, 'one, that prosecutor and prisoner ought to proceed upon perfectly equal terms; another, that the sole object in criminal trials is to ascertain the truth'.[1] The second part of Calvert's statement is acceptable although there was, of course, virulent disagreement over the best means to achieve this objective. The first part is too precise to claim universal consent and would be more accurate if 'fair' were substituted for 'perfectly equal'. Fairness rather than equality was the ideal to which speakers usually appealed, although by fairness they often meant equal treatment for the prosecution and the defence. Calvert's first principle is an overstatement, but does draw attention to this undercurrent of concern with equality in the Prisoners' Counsel Act debate.

The complaint that the felony counsel restriction was unfair in allowing a speech to one counsel and not to the other, and that this unfairness inclined juries to acquit presupposed an expectation of equality between counsel. Similarly, the frequent comparisons reformers made between the professionally assisted prosecutor and the helpless prisoner struggling to defend himself derived their rhetorical force from their stark portrayal of an inequality. Sydney Smith called for equality, without using the term, when he wrote: 'We want only fair play. Speech for both sides, or speech for none. The first would be the wiser system, but the second would be clear from the intolerable cruelty of the present'.[2] Similarly the subsidiary questions of the last word and the deposi-

[1] Calvert (1836) 8. In this pamphlet Calvert argued that neither prosecution nor defence counsel should be allowed to address the jury in criminal trials.

[2] Smith (1822) 368. Sydney Smith makes particularly effective use of comparisons which emphasise prisoners' inequality in his two discussions of full defence by counsel. For an excellent example see Smith (1826–27) 77.

tions clauses manifest a concern with equality. The various proposals between 1834 and 1836 for the last word clause all ensured the prisoner's and the prosecutor's counsel the same number of speeches to the jury and the same freedom to call evidence without conceding a procedural advantage to the other side. The depositions clauses promised the prisoner the same access as the prosecution to the official record of the evidence taken by the justices of the peace in committing the prisoner to trial.

Defenders of the felony counsel restriction tended to separate fairness from equality, preferring to identify fairness with the decorum of the proceedings, the restraint of prosecution counsel, the paternalism of the judge and the virtues of the jury. However, in the later stages of the debate, when the efforts of opponents of change were increasingly dominated by the need to defeat full defence by counsel rather than to justify the status quo, equality emerged, as in Calvert's pamphlet, as an argument against reform.

Calvert's two principles were not the only matters upon which there was almost universal consent during the debate. Both sides also agreed that two important consequences were likely to follow the enactment of full defence by counsel. First, they accepted that prosecution and defence counsel would conduct their cases contentiously, with the result of some loss of decorum at trials. Opponents of change predicted alarming excesses in the speeches of counsel. Reformers responded that these claims were exaggerated, but admitted that some abuses would occur. Both the conservative *Law Magazine* and Sydney Smith in the *Edinburgh Review* anticipated the use of professional 'tricks' in counsel's speeches.[3] Secondly, both sides expected full defence by counsel to increase the conviction rate. Reformers welcomed this result as the fruits of the improved investigation of the truth and the greater confidence of juries in their verdicts, while their opponents lamented the vulnerability of prisoners under a procedure which sought truth in an unequal contest of forensic skill.

Full defence by counsel disturbed an established order in the criminal trial and ushered in a short period of uncertainty and adjustment. The procedure at the trial had to accommodate the new speech of defence counsel which, on the analogy of civil litigation, would require new rules to define its relationship to defence evidence and the speeches of prosecution counsel. The purpose of the prisoner's statement to the jury required clarification to justify the apparent duplication of addresses to the jury from the prisoner and his counsel. The traditional judicial

[3] 'The Prisoners Counsel Bill' (1836) 15 *Law Magazine* 394 at 400; Smith (1826–27) 87.

paternalism towards the prisoner was no longer self-evidently necessary, and both judge and counsel had to adapt to the new adversarial environment. This chapter considers the novel questions raised by full defence by counsel, and their settlement by degrees in the final stages of the Prisoners' Counsel Act debate and in the first years of the Act's operation.

The starting point for discussion of the implications of full defence by counsel is adversarialism. Opponents of reform gave considerable attention to the pressures adversarialism placed on counsel, and its temptations, which are considered in the first section of this chapter. Adversarialism gave a new importance to equality between counsel but, for the reasons discussed in the second section, the prisoner's counsel usually had to conduct the defence at a considerable disadvantage. The right to the last word to the jury, which could be neither divided nor shared, was the most intractable inequality between prosecution and defence counsel.

The traditional role of the judge in the felony trial presupposed the inequality of counsel, the weakness of the defence, and the need for the active judicial participation in the trial to ensure fairness and the discovery of the truth. The impact of adversarialism on this role was minimised if some subordination of the defence to the prosecution were retained, which might explain the deletion of the last word clause by the House of Lords. The tangled threads of judicial impartiality and paternalism, equality of counsel, and the last word to the jury are considered in the third section of this chapter.

The fourth and fifth sections consider the judicial implementation of the Act, both in the 1837 Practice Memorandum and in case law. The Memorandum and contemporaneous judicial decisions relating to procedure under the Act exacerbated the unequal position of the prisoner's counsel. The last word was again involved, this time in the context of the subsidiary question in the Prisoners' Counsel Act debate of the defence access to the depositions.

The discussion of the implications of full defence by counsel for the judicial role in the trial raises the difficult question of the attitude of the judges themselves to this reform. Their views are not easily discerned in the public record. Lords Abinger and Denman, respectively Chief Baron of the Exchequer and Chief Justice of King's Bench, had places in Parliament, but they spoke personally and not for their brethren when they supported the principle of full defence by counsel. The judges did not give evidence before the Criminal Law Commissioners, although three judges did make some interesting observations on full defence by counsel in giving evidence to a select committee on county rates in 1834. However, considerable insight into the concern at the highest level of the legal profession with the implications of full defence by counsel is offered by Lord Brougham's correspondence at this time. Lord Brougham did not take part in the debates in the House of Lords during the final stages of the Prisoners' Counsel Bill, being estranged from his party and no longer the Lord Chancellor, but was written to about the bill by Lords Lyndhurst and Denman and Mr Justice Williams.[4]

The *Brougham Papers* also contain a large and useful collection of correspondence between Lord Brougham and Charles Phillips. Phillips was a criminal barrister whose career travelled a curious orbit around Henry Brougham, deflected and accelerated in its course at different times by the influence of that much weightier body in the legal firmament. Phillips had been admitted to the Irish Bar in 1812, where his blazing oratory brought him spectacular early success and enabled him to publish a volume of collected speeches after only six years of practice. His style attracted attention in England, including two critical articles by Brougham in the *Edinburgh Review.* He arrived in England with an established literary and forensic reputation, was admitted to the English Bar on 10 February 1821—making five separate speeches that night at dinner in Middle Temple Hall—and soon attracted briefs in common law actions. Brougham crossed his path again in 1823 as defence counsel in *Shaw v Williams,* a seduction case where Phillips appeared for the plaintiff. Brougham mocked and ridiculed the dazzling exorbitance of Phillips' opening and invited the jury to bring in a derisory verdict, which they did. Phillips' reputation as an advocate in civil cases never recovered, but he developed a highly successful practice in the criminal sphere. He entered Brougham's confidence–'kissed the rod that had chastised him' a fellow barrister remarked—and during Brougham's Lord Chancellorship wrote assiduously to him on matters relating to criminal law reform, including the Central Criminal Court Act, the Prisoners' Counsel Act, and a proposal, raised by Phillips with himself in mind, to appoint a public prosecutor at the Old Bailey. He appeared before the select committee of the House of Lords on the Prisoners' Counsel Bill in 1835, where he gave evidence against the Bill. In 1842 Phillips asked Lord Brougham to approach Lord Lyndhurst, by this time again Lord Chancellor, to find him a judicial position, and shortly afterwards retired from the Bar to a Commissionership of Bankruptcy. He maintained an interest in law reform, corresponding on legal subjects with Lord Brougham and towards the end of

[4] *Brougham Papers,* University College Library, London. There is also a letter from Lord Brougham to Lord Lyndhurst on the Prisoners' Counsel Act amongst the *Lyndhurst Papers,* Trinity College Library, Cambridge, quoted in Martin (1884) 371–2.

his life producing a widely read pamphlet urging the total abolition of capital punishment.[5]

Phillips opposition to full defence by counsel is important for three reasons. First, he was among the most successful criminal barristers of the time, so his opinion carries the weight of experience. '[Y]ou must remember', he wrote to Lord Brougham, 'that I have literally been toiling night & day, for sixteen long years, in the proposed scene of this experiment. I have had ample means of anticipating its operation'. The extent of his practice is apparent from details he gave to the select committee of the House of Lords. 'In the year 1828', he said, 'it fell to my Lot to defend no less than 800 Prisoners at the Old Bailey and on the Oxford Circuit...In the September Sessions [at the Old Bailey] of that year I had 110 separate Briefs'. He derived his opposition to full defence by counsel from this experience: 'all Theory is for this Measure' he believed, 'all Practice against it'.[6] Secondly, Phillips seemed peculiarly well placed to benefit from full defence by counsel, so that his opposition was against self-interest. He had a large criminal practice, was popular with juries and was a more accomplished speaker than most of his contemporaries in the criminal courts. Sir John Campbell in a letter to Lord Brougham wondered how an overcautious judge like Mr Justice Gasalee would ever control the oratory of Charles Phillips in a trial for murder.[7] Thirdly, there is in Phillips' opposition a sense of foreboding

[5] **Phillips' forensic style**: Brougham (1815); Brougham (1817); 'JPT' (1821); **Phillips' admission to the English Bar**: 1 Robinson (1872) 369; cf. Talfourd (1821a) which possibly describes the same evening; **Shaw v Williams**: *The Times*, 21 June 1823, (1823) *Annual Register* (Chronicle) 40. **The effect on Phillips' career of Shaw v Williams**: Ballantine (1883) 58–9, quotation at 59, and *Brougham Papers, No. 28,437* (3 July 1834); **The Central Criminal Court Act:** *The Times,* 3, 7 and 10 November 1834, and *Brougham Papers, No. 26,359* (16 March 1834), *No. 26,409* (1834), *No. 13,396* (undated), *No. 46,711* (15 January 1834); **The Prisoners' Counsel Act:** *Brougham Papers No. 36,815* (26 August 1834), *No. 26,364* (August 1835), *No. 28,444* (1 May 1836), *No. 28,446* (June 1836), and Brougham to Phillips, unnumbered, 14 April and 15 July 1836; **The proposal to appoint a public prosecutor:** *Brougham Papers No. 28,437* (3 July 1834), *No. 36,815* (26 August 1834), and O'Connell to Phillips, *No. 26,362* (attachment, 5 September 1834). Cf. Kurland and Waters (1959) 498. **Phillips' request that Brougham approach Lord Lyndhurst:** *Brougham Papers No. 5768* (undated, probably 1841 or 1842). (All letters Phillips to Brougham unless otherwise stated).

[6] Phillips to Lord Brougham, August 1835, *Brougham Papers No. 26,364; Prisoners' Defence Bill. Minutes of Evidence taken before the Select Committee of the House of Lords etc*. (1836) Lords' Papers 119, at 3 and 6. The 1828 September Sessions at the Old Bailey lasted nine days.

[7] Campbell to Lord Brougham, 30 October 1833, *Brougham Papers No. 14,288.* Phillips was accused in the House of Commons of opposing the Prisoners' Counsel Bill for financial reasons: see (1836) 31 P. D. 498–9 and 1149–52, and Phillips to Brougham, undated, *Brougham Papers No. 28,448* and *No. 28,449.* The financial implications for the Bar of full defence by counsel were little discussed publicly. Prisoners were often unable to afford more than the minimum fee for counsel of one guinea. Many practitioners in criminal courts were underemployed, and ready to appear for one guinea. In such circumstances fees were unlikely to increase to compensate barristers for the additional service of an address to the jury or the additional living expenses of prolonged circuits.

that full defence by counsel would darken the administration of justice. He thought that counsel would prejudice the trials of prisoners without advancing the investigation of the truth. 'Some Persons', he said, 'advocate this Bill as if it went to protect Prisoners; I have no Doubt it will do them Mischief'. He predicted that it would be a curse for judges, and also for advocates, who would be forced to treat human life and liberty as matters for sophistry. In this latter respect he anticipated the public vilification the defence of prisoners would bring to the Bar, and himself, in the 1840s, which is considered in Chapter 6.[8]

Forensic Gladiators

Both sides in the Prisoners' Counsel Act debate believed that full defence by counsel meant the advent of the adversarial felony trial. Reformers anticipated a more thorough scrutiny of the facts and more reliable verdicts, while their opponents thought that the contention of counsel would disorder the trial and confuse the investigation of the truth. The opponents believed that adversarialism and the felony trial had mutually antagonistic qualities which would never form a stable union. The gravity of the felonious crimes and their punishments would add unacceptable volatility to adversarialism, and the competition of counsel inseparable from adversarialism would aggravate this reaction.

Under the felony counsel restriction prosecution counsel was expected to open with restraint, confining himself to a narrative of the facts and avoiding eloquence or argument. On the introduction of full defence by counsel, however, defence counsel could not be expected to show similar restraint. There could not be any relaxation in the exertions of counsel, to the limits of the law and his professional duty, in a case involving the life or liberty of a prisoner. The level of commitment required from the early nineteenth century defence counsel in a case involving life and death was well expressed by John Curran in an Irish trial:[9]

> It is the privilege, it is the obligation, of those who have to defend a client on a trial for his life, to exert every force, and to call forth every resource that zeal, and genius, and sagacity can suggest. It is an indulgence in favour of life; it has the sanctity of usage; it has the permission of humanity; and the man who should linger one single step behind the most advanced limit of that privilege, and should fail to exercise every talent that Heaven had given him, in that defence, would be guilty of a mean desertion of his duty, and an abandonment of his client.

[8] *Lords' Evidence* (*supra* n. 6) 6–9 (quotation at 6); Phillips to Lord Brougham, August 1835, *Brougham Papers No. 26,364*.

[9] *R v Hayes*, 1803, quoted in Phillips (1857) 304–5.

This commitment might be a matter of conscience as well as professional duty for an advocate like Charles Phillips, who had strong objections to the death penalty. Phillips was later to write to Lord Brougham of 'the physical labour & mental anxiety' of speaking in the defence of prisoners. '[A] fellow creature', he wrote, 'standing before you, not only seems to have, but very often has, all that is dear to man depending. Under such circumstances, to spare one's-self would be an actual crime'.[10]

The sole object of defence counsel, opponents of reform believed, would be to obtain a not guilty verdict. They expected defence counsel to bring this attitude to every defence, irrespective of its merits. If, as the opponents of reform believed, the truth was usually obvious from the evidence then the worst excesses of defence counsel would occur in cases where the facts plainly showed the prisoner's guilt. Without a factual basis for a defence, counsel would work on the passions and prejudices of the jury and seize any opportunity to conceal or confuse the truth.[11] They would 'substitute sophistry for fact', engage in 'vicious eloquence', make speeches 'full of inflammation and exaggeration', make animated appeals to the passions of the jury, and decorate their speeches 'with every ornament of fancy that was calculated to bewilder the jury and lead them away from the real merits of the case'.[12] Three of the most senior lawyers amongst the reformers—Lords Lyndhurst, Abinger and Denman—responded that in cases of flagrant guilt the prisoner's counsel would act responsibly by remaining seated and saying nothing. Lord Abinger, for example, said that 'in cases where the prisoner's guilt was clearly proved, no counsel of the least discretion would think of addressing the jury to assert his innocence'. 'They would' he said on another occasion 'in many cases, when they saw they could make no defence, allow a conviction'.[13] Opponents of reform believed that this course was impossible because, as Copley himself had said in the first phase of the debate, if the prisoner's counsel 'did not speak, he would by his silence pronounce a verdict of guilty'.[14] Further, prisoners and their attorneys

[10] Phillips to Lord Brougham (undated, probably 1841 or 1842), *Brougham Papers, No. 5768*. Cf. Phillips' comments at *Lords' Evidence* (*supra* n. 6) 7.

[11] The premise of this argument is the 'plain facts' view of the relationship between evidence and truth, discussed in Chapter 4. The case of plainly apparent guilt or innocence was the paradigm for defenders of the status quo, while reformers constantly emphasised the need for counsel in cases of complex facts and uncertain guilt or innocence.

[12] *Lords' Evidence* (*supra* n. 6) 9 (Phillips); *Second Report of this Majesty's Commissioners on Criminal Law* (1836) Parl. Papers XXXVI App. 2 (Sjt. Spankie); (1824) 11 P. D. 207 (Copley) and 190–1 (North).

[13] (1836) 35 P. D. 183; (1826) 15 P. D. 624. See also (1836) 34 P. D. 769 (Lyndhurst) and (1826) 15 P. D. 630 (Denman).

[14] (1824) 11 P. D. 207. See also (1836) 35 P. D. 184 (Earl Devon), *Lords' Evidence* (*supra* n. 6) 9 (Phillips).

would quickly learn to avoid over-scrupulous counsel and give their briefs to a class of barristers—the young, the ambitious, the quacks—prepared to make a speech in every case. 'There would be no want of volunteers', a senior barrister observed, 'in this field of fame'.[15]

The same combination of duty and ambition would seize prosecution counsel and overthrow the duty of restraint. He would feel compelled to go beyond a simple narrative of the facts into argument and discussion of the merits in order to pre-empt or correct the excesses of defence counsel. Professional pride would prick him to match the zeal of the other side. Barristers, Phillips explained, are judged on their success and if a barrister 'is generally unsuccessful he will not be employed'. 'I know very well', he continued, 'this is not a very flattering Theory, but it is true nevertheless'.[16]

In this way opponents of reform reached the same conclusion as reformers that full defence by counsel would lead to an aggressive adversarialism. However, they reasoned without the assumption, which reformers derived from 'civilisation' and 'individual experience', that adversarialism was conducive to the discovery of the truth. Without this element adversarialism seemed to debase the trial to a mere contest or competition between counsel, with counsel casually indifferent to truth in the pursuit of victory. In the 1826 debate Sir John Copley contrasted this view of the criminal trial with the status quo:[17]

> Instead of the calm and deliberate justice with which criminal prosecutions were at present carried on, the effect of allowing counsel to speak for the defence would be to convert the court into an arena, where opposing advocates might meet in professional conflict, and where, instead of endeavouring to elicit the truth by a reference to plain facts, or the real merits of the case, the time of the public would be wasted by contests between the counsel on either side, animated, as they would be, by all the excitement, zeal, and pertinacity, which such contests usually inspired.

Opponents of reform often employed martial metaphors—'arena', 'gladiators', 'combatants', 'war'—to evoke the character of adversarialism. These metaphors captured the iron qualities of loyalty, ambition, and a willingness to fight, and the baseness of a struggle over human life, which they believed adversarialism would bring to the criminal trial.[18]

15 *Second Report* (*supra* n. 12) App. 2 (Sjt. Spankie).

16 *Lords' Evidence* (*supra* n. 6) 7. See also (1826) 15 P. D. 617–18 (Tindal); *Second Report* (*supra* n. 12) App. 2 (Sjt. Spankie).

17 (1826) 15 P. D. 599.

18 *Ibid*, and at 625–6 (Wetherell); (1824) 11 P. D. 208 (Copley); *Lords' Evidence* (*supra* n. 6) 7 (Phillips); (1834) 24 P. D. 162–3 (Sjt. Spankie).

The Unequal Struggle

This aggressive adversarialism meant that the Prisoners' Counsel Act was likely to add much more than an address to the jury to the responsibilities of defence counsel. He would also need to counter the prosecution aggression, compensate for any loss of judicial sympathy, meet the heightened expectations of vigilance and combativeness on the prisoner's behalf, and accept that the success or failure of the prisoner's case depended on his advocacy more than ever before. Adversarialism would so affect the conduct of both counsel that the elimination of all inequalities would become imperative to the fairness of the proceedings. The increased aggression of prosecution counsel, the new responsibility of defence counsel, and the acceptance of a philosophy which sought truth in the contention of counsel demanded that the prosecution and defence met on equal terms. If either counsel enjoyed any advantage then this advantage rather than the merits of the case might determine the verdict.

Opponents of reform argued that full defence by counsel was likely to make prisoners the victims of inequalities between the prosecution and the defence which had previously been negated by the restraint of prosecution counsel and the paternalism of the judge. These inequalities fell into three broad categories, which may be called representative inequalities, preparative inequalities and, most significantly, the tactical inequality.

The representative inequalities involved the quality of the legal representation prisoners were likely to enjoy under full defence by counsel. '[T]he immediate effect' of permitting defence counsel to make speeches, said the *Law Magazine*, 'would be to make trials more and more dependant upon advocacy, and the best advocacy would be ordinarily on the side of the prosecution, because the prosecutor is ordinarily the richer party, and has the first choice to boot'. Even an impoverished prosecutor could expect some reimbursement from the county of the cost of employing an attorney and counsel, and for the attendance of witnesses, but prisoners had to meet all these costs themselves. The poverty of prisoners would compel them to employ the younger and less successful members of the bar whose ambition and eagerness for personal distinction would lead them, opponents of reform claimed, into flashy oratory, confrontations with the Bench, and other misguided displays of zeal on the prisoner's behalf. The balance of talent, experience, and circumspection in legal representation was likely to be decidedly against the prisoner.[19]

[19] 'The Prisoners' Counsel Bill' (1836) 15 *Law Magazine* 394 (quotation at 398); *Second Report* (*supra* n. 12), App. 2 (Sjt. Spankie); *Lords' Evidence* (*supra* n. 6) at 6 (Phillips); (1826) 15 P. D. 618 (Tindal); (1824) 11 P. D. 208 (Copley).

The preparative inequalities refer to the disadvantages of prisoners in collecting evidence and preparing their cases for trial. The poverty of prisoners and in many cases their imprisonment pending trial created difficulties for the organisation of the defence, which were exacerbated by procedural restrictions denying the defence copies of the indictment and the depositions. Some opponents of full defence by counsel argued that pre-trial assistance, such as the depositions clauses in the Prisoners' Counsel Act, would be more helpful to the prisoner than a speech from his counsel. This was the view of Charles Law, the Recorder of London during the second phase of the debate:[20]

> My Opinion is, that to give the Prisoner a fairer and fuller Opportunity of Defence you would not resort so much to the Speeches of Counsel as affording him Facilities before the Trial of distinctly understanding the Sort of Charge made against him. I think the Depositions taken before Magistrates should be delivered to him (they are in the hands of the Prosecution) and a Copy of the Indictment. I think that every Means of thoroughly understanding and meeting the Charge should be given to the Prisoner, and that on the Trial he should be put on a Perfect Equality with the Prosecutor.

Alternatively, Frederick Calvert suggested improving the pre-trial assistance to prisoners through the employment by each county of an attorney to enquire into charges on behalf of prisoners.[21] Both Law and Calvert proposed to complement this increased preparative equality for prisoners with equality between counsel at the trial by eliminating the address to the jury of prosecution counsel.

Opponents of reform saw the representative and preparative inequalities, though not created by full defence by counsel, as assuming an unacceptable significance in the adversarial criminal trial. By contrast, tactical inequality would be the direct result of adversarialism if, as in fact occurred, it introduced into criminal trials the rules of civil procedure concerning the relationship between evidence and counsel's speeches. In civil actions (and in misdemeanour trials which already followed civil procedure in this respect) the plaintiff's counsel had the advantage of a right of reply to the defence case, although the defence counsel could deprive the plaintiff of this right, and secure the last word to the jury for himself, by dispensing with evidence and instead closing his client's case at the conclusion of his 'opening' address. The Bar at this time placed such faith in the persuasive power of the last speech to the jury that defence counsel were often prepared to withhold relevant and favourable evidence in order to secure the last word, preferring this course to the production of witnesses and the concession to the plaintiff

[20] *Lords' Evidence* (*supra* n. 6) 20. [21] Calvert (1836) 18–26.

of a potentially fatal reply. The Common Law Commissioners of the early 1850s described in these terms this choice defence counsel were required to make between evidence and last word eloquence:[22]

So great is the advantage of the reply felt to be in practice, that, generally, one great object of a counsel for a defendant is, if possible, to avoid calling witnesses, even though conscious that, otherwise, his witnesses would improve his case. The exercise of a sound discretion on this point is one of the most difficult parts of the duty of the advocate; and many verdicts are doubtless lost, on the one hand, by exposing the case to the danger of a reply, and on the other, by the fear of it operating to the keeping back of evidence which might have been decisive with the jury.

A related disincentive to the production of witnesses by the defence was the lack of any opportunity to correct or explain any inconsistencies between defence witnesses, or between these witnesses and the opening address of defence counsel, by means of a closing address. The defence counsel only had one speech, at the opening of his client's case, and so could not comment on subsequent unexpected developments, which the plaintiff's counsel might ruthlessly exploit in his reply.

In the first phase of the Prisoners' Counsel Act debate Sir John Copley turned the tactical inequality of civil procedure into a powerful argument against full defence by counsel in criminal trials. Under civil procedure, he said in 1824, 'the odds were always in favour of the plaintiff'. Should this 'defect' of civil procedure, he asked, 'be introduced into our criminal system?' He argued in his 1824 and 1826 speeches that the introduction of this defect into criminal trials would lead to the exclusion of defence evidence, to the prejudice of both the prisoner and the investigation of the truth:[23]

it was necessary to consider what was the most essential requisite to the due administration of justice. That he conceived to be, that no obstruction should be opposed to the fullest inquiry and investigation. If, however, counsel were allowed to speak for the defence, and, having done so, to call evidence, the inevitable consequence would be, that the counsel for the prosecution would be entitled to a speech in reply...In civil cases, where the counsel for the [plaintiff] was allowed the liberty of reply, how frequently was the counsel for the [defendant] deterred from bringing forward witnesses material to his cause, from a fear of the impression which might be made upon the minds of the jury by the opposing counsel's speech to the evidence!...As far, therefore, as the investigation

[22] *Second Report of Her Majesty's Commissioners for Inquiring into the Process, Practice and System of Pleading in the Superior Courts of Common Law etc.* (1852–53) Parl. Papers XL. 701 at 711.

[23] (1826) 15 P. D. 600–1, and (1824) 11 P. D. 207–8. The words in brackets in the quotation were juxtaposed either by Copley or the Hansard reporter, and have been restored to their clearly correct positions.

of the truth was concerned, it would, in his opinion, be much better to leave the system as it was.

In the second phase of the debate the reformers accepted the validity of this criticism, but suggested that it could be overcome by including in the legislation a clause which granted the prisoner's counsel the last word to the jury. The Criminal Law Commissioners, for example, conceded 'that the introduction into Criminal Courts of the Nisi Prius practice ought greatly to be deprecated. One great cause of complaint attending that system, is the undue advantage given to the Plaintiff in a cause'. The Commissioners continued to explain the dangers to the defence of the reply and of unforeseen variances between the speech of defence counsel and the evidence of defence witnesses, which could be avoided only by declining to call evidence. 'We deem it', they concluded, 'to be of the highest importance to exclude all such apprehensions from criminal trials...and with that view we suggest the propriety of admitting the Prisoner's Counsel in all cases the privilege of making the last address'.[24] It required some discussion to settle the form of the last word clause, but the different proposals all ensured an equal number of speeches to the prosecution and the defence, and the uninhibited production of evidence by guaranteeing the defence the last word.

The Prisoners' Counsel Bill passed by the House of Commons in 1834, 1835, and 1836 included last word clauses, and for the sake of consistency throughout the common law these clauses were framed to extend to treason and misdemeanour trials.[25] Supporters and opponents of full defence by counsel in the Commons were united in the view that the tactical inequality of civil procedure should not be introduced into felony trials. Some of the principle's strongest supporters believed the status quo preferable to the introduction of counsel into felony trials on such unequal terms. Frederick Pollock, for example, was of this view, to which he added an astonishing estimate of the responsibility of this tactical inequality for wrongful verdicts in misdemeanour trials:[26]

He [Pollock] thought it would be even better to allow the law to remain as it was, than to permit the prosecutor's Counsel to reply. He could state that, in conse-

[24] *Second Report* (*supra* n. 12) 16–17.

[25] The last word clause passed by the Commons in 1836 is set out in Appendix 1.2. This clause allowed the prisoner's counsel an answer to any reply made by the prosecution counsel. This meant that a trial would require either four speeches (two opening speeches, the prosecution reply and the defence answer) or, if the prosecution counsel chose not to reply, two speeches (the openings) but in either event the defence would enjoy the last word. For discussion of alternative formulations of the last word clause, including Scottish practice, see (1834) 24 P. D. 159–60 (Ewart) and 821; *Second Report* (*supra* n. 12) App. 1 (evidence of Ewart); (1835) 28 P. D. 872 (Sandford and Campbell); and (1836) 31 P. D. 1152.

[26] (1834) 24 P. D. 169.

quence of the prosecutor's Counsel being allowed to reply in some cases of misdemeanours—as conspiracy—four defendants out of five were unjustly convicted.

There were even calls at this time to reform civil procedure within its own sphere. The Common Law Commissioners in their *Third Report* of 1831 recommended the introduction of a closing speech for defence counsel in civil trials, a suggestion repeated by the next generation of Common Law Commissioners in 1853, and enacted by the Common Law Procedure Act of 1854.[27] However, the defective civil procedure—already believed to require amendment, condemned for its unfairness to the defence, expected to produce wrongful convictions—became part of all criminal trials in 1836, when the Prisoners' Counsel Act was enacted without the last word clause.

The last word clause was struck out of the Prisoners' Counsel Bill by the House of Lords, largely because of the opposition of James Scarlett, now Lord Abinger, and Lord Lyndhurst. Lord Abinger insisted, and after some initial ambivalence Lord Lyndhurst agreed, that the civil procedure must be followed in order to avoid 'anomalies' and to ensure that the proceedings were consistent with the investigation of the truth.[28] This fidelity to the civil analogy begged the question of whether the rules regulating speech order in civil trials were consistent with the truth, and ignored the persuasive arguments that they were not, arguments that had been so forcefully made by Lord Lyndhurst himself in 1824 and 1826. The next section shows that the dogmatic opposition to the last word clause might reflect an anxiety to minimise the impact of full defence by counsel on the duties of the judge, and to placate judicial opposition to the Act.

The Duties of the Judge

The discussion during the Prisoners' Counsel Act debate of the aphorism that the judge was the counsel for the prisoner showed some of the

[27] *Third Report Made to His Majesty by the Commissioners Appointed to Inquire into the Practice and Proceedings of the Superior Courts of Common Law* (1831) Parl. Papers X. 375 at 442–3; *Second Report of Her Majesty's Commissioners for Inquiring into the Process, Practice and System of Pleading in the Superior Courts of Common Law etc.* (1852–53) Parl. Papers XL. 701 at 711; The Common Law Procedure Act (17 & 18 Vict., c. 125), s. 18. The practice under this Act was eventually extended to criminal trials by the Criminal Procedure Act 1865 (28 & 29 Vict., c. 18), s. 2.

[28] (1836) 35 P. D. 177, 183–4, 1248. The last word clause was initially struck out by a Select Committee of the Lords, which did not give reasons for its amendments. A letter from Lord Denman to Lord Brougham, undated, *Brougham Papers No. 14,280,* indicates that Lord Abinger influenced the Committee ('Abinger...proposed in Committee that the 1st clause [ie the bare principle of full defence by counsel] should pass, but this alone. With this all must be contented').

qualities contemporaries expected from a judge. Reformers assailed this aphorism for confounding the roles of the judge and the advocate, and emphasised the need for judicial impartiality. It was the office of the judge 'to prepare the minds of the Jury for correctly forming their own conclusion', and not to urge them to find a particular verdict.[29] 'The judge stood high and independent', said Lord Lyndhurst, speaking from experience as Chief Baron of the Exchequer, 'and was looked up to by the jury. They had a reliance on his wisdom and experience; and above all they had a reliance on his impartiality'.[30]

Impartiality is the proper state of judicial independence from the parties and issues before the court. A deficiency of independence in the judge is the vice of bias, which involves either favouritism or prejudice. There is also a judicial vice of an excess of independence, which may be called remoteness. The remote judge evades responsibility for the conduct or the outcome of proceedings. He does not interfere in the trial, listens without comment to the evidence and argument, restates the evidence without observation to the jury, and applies the law with a slavish legalism. The remote judge entrusts the justice of the proceedings to precedents, procedure and the jury. His exalted independence enables him to ignore all differences between the parties, so that even a criminal prosecution between the powerful and the weak, the resourceful and the helpless, one seeking advantage from a moribund law and one unexpectedly snared by it, or one with nothing at stake and one whose life hangs by a thread, is heard by him as if between equal parties, who must be allowed to conduct their cases as they think fit, without interference or assistance from him.

Impartiality is therefore the virtuous state of judicial independence that stands as a mean between the vices of bias and remoteness, respectively a deficiency and an excess of independence. The judge may slip from impartiality into bias through over-involvement in the trial, and from impartiality to remoteness through passivity. Impartiality is an active quality, requiring the judge to contemplate constantly the need for his intervention in the trial, and to intervene when the occasion requires.[31] Bentham took this view when he said that the judge should 'be equally active in his endeavours to search out the truth on both sides,—that is the true impartiality, the only true and proper sort of impartiality, befitting the station of the judge'.[32]

The impartial judge may need to intervene in the trial to ensure that the truth appears, as Bentham suggested, or to ensure the fairness of the

[29] *Second Report* (*supra* n. 12) 8. [30] (1836) 34 P. D. 770.

[31] This conception of a virtue as the mean between vices of deficiency and excess is derived from Aristotle's *Nicomachean Ethics* Book II, in Ross (1990) 36–47.

[32] *The Rationale of Judicial Evidence* in 6 Bentham (1843) 350.

proceedings. If one party possesses advantages entirely extraneous to the merits, then to ensure a fair trial and a verdict based upon the truth the judge should intervene to prevent these advantages from influencing the verdict. The impartial judge not only holds the scales of justice evenly between the parties, but also ensures that nothing is placed in the scales which should not be weighed.

Impartiality is not incompatible with assistance, even regular assistance, to one party. Such assistance may be justified by the disadvantages or vulnerability of one party, and so exemplify the active intervention of the impartial judge. Christopher St. German assumed the compatibility of impartiality and assistance when he first said that judges in criminal trials must 'be indifferent bytwene the kynge and the partye' and immediately added that they were also 'bounde in conscyence' to help the unrepresented prisoner with his pleading. Francis Bacon nearly a century later argued that the exemplary judge might need to provide substantial assistance to one party. 'A judge', he wrote, 'ought to prepare his way to a just sentence as God useth to prepare His way, by raising valleys and taking down hills; so where there appeareth on either side a high hand, violent persecution, cunning advantages taken, combination, power, great counsel, then is the virtue of a judge seen *to make inequality equal*'. Jeremy Bentham, writing in the early nineteenth century of the aphorism that the judge was counsel for the prisoner, readily accepted that the duty of 'active impartiality' might require the judge to assist the prisoner. However, he added, the judge should be equally prepared to assist the prosecution if the circumstances so required.[33]

The impartial judge of the early nineteenth century was likely to exhibit a 'favourable disposition' towards the prisoner because, almost inevitably, the prisoner rather than the prosecutor began the felony trial at a disadvantage. The prisoner laboured under the preparative disabilities of imprisonment pending trial and the denial of copies of the indictment and depositions, was not permitted to address the jury by counsel and often had no counsel at all, usually faced the death penalty for a minor crime, and in addition to these burdens of the common law might falter in even the simplest defence through poverty or ignorance.

[33] *Doctor and Student* Second dialogue, ch. 48, in Plucknett and Barton (1974) 285; *Essays and Counsels Civil and Moral (Of Judicature)* in 2 Bacon (1819) 383 (emphasis added); *The Rationale of Judicial Evidence* in 6 Bentham (1843) 350. The aphorism that the judge was counsel for the prisoner confused this impartial assistance, properly part of the judicial office, with the role of counsel. It was premised on an indisputable truth, but nevertheless expressed a fallacy. The aphorism was discredited and discarded during the debate, but not the judicial duty to assist the prisoner if the circumstances required, which was sometimes affirmed even as the aphorism was denounced; see for example (1826) 15 P. D. 599 and 601 (Copley).

By the early nineteenth century the common law judges were long accustomed to equalising some of the inequalities of the felony trial. One form of judicial assistance inhabited the husk of the medieval doctrine that the church disciplined its clergy, another appeared in the technical rules for the construction of indictments, a third in the gaudy aphorism that the judge was the counsel for the prisoner, but there were also countless other opportunities to help the prisoner in every trial, if the judge believed it necessary, through the control of procedure and evidence, questions from the bench, and the summing-up. This *ad hoc* assistance was likely to possess two characteristics. First, it became the judicial office, and avoided the appearance of over-involvement in the trial or indulgence to the prisoner, if the judicial assistance was discreet, which meant that the effect of a helpful comment or ruling might not be immediately apparent to the spectators at the trial.[34] Secondly, judicial assistance was likely to be effective. The judge was the central actor of the assize, distinguished in court by his dress and his elevated position, embodying the majesty of the law and the royal concern with justice, bringing together around his person the dignitaries of the county and attended by a train of lawyers, officials and liverymen. He had much greater influence over the jurors than counsel. Jurors might listen attentively to counsel but, as Lord Lyndhurst said, they looked up to the judge, and relied upon his wisdom and experience. Mr. Justice Williams, in a letter discussed below, remarked that 'one minute from the judge is...worth an hour from the Councel'. Even the part-time chairmen of the courts of quarter sessions, in conducting minor felony trials, could, said Lord Denman, 'beat the council hollow'.[35]

Full defence by counsel would complicate the exercise of the duty of active impartiality in two ways. First, it would require the judge for the first time to comment on the speeches of counsel in his summing-up. It would add one and perhaps two speeches between the close of the evidence and the jury's deliberations, so that the judge would need to watch, and if necessary respond to, not only the presentation of the evidence, but also counsel's interpretation of the evidence. Secondly and more importantly, it would powerfully increase the voice of the prisoner's counsel in the criminal trial, and so the possibility that the judge might need to exert his influence against the prisoner. The judges

[34] Cf. Sir Archibald MacDonald's statement that as a judge he 'would always desire to give the prisoner the benefit of every thing that I could discover in his favour. I knew it perhaps when he did not': *Report from the Select Committee appointed to consider so much of the Criminal Law as relates to Capital Punishments in Felonies* (1819) Parl. Papers VIII. 1 at 50. MacDonald was the Chief Baron of the Exchequer from 1793 to 1813.

[35] (1836) 34 P. D. 770 (Lyndhurst); Williams to Lord Brougham, July 1835, and Lord Denman to Lord Brougham, undated, *Brougham Papers No. 14,438* and *No. 14,280.*

were accustomed to assisting the prisoner rather than the prosecutor, but were well aware that their duty of active impartiality required them to intervene against prisoners who seemed likely to escape for reasons extraneous to the merits. The prospect of regular judicial intervention against prisoners concerned many senior lawyers, especially judges. Mr Justice Williams, for example, wrote to Lord Brougham that the inevitable judicial response to the speech of the prisoner's counsel would be detrimental to both the prisoner and the judicial reputation:[36]

This [i.e. the Prisoners' Counsel bill] is all very well...I voted for it myself, in the house, upon the *surface* reason (a reason however undoubtably) that the administration of the law may, probably, appear more equal, &, therefore more satisfactory, with counsel...The great lawgivers, with whom this sublime improvement originated...have, probably, overlooked an important consequence...I allude to the necessarily changed position of the judge...Suppose the case a strong one against the prisoner, with features in it, however, of a contrary tendency (and how few there are without some such?) & further that the Counsel has really made a clever & powerful speech,—bringing forward all the favourable 'matters and things' & [illegible], or perverting the great & leading facts of the Case: If the Judge have anything in him, can, ought this state of things be left without correction? Probably, you will say no. And if so, then I say, that, call it what you please, there will be, in effect, a *Reply* by the Judge, and, thereby, almost inevitably, will follow as a consequence of setting the Case straight before the jury the straightening of a rope by the councelled prisoner at one end of it. Because (& I am sure you will not think I say this because I wear a wig as big as myself) one minute from the judge is...worth an hour from the Councel...My final opinion, therefore, is that the number of convictions will be greater, & the danger considerable that the position of the judge will not be quite so amiable in the eyes of the people...as heretofore.

In a similar vein Mr Justice Park, in giving evidence before the Select Committee on County Rates, argued that the traditional judicial attitude to the prisoners would be reversed by the irresponsibility of defence counsel:[37]

If you have speeches for prisoners, you change immediately the nature of things; it is the duty of the judge to watch for the prisoner's benefit, and take every objection for their benefit; instead of that, there will be some young gentleman making speeches, and talking of things quite extraneous, and that will turn the

[36] Williams to Lord Brougham, July 1835, *Brougham Papers No. 14, 438* (emphasis original). This letter is particularly interesting because Williams had spoken in favour of full defence by counsel in the 1826 debate in the House of Commons, during which he dismissed the assistance provided by the judge as 'counsel for the prisoner' as of 'little practical advantage' to prisoners: (1826) 15 P. D. 603–5. At the Bar he asserted the value of counsel; but from the Bench, as this letter shows, he discovered the power of the judge.

[37] *Report from the Select Committee on the Receipt and Expenditure of County Rates* (1834) Parl. Papers XIV. 1 at 143.

judge immediately into the prosecutor's counsel, to prevent false topics being made use of to the defeat of justice.

The comparison in this passage between the judicial solicitude for the prisoner under the status quo and the judicial strictness full defence by counsel would bring was a common theme of opponents of reform. Under the proposed reform juries would regularly observe the authority of the judge arrayed against the prisoner, and the damage to the defence of this impression might outweigh the assistance of his counsel. Thus, argued Sir John Copley in 1826, all the advantage which the prisoner had under the established procedure 'in the favourable disposition of the judge, might be taken from him, and his situation be made infinitely worse by the ill-directed zeal, or the indiscretion of his advocate'.[38]

The alarmist expectations of adversarialism intensified these apprehensions of a changed judicial role. The zeal and excesses of defence counsel would create a corresponding necessity for judicial intervention against the prisoner. Further, adversarialism presupposed counsel on both sides, but in many felony trials of the 1830s, particularly at the Old Bailey, there was no prosecution counsel. In such circumstances the prisoner's counsel would address the jury without any adversary to give the jury an alternative interpretation of the evidence. The duty of active impartiality would require the judge to equalise this inequality, and again the jurors and spectators would gather the impression of the judge pressing his authority against the prisoner.[39] Some opponents of reform raised the spectre of the 'prosecuting judge', with its sinister implications for the liberty of the subject and the judicial reputation in the eyes of the people, as the inevitable consequence of allowing the prisoner's counsel to address the jury.

Lord Lyndhurst felt it necessary to respond to these concerns in moving the second reading of the Prisoners' Counsel Bill in the House of Lords. He argued that the judicial influence with the jury, rather than weighing against the defended prisoner, would enable the judge to preserve the integrity of the adversarial trial without giving an advantage to either

[38] (1826) 15 P. D. 601. See also (1824) 11 P. D. 207.

[39] (1826) 15 P. D. 619 (Tindal, who estimated that in nine-tenths of cases at the Old Bailey there was no prosecution counsel); Phillips to Lord Brougham, August 1835, *Brougham Papers No. 26,364*, where Phillips estimates prosecution representation in this court at one case in 20, and continues: 'The consequence is that the burthen [sic], not only of trying a prisoner, but, of prosecuting him also, falls upon the Judge...By this bill increased exertion will certainly be required from the counsel for the defence; a corresponding activity will, of course, be requisite on behalf of the prosecution. If this office is to devolve upon the judge he must...reply upon the prisoners' counsel...Now to metamorphise the judge into an advocate is surely not the way to make him respected. This bill allows him no alternative. If there be no counsel for the prosecution, it will be the odious, but bounden duty of the judge to unwind the web of the defence and expose the guilt of the prisoner'.

side. Such was the mastery of the judge that he could express his authority discreetly and remain effective. The judge did not need to appear any less than impartial in performing his duty of active impartiality:[40]

> It was not necessary for the judge to embark with zeal in the case. If he dealt in a mild manner with the sophistries of the counsel for the prisoner and felt it necessary to expose his inconsistencies in argument, and to correct his errors as to facts, by drawing the attention of the jury to his notes of the trial, that would be abundantly sufficient for the purposes of justice. What did experience teach on these points? In trials for misdemeanours the judge...appeared as an arbitrator and a mediator, acting evenly between the parties; presenting the case fairly and impartially to the consideration of the jury. He [Lord Lyndhurst] had no apprehension of that result which had always been insisted upon in the discussion of this question.

Notwithstanding Lord Lyndhurst's confidence, a sense of doubt about the implications of full defence by counsel for the judge persisted throughout the debate. The deletion of the last word clause perhaps owes more to legislative caution engendered by this doubt than to the acceptance of any argument or principle. There was a willingness to defer decision on this difficult clause, by omitting it from the Act on the assumption that it could be enacted separately at a later date if experience showed it was necessary.[41] In addition, the omission of the last word clause preserved the buffer of a prosecution reply between the speech of the prisoner's counsel and the summing-up in cases where the defence called evidence, and to this extent softened the impact of full defence by counsel on the traditional judicial role. In such cases prosecution counsel would be able to reply to any excesses or inaccuracies in the speech of defence counsel, allowing the judge to restore the balance between counsel in his summing-up. If prosecution counsel abused his advantage he could be criticised or even silenced by the judge intervening, in traditional fashion, on the prisoner's behalf.

In general the judges themselves maintained a dignified public silence during the Prisoners' Counsel Act debate. Lords Abinger and Denman were members of the House of Lords and spoke publicly on the Act in this capacity, and three judges made passing reference to full defence by counsel in evidence before the Select Committee on County Rates in 1834, but this was the limit of the judicial pronouncements. They were not apparently so reticent within their close professional circle. Lord Campbell's memoirs record that 12 of the 15 judges opposed the Act,

[40] (1836) 34 P. D. 770.

[41] (1836) 35 P. D. 182 (Lord Plunket), 186 (Lord Cottenham LC), 1324–5 (Lord John Russell). Even Lord Lyndhurst admitted to indecision on the merits of the last word clause: see (1836) 35 P. D. 171.

and that Mr Justice Park felt so strongly on the issue that he threatened to resign if the Act were passed. Lord Denman's correspondence with Lord Brougham describes the attitude to the Act of some unidentified judges as 'rabid', indicates that Sir Nicholas Tindal, the Chief Justice of Common Pleas, and Mr Justice Park were 'most violent against the bill', and confirms that Mr Justice Park was threatening to resign. Mr Baron Garrow also opposed the Bill, and Mr Baron Alderson apparently had no enthusiasm for the proposal. The limited disclosures of these memoirs and the *Brougham Papers* establish that Mr Justice Williams had written to Lord Brougham about the Act, Mr Justice Park had written to Sir John Campbell, then Attorney-General, Sir Nicholas Tindal and Mr Justice Park had contacted Lord Lyndhurst, and that Lord Denman was well aware of the opinions of his brother judges.[42] The objects of this judicial attention all supported full defence by counsel but, excepting Lord Brougham who never expressed an opinion on this issue, none of them defended the last word clause.

The Implementation of the Prisoners' Counsel Act

The Prisoners' Counsel Act came into effect on 1 October 1836, to be first applied at the remaining Old Bailey sessions of 1836, and by magistrates throughout the country at adjourned sessions or at the Epiphany Quarter Sessions of 1837.[43] Late in 1836 Lord Lyndhurst, writing to Lord Brougham from Paris, enquired of the effect of the Act on criminal trials. Lord Brougham replied that at the Old Bailey the Act had been found to increase acquittals against the evidence, and suggested that this was not the fault of the Act but of the absence of prosecution counsel in this court:[44]

there is a general belief & I think from all I can learn a well founded one that it [the Act] has led to acquittals in no small number agst the truth of the case. This is the fault, however, not of the bill but of there being no council for the prosecution. The judge cannot (if he chose) do the business of the Prosecution & he ought not to choose to place himself in so odious a position. Tho' the Bill had never passed, I should have said a prosecution without council ought not to be but the [Prisoners' Counsel] Bill makes it quite clear Something must be done to remedy this glaring

[42] 2 Hardcastle (1881) 106–7; Lord Denman to Lord Brougham, undated and May 1836, Mr Justice Williams to Lord Brougham, July 1835, *Brougham Papers, Nos. 14,280, 14,281* and *14,438*. For Mr Baron Garrow's opposition see Denman (1851) at 352–3. Mr Justice Park did not fulfil his threat to resign when the Act passed.

[43] The first case under the new Act in London was at the Westminster Sessions on 13 October 1836: see (1836) 12 *Legal Observer* 497.

[44] Lord Lyndhurst to Lord Brougham, undated, *Brougham Papers No. 13,357;* Lord Brougham to Lord Lyndhurst, 20 December 1836, *Lyndhurst Papers No. 121* (quoted in Martin (1884) 371–2).

defect...I need hardly add (after what I have said) that there has been no instance of wrong conviction, owing to the Bill. It has been all the other way.

The royal judges had over six months to observe the Act in operation before setting out on their first circuit since its enactment, the Spring Circuit of 1837. At a meeting of the judges prior to this circuit 'a discussion took place as to some points which were thought likely to occur at the assizes, in consequence of the recent act for allowing prisoners, indicted for felony, to make full defence by counsel', and a five clause practice memorandum was issued. The first three clauses regulated the defence use of the depositions at the trial by giving the prosecution a right of reply to the entire defence case if the prisoner's counsel referred to them. The remaining two clauses provided that the prosecution counsel was entitled to a reply in state prosecutions, irrespective of whether the defence called evidence, and in all cases was permitted to reply to purely character evidence. The depositions clauses applied an existing rule of evidence to the use of the depositions, and the other two clauses confirmed the existing practice of misdemeanour trials. The effect, however, was to give maximum scope to the prosecution right of reply, and to create an incentive for the prisoner's counsel to dispense with the use of the depositions at the trial and, to a lesser extent, with character evidence.[45]

The application of established practices in civil and misdemeanour trials to any points of procedure arising from the Prisoners' Counsel Act also appears in the judicial decisions of the first years of its implementation. It was held, following the practice of misdemeanour cases, that the defence was entitled to address the jury only once, and so had to choose between a prisoner's statement and a speech from counsel.[46] Secondly, following the practice in civil trials it was held that defence counsel could not refer to any matter in his speech that the defence was not in a position to prove. This meant that defence counsel could not refer to matters solely within the prisoner's knowledge, because the prohibition on the prisoner testifying meant the defence had no evidence of them.[47] The difficulties that these two rules might cause for the defence in even the simplest of cases are well illustrated by the facts of *R v Malings*. The prisoner was indicted for malicious wounding. The prosecutor gave evidence that he was violently assaulted by the prisoner, without any provocation or cause, as they walked home together one night from a

[45] The Practice Memorandum is reproduced in Appendix 1.3. The depositions clauses are considered in more detail in the next section of this chapter. Where the only evidence called by the defence was as to the prisoner's character the usual practice was for the prosecution not to reply. Clause 4 acknowledged this practice but said the strict position was that the prosecution was entitled to a reply.

[46] *R v Daniel Boucher* (1837) 8 C. & P. 141; *R v Burrows* (1838) 2 M & Rob. 124.

[47] *R v Henry Beard* (1837) 8 C. & P. 142.

public house. No one else was present or saw the assault. The defence was that the prosecutor had threatened to shoot the prisoner, had snapped a gun at him, and the prisoner had responded in self-defence. If the prisoner made a statement to this effect to the jury then he had to forgo a speech from his counsel. If counsel addressed the jury then he could not refer to the facts supporting self-defence as he was not in a position to call evidence to prove them.[48]

The ruling that the prisoner could not address the jury in person and by counsel ignored the traditional 'testimonial' function of the prisoner's statement. It assumed that the statement had a 'defensive' character, and so served the same function as a speech from counsel.[49] In *R v Rider* Mr Justice Patteson treated counsel's speech and the prisoner's statement as identical when he indicated, *obiter dicta,* that the prisoner in his statement could not refer to matters not established by other evidence:[50]

> The general rule certainly ought to be, that a prisoner defended by counsel should be entirely in the hands of his counsel...If the prisoner were allowed to make a statement, and stated as a fact anything which could not be proved by evidence, the jury should dismiss that statement from their minds; but if what the prisoner states is merely a comment on what is already in evidence, his counsel can do that much better than he can.

This view denied any testimonial function to the prisoner's statement, and so any reason for the defended prisoner to address the jury. The prisoner was usually distinguished from the other participants in the trial not only by his name at the head of the indictment, his place in the dock, and his stake in the verdict, but also by his intimate knowledge of the events in issue. The implementation of full defence by counsel together with the long-standing prohibition on the prisoner giving evidence denied him the opportunity to speak at his own trial. In the aftermath of the Prisoners' Counsel Act the defended prisoner stood or sat in silence while his counsel conducted his defence and the jury reached their verdict without the benefit of hearing him tell the court his version of events.[51]

[48] (1838) 8 C. & P. 242. Mr Baron Alderson in this case permitted a prisoner's statement and an address by his counsel, but this was subsequently recognised as a very exceptional course: see *R v Walking* (1838) 8 C. & P. 243; *R v Manzano* (1860) 2 F. & F. 64.

[49] On the testimonial and defensive functions of the prisoner's statement see Chapter 2.

[50] (1838) 8 C. & P. 539.

[51] The prisoner became competent though not compellable to give evidence by the Criminal Evidence Act 1898 (61 & 62 Vict., c. 36). Prior to this Act there seems to have been a shift in the judicial attitude towards prisoners' statements, involving some recognition of a testimonial function: see, for example, Stephen (1890) 187, Stephen's comments, as presiding judge, in *R v Maybrick* (1889) as reported in Irving (1912) 183–4 and 334–5, and Cave J. in *R v Shimmin* (1882) 15 Cox C. C. 122. For the later history of unsworn statements see Cowen and Carter (1956).

The Depositions: A Case Study in Tactical Inequality

The history of the depositions sections of the Prisoners' Counsel Act illustrate the difficulties created for defence counsel by the deletion of the last word clause and the restrictive judicial attitude to the implementation of the Act. These sections granted the prisoner the advantage, already enjoyed by the prosecution, of copies of the depositions prior to the trial. However, the rules of practice for the implementation of these sections in the Practice Memorandum linked the defence use of the depositions to the right to the last word to the jury in a manner prejudicial to the defence. The result was that an inequality apparently eliminated by legislation was entrenched by the judicial application of that legislation.

Sections 3 and 4 of the Prisoners' Counsel Act enabled prisoners to have copies of and to inspect the depositions against them. These sections had a short and quiet legislative gestation, first appearing in 1836 amongst the amendments of a select committee of the House of Commons to the Prisoners' Counsel Bill. The select committee's proposals were accepted by the House of Commons and, with the addition of a proviso to section 3, by the House of Lords.[52] Lord Abinger provided the strongest opposition to these clauses, on the grounds of inconvenience and the opportunity the depositions would give prisoners to concoct defences.[53]

At the time of the Prisoners' Counsel Act it was established at common law, although only recently, that the prisoner had a right to be present when the depositions were taken, and to question the witnesses. The prisoner was usually permitted to be accompanied by an attorney to advise him, to cross-examine witnesses, and to take notes. Some magistrates in their discretion would allow prisoners copies of the depositions.[54] Sections 3 and 4 in most cases simply entitled the prisoner to copies of an official record of evidence taken in his own and his attorney's presence and already recorded by them. Nevertheless these clauses protected prisoners from magisterial caprice and to an extent from bewilderment or lack of representation at pre-trial hearings, and gave them a significant benefit at the trial, where a copy of the 'official'

[52] See (1836) Parl. Papers IV 697; (1836) 31 P. D. 1159; (1836) 35 P. D. 249. An amendment relating to depositions had been proposed in debate in 1834, but was withdrawn after a short discussion: see (1834) 24 P. D. 1098 (O'Dwyer).

[53] Lord Abinger convinced a select committee of the Lords to strike out the depositions sections, but his comments in debate suggesting depositions were sometimes taken in the absence of prisoners provoked a strong reaction in their favour, and they were restored during the third reading of the bill: see (1836) 35 P. D. at 184–6, 228–32 and 249.

[54] *Arnold* (1836) 8 C. & P. 621; Beattie (1986) 276–7; (1836) 35 P. D. 184–5 (Duke of Richmond), and 250 (Lord Cottenham LC).

record was much more useful to counsel than an attorney's instructions as to what passed at the pre-trial hearing. The depositions would enable counsel to identify immediately and with confidence any discrepancies between the evidence at trial and the evidence of the witness before the examining magistrate, and so enable him to challenge the recollection or credibility of a witness in cross-examination, and to press reasonable doubt in his address to the jury.

The Practice Memorandum declared that the prisoner's counsel could not refer to the depositions, or more generally to any statement made by a witness before the magistrate, in either cross-examination or his address to the jury until the deposition had been read *as part of the evidence of the defence.* When the defence called any evidence then the prosecution counsel was entitled to a reply—to a second speech and the last word to the jury. The last word, as already discussed, was so highly prized by barristers that the prisoner's counsel was unlikely to exchange this advantage for the discrepancies in prosecution evidence which the depositions might establish. The Prisoner's Counsel Act granted the defence access to the depositions but the Practice Memorandum, by encumbering their use with the loss of the last word, ensured that in most cases the defence would not use them.[55]

The reluctance of the defence to concede the last word, the consequent loss of use of the depositions, and the struggle of a defence counsel against the restrictive clauses of the Practice Memorandum are illustrated by the trial of François Courvoisier. Courvoisier was the valet of Lord William Russell, who was murdered in his bed on 6 May 1840. There were signs that the victim's house had been broken into, and some plate had disappeared. The prosecution claimed that Courvoisier, who lived in the house, had created the impression that the house had been robbed by intruders to conceal his guilt. The defence case was that a person or persons unknown had broken into and robbed the house, and in doing so had committed the murder. Courvoisier's counsel were prepared to explore the possibility that one of the other servants had

[55] The Practice Memorandum treated the depositions as documentary evidence produced by the defence. *The Queen's Case* had decided that where cross-examining counsel wished to put statements in a letter to a witness then the letter must be read immediately or when counsel opened the defence, but, in any event, 'as part of the evidence of the counsel proposing it, and subject to all the consequences of having such letter considered as part of his evidence'. The purpose of this rule was to ensure the court was possessed of the entire written document, and not simply the parole responses of a witness to statements in the document selected by counsel. A premise of the rule, therefore, was that the court did not possess the document, which did not apply to the depositions. In fact, the status of the depositions prior to the Prisoners' Counsel Act had usually been the exact opposite of the letters in *The Queen's Case;* they had been in the possession of the court, and used by the judge to question witnesses, but not available to the prisoner or his counsel: see (1820) 2 Brod. & B. 284 at 286–90 (quotation at 290).

assisted the break-in, perhaps the housemaid Sarah Mancer who seemed to precognise some injury to Lord William Russell before his death was discovered. She had disposed before the coroner that the first thing she saw on entering the victim's bedroom was 'his lordship murdered in bed'. Her evidence at the trial did not contain this immediate conclusion of murder—she said instead that she had entered the room to near the foot of the bed, had addressed his lordship, then seen blood on the pillow and had run from the room screaming.

The leading counsel for Courvoisier was Charles Phillips. He interrupted the examination of Sarah Mancer at an early stage, and the following exchange took place:[56]

Mr C. PHILLIPS suggested it might be as well for their Lordships to have the depositions before the coroner and the magistrates to refer to.

Mr ADOLPHUS [Counsel for the prosecution] said, if the depositions before the coroner and the magistrates became at any time necessary for the defence of the prisoner, either in examination, cross-examination, or in addressing the jury, whatever objection he might offer to their production on other occasions, he should urge none in a case like the present.

Mr Baron PARKE saw no reason why this case should be conducted on principles different from any other. Every case must proceed according to the established rules of law, and no counsel was entitled to take credit for any relaxation.

Mr C. PHILLIPS: All I ask for the unfortunate prisoner at the bar is that justice which the law entitles him to. I only suggested that the depositions taken before the coroner should be before your Lordships.

Adolphus' offer was understood to waive the right of reply to which the Practice Memorandum would entitle him if Phillips referred to the depositions.[57] Mr Baron Parke, however, insisted that counsel adhere to the rules of practice, notwithstanding that in other circumstances the prosecution counsel could waive his right of reply.[58] By this exchange Phillips drew the jurors' attention to the depositions, and so prepared their minds for his cross-examination of Sarah Mancer during which he was going to draw upon the depositions but be unable to refer to them directly.

Phillips began his cross-examination by establishing from Sarah Mancer that she had been examined 'many times' by a magistrate and the coroner. He then switched to her discovery of the victim. He put to her

[56] *The Times,* Friday 19 June 1840.

[57] Phillips interpreted Adolphus' vague language (perhaps poorly reported) in this way: see *infra* n. 60.

[58] For example, see clause 4 of the Practice Memorandum in Appendix 1.3. The practice was for prosecution counsel not to reply to character evidence, and Adolphus did not do so in *Courvoisier.*

six times that she had previously said she had seen his lordship murdered in his bed, without extracting the admission he wanted. He avoided reading her deposition to her or, until the sixth attempt, identifying the coroner's inquest as the occasion she had made the statement. When Phillips mentioned the coroner the Court intervened and he had to leave the point unproved:[59]

Mr Phillips: Did you never say you saw him murdered in bed; you were examined before the coroner, now I give you warning.

Mr Baron Parke said that if anything that passed before the coroner should be enquired into, the depositions would have to be produced.

Mr Phillips: Well you say you always gave the same account of the transaction that you do now?—Witness: Yes.

The jury were treated to the browbeating of a confused housemaid by an experienced criminal barrister, at the end of which they did not have the benefit of either knowing what Sarah Mancer had said before the coroner, or hearing her explanation of it. All this time the depositions were in the court, but the effect of the Practice Memorandum was to keep them from the witness and the jury.

In his address to the jury Phillips could not read Sarah Mancer's deposition or state there was a contradiction between her evidence at the trial and the deposition, without conceding the last word. Again he resorts to circumlocution to make a simple point, and probably transgressed the Practice Memorandum in doing so:[60]

The depositions taken before the coroner were now before the learned judges, and perhaps they would consider it their bounden duty to tell the jury whether that woman [i.e. Sarah Mancer] swore before the coroner as she did before the court. His conscience was clear; he [Phillips] had discharged his duty by throwing out that suggestion. The question he had put to the witness was this—'Upon the oath you have taken, did you not tell the coroner that you saw—instead of some blood on the pillow—his Lordship murdered on the bed?' That was matter for the jury to consider: he would now pass on.

The summing-up of the Chief Justice of Common Pleas, Sir Nicholas Tindal, upheld the rules established by the Practice Memorandum by not revealing the contents of Sarah Mancer's deposition. He instructed the jury that there was no evidence to contradict Sarah Mancer's evidence in court on this point, but added that if the alleged words had been used at

[59] *Morning Chronicle*, Friday 19 June 1840.

[60] See Appendix 3.7 (*The Times*, Monday 22 June 1840). In the *Morning Herald* of the same day Phillips is reported as introducing the above passage with a comment to disarm possible objections: 'Mr Adolphus has said he would allow me to use every deposition, and that he will not insist on the right of reply'.

an earlier time they 'really appeared to be a trivial expression, and could scarcely amount to a contradiction'.[61]

Conclusions

Adversarialism sought the discovery of the truth through the contention of counsel. Where each party had counsel, and each counsel put its party's case in the best possible light, then the court would have the benefit of the fullest investigation and interpretation of the facts in reaching its verdict. The discussion in this chapter shows that the ambition and conscience of counsel, the inevitable inequalities between the parties, the right to the last word, the nature of the judicial involvement in the trial, and the implementation of the legislation might interfere with the emergence of the truth through adversarialism.

Perhaps the most serious impediment to the ideal of adversarialism was the question of the last word. The attractive portrayal by reformers of the truth emerging through the contention of counsel had to accommodate the reality that one counsel or the other had to speak last and that counsel, experienced lawyers agreed, would possess a considerable advantage. The loss of the last word clause in the final stages of the Prisoners' Counsel Act debate meant the introduction of the practice of civil trials into all criminal trials, by which the prosecution had a second speech and the last word if the defence called evidence. The Practice Memorandum strengthened the prosecution's hold on the last word in providing for a reply to any use of the depositions by the defence. The last word factor compromised the discovery of the truth by creating a significant incentive for the voluntary exclusion of defence evidence.

The full disclosure of the facts on the defence side was further compromised by the restrictions on the prisoner addressing the court. The prisoner was not competent to give evidence, and after the Prisoners' Counsel Act could only make a statement from the dock by forgoing the benefit of a speech from his counsel. The result was that prisoners were increasingly likely to remain silent throughout the trial.

After the Prisoners' Counsel Act, therefore, defence counsel often had to address the jury without the assistance of any defence evidence,

[61] *The Times*, Monday 22 June 1840. Another problem with the depositions sections of the Prisoners' Counsel Act was that the defence was encouraged to prepare to meet the case in the depositions, and was often surprised at the trial by the appearance of a number of witnesses who had not made depositions. For comment on this misleading practice of prosecutors see (1838) 16 *Legal Observer* 313 and 449. The defence in *Courvoisier* was embarrassed by the appearance of unexpected witnesses and evidence at the trial, although in this case it seems the new evidence was genuinely discovered at the last moment: see Appendix 3.13, Henderson (1871) 205–6. *Courvoisier* is considered further in Chapter 6.

except perhaps on the collateral question of the prisoner's character. He had to meet the new responsibilities of a speech without reference to the depositions, and without the factual foundation of a statement from the prisoner or the testimony of witnesses favourable to the prisoner. He was forced to base the defence on the rebuttal of the prosecution case, which meant drawing out the improbabilities, inconsistencies and omissions in the prosecution evidence. It meant proposing alternative explanations of the evidence compatible with the prisoner's innocence. The delineation of doubt and the alternative hypothesis would become the staple logic of defence speeches. Eloquence might add persuasiveness to this logic, and gloss over its deficiencies.

Senior lawyers did not agree on the implications of full defence by counsel for the judge. There were concerns that the traditional judicial paternalism would be reversed by the need to respond to the irresponsibility of defence counsel, which would damage the credibility of prisoner's defences with juries, and also the judicial reputation in the eyes of the people. The more confident view was that the judicial mastery of proceedings would enable the judge to control defence counsel without appearing to favour the prosecution. Whichever view proved correct the need for judicial intervention against the prisoner was minimised if the defence were denied the last word, which the deletion of the last word clause and the Practice Memorandum sought to do.

Notwithstanding the impediments placed in their path, defence counsel were reluctant to relinquish the last word. After the Prisoners' Counsel Act counsel's speech often constituted the entire defence case, as all evidence was sacrificed to retain this advantage. The nature and importance of this speech encouraged aggressive advocacy, which was likely to be anticipated and matched by prosecution counsel. This forensic aggression accorded with the adversarial ideal, but without the foundations of equality between the protagonists and the complete disclosure of relevant evidence it may be doubted whether the emergence of truth would always be the outcome.

6

The Limits of Adversarialism

The Licence of Counsel Controversy

The enactment and implementation of the Prisoners' Counsel Act was followed almost immediately by controversy. The public and the press did not share the unqualified enthusiasm of the Act's promoters for adversarialism, and condemned some of the more zealous displays of defence advocacy under the new procedure as distasteful, deceptive, and immoral. The recurring criticisms in the press of forensic morality prompted an examination in legal literature of the duties of counsel. Some lawyers, particularly Lord Brougham, advocated an uncompromisingly adversarial conception of the duties of counsel which made commitment to the client the first forensic virtue and demanded that counsel exploit all expedient means to obtain the verdict. The predominant view was that there were moral qualifications on counsel's duty to his client, but the limits of adversarialism under this view were difficult to identify with precision.

Some of the issues of the Prisoners' Counsel Act debate re-emerge in the licence of counsel controversy, especially the merits of advocacy, the best means to elucidate the truth in criminal trials, and the need to prevent the escape of the guilty. There was even a call for the reconsideration of the Prisoners' Counsel Act, but generally the debate of the 1840s assumed full defence by counsel to be justified and concentrated on the character of defence advocacy. The emphasis passed from criminal procedure to the standards of the legal profession, from the necessity for counsel to their responsibilities. At the same time, the press and professional literature replaced parliamentary debate and official inquiry as the primary medium of discussion.

The licence of counsel controversy involved an intensification of the periodic rumblings of the 1830s against the forensic practices of the Bar. These years saw concern at the abuse of cross-examination at the Old Bailey, as discussed in Chapter 2, and also at abuse of the Bar's privilege of free expression. This privilege secured the uninhibited presentation by counsel of their clients' cases, and so was an important corollary to full defence by counsel on its introduction in 1836. However, shortly after the passage of the Prisoners' Counsel Act it began to attract criticism. Charles Dickens paraded the abuse of the privilege of free speech by rhetorical excess and gratuitous insults in the advocacy of Serjeant Buzfuz in his *Pickwick Papers* published in 1837. Benjamin Disraeli lashed out at forensic licence in 1838 after learning that at the hearing of an election petition Charles Austin, a rising star of the parliamentary bar, had accused him of bribery. In a letter to the *Morning Post* Disraeli attacked 'the privilege of circulating falsehoods' which, he said, 'is delicately described as doing your duty towards your client'. He concluded by calling Austin 'a rhetorical hireling' who had made a statement he knew to be false. Austin responded by issuing proceedings for criminal libel and the matter concluded in King's Bench when Disraeli, appearing on his own behalf, retracted the slur on Austin's character. However, he took the opportunity to reiterate, though in more temperate language, his criticism of the Bar itself. 'I believe at this moment', he told the court, 'that there is in the principles on which the practice of [the] bar is based, a taint of arrogance...of that reckless spirit, which is the necessary consequence of the possession and exercise of irresponsible power'. The 1840s inherited this fragile public patience with forensic licence, which was to erupt into virulent condemnation as a result of the defence advocacy in some highly publicised criminal trials.[1]

Notwithstanding these links with the previous decade, the licence of counsel controversy owes much to the circumstances of the 1840s. It was a difficult decade for the Bar, a time of press hostility and public antipathy; of unwelcome scrutiny, exposed shortcomings and demands for it to justify its prerogatives. Legal education was investigated by a parliamentary select committee which attributed a wide range of contemporary professional problems, including incompetent senior counsel and judges, intellectual narrowness and a hypercritical attention to technicalities in court, to the absence of systematic training for the Bar. There were complaints, which reached the level of parliamentary debate, of senior barristers accepting more briefs than they could possibly attend to, and then either attempting to run from one court or parliamentary committee to another 'to the great confusion and delay of business, as well as to the damage of their clients' or simply not appearing at all, but invariably retaining their fees. There were struggles with solicitors, especially over rights of audience in county courts and before courts of quarter sessions, and the parliamentary bar sought to implement a

[1] *Morning Post*, 2 (Austin's remarks) and 6 (Disraeli's letter) June 1838; Stammers (1838), quotation at 10.

collective refusal to deal against slow paying parliamentary agents. The Oxford and Western Circuit messes plunged the Bar's relations with the press to their nadir in 1845 by banishing from their company any practitioners who provided law reports for newspapers. In response, the press abused any professional target available. *Fraser's Magazine,* for example, marked the early death of Sir William Follett, which extinguished a brilliant political and legal career on the threshold of judicial office and in sight of the Lord Chancellorship, with recollections of his greed, his practice of 'taking briefs that he could never read, and for pocketing retainers in causes he could never plead', and his ability to 'play the artful dodge' with affidavits—that is, to read them in such a dextrous way as to misrepresent their meanings. *Punch* portrayed the honour and integrity of the Bar in scornful terms:

> They'll [i.e. Barristers will] turn a man from their mess who reports in a paper; they'll expel a man from their spotless society for reporting in the *Times* or the *Morning Chronicle.*
>
> They do not expel a man for disgusting hypocrisy; for bearing false witness; for the 'artful dodge'; for keeping 'fraud and falsehood' out of view—they load him with honours for it.

The impact of this criticism on the Bar is apparent in its literature during this decade, both in the defensive articles and editorials in professional journals on 'the state of the profession', and in the many works devoted to the traditions and the 'great men' of the Bar.[2]

There were various means available to an unscrupulous counsel, in cross-examination and the address to the jury, to abuse the privilege of free expression. Three abuses of the address to the jury were rhetorical excess, presenting a case counsel knew to be false, and needless attacks on the character of witnesses or parties. These abuses could occur in either civil or criminal trials, but their consequences were much more serious in a criminal trial where they might save a murderer or threaten the life of an innocent, and it was in criminal trials that they aroused the fiercest indignation and brought the greatest vituperation to the Bar. The

[2] **Legal Education**; *Report from the Select Committee on Legal Education in England and Ireland* (1846) Parl. Papers X. 1; **Counsel accepting excessive briefs**: (1842) 62 P.D. 309 (quotation at 310); **Struggles with solicitors**: (1845) 4 L.T. 263, 300, App. 50, (1845) 5 L.T. 61, 64, 85, 304, (1846) 7 L.T. 256, (1846) 8 L.T. 76, (1847) 10 L.T. 60, 253, (1848) 12 L.T. 203, 227, (1850) 14 L.T. 240, 490; **Parliamentary bar and parliamentary agents**: (1848) 11 L.T. 162; **The Bar and the press**: *The Times,* 29 July 1845; *The Examiner,* 16 August 1845; (1845) 5 L.T. 163 and 183; 'Events of the Quarter' (1845) 33 *Law Magazine* 421; 'Newspapers and the Bar' (1845) 34 *Law Magazine* 163; 'Events of the Quarter' (1846) 35 *Law Magazine* 218 and 368; 'The Bar and the Press—the State of the Profession' (1846) 3 *Law Review* 27; Kirwan (1845), quotation at 172 (Follett article); (1845) 9 *Punch* 64 (quotation), 101, 104, 108, 113, 114, 121, and 128. On the Bar's responses to the problems of the 1840s see Cocks (1983) ch. 3.

public and the press were quick to ascribe these forensic excesses to the irresponsibility of counsel, but they might also be the result of errors of judgement as counsel struggled with the novel tactical and moral difficulties of full defence by counsel. The pressures of defence advocacy after the Prisoners' Counsel Act are well illustrated by *Courvoisier,* which was the most controversial criminal trial of the 1840s and to many people the epitome of pernicious advocacy.

The status of Courvoisier's victim, a younger brother of two dukes of Bedford, ensured his trial immense attention. On the opening day of the trial 'the anxiety to witness the proceedings', said *The Times,* 'particularly by those who compose the higher classes of society, was beyond all precedent'. The nobility and dignitaries on the Bench or in the court included a royal duke, five earls, the Dutch and Portuguese ambassadors, and numerous noble ladies whose 'extensive draperies' Serjeant Ballantine later recalled, so hemmed in the Chief Justice 'that he had scarcely room to move'. The defence was expected to argue that the victim, Lord William Russell, was murdered by unknown housebreakers and not by Courvoisier. As noted in the last chapter, there were signs of forced entry to the victim's house, and a quantity of plate had disappeared. An exhaustive search had not discovered the plate in the house and Courvoisier, who as the victim's valet lived with him, had been under observation since the murder and had not removed it. There were bloodstains on items in a trunk of Courvoisier's clothing, but the suspicious circumstances of their discovery would enable the defence to argue they were placed there by reward hungry police officers. Courvoisier's senior counsel, Charles Phillips, firmly believed in his client's innocence.[3]

The senior counsel for the prosecution, John Adolphus, opened aggressively, without any of the restraint expected from prosecution counsel prior to the Prisoners' Counsel Act. He minutely examined and connected the circumstantial evidence against Courvoisier, 'pausing frequently', observed the *Annual Register,* 'to remove any impression favourable to [the prisoner], and suggesting a guilty motive for all he said and did'.[4] He anticipated and discussed the prisoner's possible defences, and even the lines of cross-examination defence counsel

[3] *The Times,* 19 June 1840 and 20 November 1849; Ballantine (1883) 61. On *Courvoisier* generally see 1 Townsend (1850) 244, and Atlay (1899) ch. 3.

[4] (1840) *Annual Register* (Chronicle) 229, quotation at 230. Adolphus even saw Courvoisier's nationality as circumstantial evidence against him (from *The Times,* 19 June 1840; Courvoisier was a Swiss national): 'Englishmen were not in the habit of considering murder as a prelude to plunder. With foreigners it was different, for they imagined that if they destroyed the life of the person they robbed, there would then exist no direct testimony against them. It therefore was a natural supposition that the murder was committed by the prisoner'.

were likely to pursue. In this opening, a fellow barrister wrote, Mr Adolphus 'emulated the fame of Garrow on the prosecution of Patch,...so artful and ingenious, sometimes sophistical, were his innuendoes and inferences of guilt'.[5]

On the morning of the second day of the trial the defence learnt that the prosecution intended to call seven new witnesses to prove the discovery of the missing plate the previous day in a parcel left at a Leicester Square hotel. The proprietress of the hotel, Mrs Piolaine, could positively identify Courvoisier as having deposited the parcel with her some days *before* the murder. The strongest prop of the defence—the possibility that the murder was committed during a robbery by persons unknown—collapsed. Courvoisier called his counsel over to speak with him in the dock and the following conversation, as later recounted by Phillips, took place:[6]

> 'I have sent for you, gentlemen', said he [Courvoisier] 'to tell you that I committed the murder!' When I [Phillips] could speak, which was not immediately, I said, 'Of course, then, you are going to plead guilty?' 'No, Sir', was the reply, 'I expect you to defend me to the utmost'.

Phillips and his junior were unsure of the proper course for them to pursue in light of this confession, and so sought an interview with Mr Baron Parke, one of the two judges trying the case. Phillips' account continues:

> Mr Baron Parke requested to know distinctly whether the prisoner insisted on my defending him, and, on hearing that he did, said I was bound to do so, and to use all fair arguments arising on the evidence.

At the close of the second day Courvoisier gave his solicitor another message for Phillips:

> Tell Mr. Phillips, my counsel, that I consider he has my life in his hands.

The dilemma of representing a cause known to be false is as old as the legal profession; it was, for example, addressed by the pleaders of the English Bar in the reign of Edward I.[7] Nor was it a new situation for an advocate to represent a murderer knowing of his or her guilt; there were rumours, for example, that Patch's counsel had been in that position.[8] However, the Prisoners' Counsel Act and its judicial implementation had

[5] 1 Townsend (1850) 245. Adolphus' opening is fully reported in *The Times*, 19 June 1840.

[6] Phillips gave his account of Courvoisier's confession in a letter published in *The Times* of 20 November 1849. There is an erroneous account of the confession in Ballantine (1883) which has misled some later commentators.

[7] See Statute of Westiminster, prim. cap. 29.

[8] *Patch's case* is discussed in Chapter 2. On the position of his counsel see (1840) 24 *Law Magazine* 238.

introduced and loaded so much significance on to the speech of the prisoner's counsel that Phillips faced this old dilemma—inevitably at its most difficult in a capital trial—in a particularly acute form. The Act entitled Courvoisier to a speech from counsel, the contemporary practice was to sacrifice all defence evidence to derive the maximum advantage from this speech, and the philosophy of adversarialism required the speech to be made as zealously as possible.

Phillips' predicament raised the question of the nature of the advocate's duty to his client, and his communications with the client and the court exposed their conflicting expectations of him. Courvoisier demanded unrestrained zeal from his advocate, who should defend him 'to the utmost'. Mr Baron Parke's advice 'to use all fair arguments arising on the evidence' qualified zeal for the client with the ambiguous standard of fairness. The merits of these two views—'all expedient means' or 'all fair means'—were debated by lawyers and journalists for the remainder of the decade. Mr Baron Parke's view left the individual advocate to decide the limits of 'fair' advocacy, and *Courvoisier* demonstrates the potential difficulty of this decision. Despite Courvoisier's confession there were many 'arguments arising on the evidence' which might be urged in favour of an acquittal. The evidence strongly suggested that the bloodstained items in Courvoisier's trunk were placed there by the police, the sudden appearance of the missing plate during the trial was suspicious, the integrity of an important prosecution witness, Sarah Mancer, had been impugned—before Courvoisier's confession—in cross-examination, and Adolphus' aggressive opening provided abundant topics for eloquent protest about the unfairness of the prosecution.

Phillips had given some indication of his personal views on the advocate's duties during the Prisoners' Counsel Act debate. He told the House of Lords select committee on the Bill in 1835 that it would be 'treacherous and dishonest' for defence counsel to omit any possible exertion on a client's behalf, even in a case of 'flagrant guilt'. 'Those who are employed as advocates', he wrote to Lord Brougham around the same time, 'must act as advocates—& the most awful of considerations may become the victim of sophistry'.[9] Phillips, like Lord Brougham, whose views are discussed in the next section, believed the advocate should adopt all expedient means to save his client, and his speech for Courvoisier largely manifested this attitude. It was arranged

[9] *Prisoners' Defence Bill. Minutes of Evidence taken before the Select Committee of the House of Lords etc.* (1836) Lords' Papers 119, at 7, Phillips to Brougham, August 1835, *Brougham Papers No. 26,364.* At the beginning of his speech in *Courvoisier* Phillips recalled his opposition to the Prisoners' Counsel Act, and spoke with apparent sadness of the manner it committed the life of the prisoner 'to the skill and talent of his advocate': see Appendix 3.2.

around the complementary themes of the insufficiency of the evidence and the indications that Courvoisier 'had been made the victim of an unjust and depraved conspiracy'.[10] Phillips demonstrated that Courvoisier's behaviour after the murder and under police questioning, from which the police and the prosecution had sought to draw so many inferences, was consistent with innocence,[11] and that some circumstances were wholly incompatible with his guilt.[12] He castigated the police investigation—accusing officers of carelessness, conspiracy, intimidation, tampering with evidence, equivocation and lying on oath—and denounced the pernicious effect on the investigation of a large reward.[13] He sought to discredit the last minute discovery of the missing plate with suspicions about Mrs Piolaine's character and complaints of prosecution ambush.[14] He occasionally invoked gentler emotions, making, for example, sentimental digressions on Swiss character, love of a mother country, the 'youth, beauty, innocence, virtue and talent' of Queen Victoria, only to return with renewed indignation to dubious proofs and police turpitude.[15] He warned the jurors of the magnitude of their responsibility, dwelling on the terrors of a wrong verdict, which would haunt their sleep, torture their consciences 'and confront and condemn them before the judgment seat of their God'.[16]

Courvoisier's confession to his counsel became common knowledge immediately after his conviction, and outrage at Phillips' speech, and to a lesser extent his cross-examination, swiftly followed. There was concern at his conception of the advocate's duty, which appeared to pay no

[10] Appendix 3.1. [11] Appendix 3.7, 3.8, 3.9.

[12] For example, see Appendix 3.4 and 3.14.

[13] Appendix 3.8–3.12. The Chief Justice in his summing-up said of one police constable that he gave his evidence 'in such a way that it would be dangerous in such a serious inquiry as this to give any credit to it'. (*The Times,* 22 June 1840). After the trial two constables involved in the investigation were dismissed, and an inspector was severely reprimanded for negligence: see 2 House, Storey and Tillotson (1965–93) 88n. Phillips' powerful denunciations of police misconduct, including their efforts to induce Courvoisier to confess, cast an intriguing light on the strict application of the law relating to the admissibility of confessions during the 1840s. The use of confessions by the prosecution gave defence counsel the opportunity to exploit suspicions of police misconduct in their jury addresses which, some argued, created a risk of wrongful *acquittals:* see Cornish (1978) 311–14, especially the comments of the Recorder of Newcastle referred to at 312.

[14] Appendix 3.15.

[15] Appendix 3.3, 3.4, 3.7, 3.13. Queen Victoria was a particularly emotive subject because of Oxford's attempt on her life at this time.

[16] Appendix 3.1 and 3.17. On two subjects Phillips made incongruous comments which manifest some concession to 'fair' advocacy. His comments on Sarah Mancer carried an innuendo, many observers believed, that she had foreknowledge of the murder, yet he also explicitly exonerated her from any involvement in the murder (Appendix 3.6; see also 3.7). Secondly, he undermined his attack on the evidence of the discovery of the missing plate by admitting that Courvoisier might well be guilty of robbery. Phillips seemed eager to impress upon the jury that an acquittal on the indictment for murder would spare Courvoisier's life but not absolve him from all punishment (Appendix 3.16).

regard to truth, personal reputation, or decency towards women,[17] and at the possibility that such advocacy would deter victims and witnesses from coming forward to make and assist prosecutions. There were expressions, from Albany Fonblanque, the editor of *The Examiner*, and Edwin Chadwick, of Benthamite contempt for the self-serving amorality of lawyers. The need for defence advocacy, forensic free speech, and even the defence of the guilty, was usually acknowledged, but only within limits which Phillips in *Courvoisier* and, it was asserted, many other advocates, particularly at the Old Bailey, far exceeded.

In the week following Courvoisier's conviction Charles Dickens wrote two letters to the *Morning Chronicle* about the case. In the first letter he questioned Phillips' imputations against Sarah Mancer, his vilification of the police, his 'disgraceful aspersions' on the character of Mrs Piolaine, and his frequent appeals to God. Dickens said that as a 'plain' and 'practical' man such advocacy made two impressions upon him—'firstly, that I never would stretch out my hand to arrest a murderer, with these pains and penalties before me; and, secondly, that no earthly consideration should induce me to permit my wife or daughter to give evidence at the Old Bailey'. This letter produced a reply, signed 'A Templar' and possibly from Phillips, which defended the use of all expedient means in advocacy. 'What is the duty of the prisoner's counsel?' he asked. 'I hold that his first duty is to endeavour to procure, by every means in his power, the acquittal of his client'. Dickens in his second letter repudiated this conception of the advocate's duty.[18]

Both Fonblanque in *The Examiner* and Chadwick in an article on the licence of counsel in *The Westminster Review* rejected 'the precept of all expedient means', as this idea of the advocate's duty might be called,[19] as founded on a misunderstanding of the prisoner's rights at his trial. The prisoner had no right or privilege to utter falsehoods in his own

[17] The wronged woman was an emotive image in this controversy. Phillips' cross-examination and speech tainted the housemaid Sarah Mancer with foreknowledge of the crime, and accused Mrs Piolaine of sexual immorality and running a disreputable hotel. Sarah Mancer was reportedly so traumatised by the murder and the trial that she was later committed to a lunatic asylum: see *The Examiner*, 27 October 1849.

[18] **Dickens' letters**: *Morning Chronicle*, 23 and 29 June 1840, reproduced in 2 House, Storey and Tillotson (1965–93) 86–91, which identifies Dickens as the author of these two letters signed 'Manlius'. Dickens' deep interest in the administration of the criminal law is considered in Collins (1994). '**A Templar**': *Morning Chronicle*, 25 June 1840 (2 House, Storey and Tillotson (1965–93) 491–3). This letter has stylistic affinities with Phillips' letters in the *Brougham Papers* (especially its vivid and emphatic expression, its mode of disparagement, and certain figures, such as those which introduce the fourth and eleventh paragraphs), has indications that the writer was present at the trial (e.g. the reference to the 'startling equivocation' of Mrs Piolaine), and was written from the Middle Temple, of which Phillips was a member, but attribution of this letter to him must remain tentative.

[19] The expression 'all expedient means' comes from Brougham's unqualified statement of the advocate's duties in *The Queen's Case*, which is discussed in the next section.

defence. Prisoners might often choose to lie to defend themselves, *The Examiner* said, 'but the impossibility of preventing the lie and the opportunity of the lie do not render the lie a right or a duty'. The advocate, they both argued, as the prisoner's representative, cannot possibly have any duty to uphold falsehood if no such duty is derivable from the client. They proceeded to try to define the limits of acceptable advocacy. Chadwick distinguished the *suppressio veri,* which should be permitted, from the *suggestio falsi,* which should not. '[P]erjury and false imputations on parties', he said, 'may be beneficially forbidden to the prisoner, and, by consequence, to his counsel'.[20]

There was some discussion in the aftermath of *Courvoisier* of possible means to prevent or punish such advocacy. The Bishop of London in the House of Lords lamented that the Prisoners' Counsel Act might compel an advocate to defend a guilty man against his conscience, and suggested that the Act be reconsidered, but no further action was taken.[21] Dickens said the abuse of advocacy might be restrained by public opinion, and Fonblanque seems to have shared this view.[22] Chadwick recommended implementing and extending some proposals made by Bentham to improve the utility of cross-examination. Bentham observed that the abuse of cross-examination required the acquiescence of the judge which, he reasoned, meant that the judge had a responsibility to check, with marks of disapprobation, the excesses of the advocate. The judge also had a responsibility to repair, as far as possible, the unjustified ill-treatment of witnesses in cross-examination by vindicating their character and sympathising with their irritation at the conclusion of their testimony.[23] Chadwick suggested that similar steps might be taken to rectify imputations against witnesses in counsel's speeches. He described an imaginary scenario of one of the judges in *Courvoisier* interrupting Phillips to prohibit the use of the epithets he applied to the police, and then at the end of the trial, after passing sentence on

[20] *The Examiner,* 12 July 1840, reprinted, in edited form, in De Fonblanque (1874) 338–40. Fonblanque proposed limitations on advocacy to the same effect as Chadwick; Chadwick (1841) 14. Chadwick always held strong views on the licence of counsel: see Finer (1952) 33.

[21] (1840) 55 P. D. 1401.

[22] *Morning Chronicle,* 29 June 1840 (Dickens). Fonblanque denounced forensic misconduct throughout the decade, usually in striking and provocative terms. His editorials on legal subjects often drew upon Bentham's *The Rationale of Judicial Evidence;* compare, for example, *The Examiner,* 28 June 1840 (reprinted, in edited form, in De Fonblanque (1874) 334) with 6 Bentham (1843) 350 and 7 Bentham (1843) 203, 474–5.

[23] *The Rationale of Judicial Evidence* in 6 Bentham (1843) 406–8. Cf. *ibid,* 338 ('Brow-beating is that sort of offence which never can be committed by any advocate who has not the judge for his accomplice'). Bentham also recommended, as checks to the abuse of cross-examination, publicity and the display of a table of rules in the courtroom 'in characters large enough to be legible to all eyes at once' prescribing what is proper and forbidden for 'the dramatis personae' in the 'forensic theatre': *ibid,* 408.

Courvoisier, publicly acknowledging the trustworthiness of the prosecution witnesses, regretting the accusations made against them, and thanking them for their public service. Chadwick also proposed that counsel should be subject to a duty to show a factual foundation in their instructions for any imputations against character, and that the instructing attorney should be subject to a duty to exercise reasonable care to exclude groundless imputations from counsel's brief. These duties would be enforceable by the judge or any witness injured by their breach.[24]

The readiness of the press to report and condemn suspect advocacy meant the licence of counsel was regularly discussed throughout the decade. The tears shed by Fitzroy Kelly during his speech for Tawell, who hanged for the murder of his wife, were held up as confirmation that barristers would go to any extreme for a fee.[25] The problem of imputing guilt to the innocent arose again in *Reid and M'Cabe,* a murder trial involving two accused. It was alleged that Reid had confessed to his counsel, Digby Seymour, but that Seymour nevertheless attempted to place the responsibility for the murder on the innocent M'Cabe. Seymour, in a letter to *The Times,* said the reports of his conduct were not accurate, in that Reid's confession was incomplete, contradictory and did not entirely exculpate M'Cabe. However, Seymour continued, he would have adopted the same line of defence even if he had possessed a full confession and exculpation. He argued that if the confession was not in evidence, then his duty was to ignore it and 'to throw the whole guilt upon M'Cabe if the evidence, by which the jury were bound to decide, warranted such a course'. *The Examiner* responded that if this were the morality of the law then 'it is high time that a better morality should be invented, or the profession of the law abolished altogether'. If McCabe had hanged, it said, 'we hold that Mr Seymour would have richly deserved to swing from the same gallows'.[26] The defence of co-accused also raised problems in *The Mannings,* where a husband and wife were jointly accused of the murder of the wife's lover. Serjeant Wilkins, acting for the husband, attempted to place the entire responsibility for the

[24] Chadwick (1841) 15–17. Chadwick's proposed duties would require major adjustments to legal professional privilege but, like Bentham and J. S. Mill, he probably thought the privilege should be abolished: see 7 Bentham (1843) 472–6, followed by Mill's editorial comments at 476–80.

[25] *The Times,* 13–15 March 1845; *The Examiner,* 15 and 29 March, and 16 August 1845. See also 'The Late Murders' (1845) 33 *Law Magazine* 317 at 324–7.

[26] *The Times,* 22–4 (trial) and 30 (editorial and Seymour's letter) December 1847; *The Examiner,* 25 December 1847, 1, 8, 15, 29 January 1848; (1848) 8 L. T. 276. *The Examiner* also criticised Seymour's defence for rhetorical excess: see 1 January 1848 ('maudlin rubbish', 'profanation of the name of the Deity'). Both Reid and M'Cabe were convicted, but M'Cabe's sentence was commuted to transportation: see *The Examiner,* 5 February 1848. On Seymour 's later career see Pue (1990).

murder on the wife, surpassing the prosecution counsel in his zeal to establish her guilt. Mrs Manning's counsel, Serjeant Ballantine, protested, and severe censure of the 'disgusting' defence followed in the press.[27]

Courvoisier was recalled throughout the decade, becoming the arch-example of forensic misconduct against which each new incident was to be measured. Eventually, in the aftermath of *The Mannings*, Phillips made a public defence of his advocacy in *Courvoisier* in a letter to *The Times*. He described the circumstances of Courvoisier's confession, and rebutted individually the charges against his advocacy in a manner which assumed that the precept of all expedient means was the true expression of the advocate's duty. He also published a letter from his friend Samuel Warren, which recorded that Mr Baron Parke had expressed the opinion that Phillips' speech 'was perfectly unexceptionable'.[28] These letters revived discussion of the case for a time in the press and professional journals until an article by Warren of, in Brougham's phrase, 'wholly preposterous' detail, exhausted the subject.[29] By this time, after a decade of criticism, the precept of all expedient means, so closely associated with the names of Brougham and Phillips, was discredited within the profession.

Henry Brougham and the Heroic in Advocacy

The controversial precept of all expedient means can be traced to state trials, where speeches in the defence of prisoners indicted for treason were first permitted in 1696. State trials often involved prisoners of high standing and struggles of great pith and moment, such as the defence of individual liberties or resistance to a repressive government or popular prejudice. Such trials required special efforts from the defence advocate and unflinching loyalty to his client. The precept of all expedient means was not devised in venal cases of murder for gain like *Courvoisier* or *The Mannings*, but in grand trials involving the *Rights of Man* and the wrongs of a queen. Henry Brougham gave the precept its definitive expression in the 'trial' of Queen Caroline in 1820, and then many years later the

[27] The speeches of Sjt. Wilkins and Sjt. Ballantine are reported in *The Times*, 27 October 1849. On Wilkins' conduct see *The Observer*, 29 October 1849; *The Examiner*, 27 October and 3 November 1849; (1849) 14 L. T. 177. Charles Dickens followed the trial and execution of the Mannings closely, and reputedly based the character of Hortense in *Bleak House* on Maria Manning: see Collins (1994) 235–41 and 280.

[28] *The Times*, 20 November 1849. Phillips also published a pamphlet at this time of supportive letters from participants or observers at Courvoisier's trial.

[29] See *The Examiner*, 24 November, 1, 8, 15, 22 December 1849; Warren (1850) (reprinted in 2 Warren (1855) 1). For Phillips' personal thoughts on *The Examiner* and Brougham's caustic comments on Warren's article see Phillips to Brougham, 1843, *Brougham Papers No. 26,467*, and Brougham to Phillips, undated, *Brougham Papers, undated and uncatalogued letters 1849–1858*.

Prisoners' Counsel Act created the problem of whether a self-confessed murderer like Courvoisier was entitled, in the speech from his counsel, to the standard of loyalty fashioned for Queen Caroline.

Throughout his long career Henry Brougham pursued an interest in eloquence and advocacy. He had studied and was fond of displaying his knowledge of the practitioners and commentators on oratory of classical antiquity, and published translations of Demosthenes' Chersonese oration and *On the Crown*. His contributions to the *Edinburgh Review* included articles on Demosthenes and Cicero, and reviews of the published speeches of Erskine and Phillips.[30] He was a leading advocate and parliamentary speaker himself, who excelled in the exposure and vehement denunciation of hypocrisy, pretension and fallacy, but was also capable of constructive oratory of impressive, sometimes magnificent, power and vision. He published his collected political and forensic speeches in 1838, and it was the inclusion of his speech for Queen Caroline in this collection which brought to notice, on the eve of the licence of counsel controversy, his statement of the duties of the advocate.

There is a lengthy description of Brougham's style of advocacy in James Grant's *The Bench and the Bar*. 'No two men' wrote Grant, 'could be more unlike each other than was Henry Brougham in a case of limited interest and in one of commanding importance'. In ordinary cases Brougham was often lacklustre, but in cases 'involving any great principle of civil or religious liberty' he far exceeded, in Grant's estimation, 'in the talent and energy he displayed', any contemporary at the Bar. In these cases he rose to astonishing levels of eloquence, argumentation and declamation, and would throw 'his whole soul into his speeches'. 'His principles', said Grant, 'unlike those of barristers in general, were really a part of his nature. In vindicating, or asserting them, therefore, in the person of his client, he was, in point of fact, repelling some outrage which had been offered to himself'. In these great cases Brougham completely identified himself with his client's cause.[31]

Brougham wrote many short biographical pieces on his contemporaries or near contemporaries in law and politics. He published three volumes entitled *Historical Sketches of Statesmen who Flourished in the Reign of George III* between 1839 and 1845 and contributed a number of articles on barristers and judges to the early issues of the *Law Review*,

[30] The articles on Demosthenes and Cicero and the translation of the Chersonese oration appear, with other works relating to classical rhetoric, in 7 Brougham (1872–73); Brougham (1810) and Brougham (1812a) (Erskine); Brougham (1815) and Brougham (1817) (Phillips).

[31] 2 Grant (1837) 110–19. On the character of Brougham's eloquence see Amicus Curiae (1819) 249–64; Forsyth (1858); Talfourd (1825); Hazlitt's comments in *The Spirit of the Age* (11 Hazlitt (1930–34)) and *On the Present State of Parliamentary Eloquence* (7 Hazlitt (1930–34) 8–9); and 'Mr Brougham's Speech for Ambrose Williams' (1829) 2 *Law Magazine* 102.

which first appeared in 1845. He considered that the personality and character of leading figures heavily influenced historical events. 'The history of empires', he said, 'is...the history of men', an exaltation of the individual in history which received its most dramatic contemporary expression in Thomas Carlyle's lectures on *Heroes, Hero-Worship and the Heroic in History* delivered in 1840. Brougham held up his subjects for instruction rather than worship, aiming to record, he said, 'for the warning or for the encouragement of the great, the errors or the wisdom, the vices or the virtues, of their predecessors'. He often identified his legal subjects with a particular forensic skill, and then digressed to discuss its characteristics. A notice of William Garrow in the *Law Review* led to a discussion of the examination of witnesses, and Lord Abinger provided an excuse to consider the qualities of a *nisi prius* leader. An inchoate vision of common law advocacy might be distilled from Brougham's critical articles in the *Edinburgh Review,* his *Historical Sketches,* and his biographical notices in the *Law Review.*[32]

In these writings Brougham often distinguished between legal skills, oratory and advocacy. The legal skills were knowledge of law and procedure, and proficiency in legal argument. Oratory required eloquence in jury addresses, and encompassed, in an analysis derived from classical writers, skill in the selection of material, the arrangement of topics, expression, memory, and delivery. Advocacy was the management of the cause in court, which demanded technical skills, such as the ability to examine and cross-examine witnesses, a knowledge of human nature, qualities of judgement, especially tact and decisiveness, and, above all, courage. Brougham considered that advocacy was the most important of these courtroom abilities, at least in common law actions, and admired oratory, his own forensic forte. The ideal advocate, personified in Brougham's writings by the figure of Thomas Erskine, excelled in advocacy and oratory, and harmoniously married them. The grand secret of Erskine's unparalleled success, he wrote, was 'the matchless skill with which he could subdue the genius of a first-rate orator to the uses of the most consummate advocate of the age'.[33]

[32] 1 Brougham (1838) Preface; 1 Brougham (1839–45) (quotations at 1 and 2); Brougham (1845a); Brougham (1845b). (For Brougham's authorship of this article on Garrow see Stewart to Brougham, November 1844, *Brougham Papers No. 23,878*).

[33] This distinction between law, oratory and advocacy appears in many of Brougham's 'sketches'. It is not invariably drawn, and Brougham usually concentrates on the skill or skills in which his particular subject excelled. His discussions of Erskine dwell on advocacy and oratory, with only passing references to Erskine's legal abilities: see Brougham (1810) (quotation at 117); 'Mr. Erskine' in 1 Brougham (1839–45) 236; and Brougham (1847). See also Brougham (1845a) ('Lord Abinger': consummate advocate, skilled orator); Brougham (1845b) ('Mr Baron Garrow': astonishing ignorance of law, capable orator, 'great, a very great advocate'); 'Lord Eldon' in 2 Brougham (1839–45) 54 (great lawyer, no pretences to eloquence, defective advocate); and 'Lord Ellenborough' in 3 Brougham (1839–45) 198.

The career of Thomas Erskine demonstrated the heights of achievement to which such skills might take the advocate. Erskine's forensic labours, Brougham claimed, had preserved the liberties of the press and the people during the treason trials of the 1790s, and 'saved his country from the horrors of a proscription'. 'Amidst all the struggles of the constitution', he wrote, 'in parliament, in the council, and in the field,—there is no one man, certainly, to whose individual exertions it [i.e. the country] owes so much, as to this celebrated advocate'. His career proved 'how much a single man can do against the corruption of his age, and how far he can vindicate the liberties of his country...by raising his single voice against the outcry of the people, and the influence of the Crown'. The lustre of orators and statesmen grew pale beside this 'most accomplished advocate'. In his admiration of Erskine, Brougham creates the image of the advocate as hero, a solitary man sustained by courage and talent struggling against, and triumphing over, oppression and prejudice.[34]

The Queen's Case brought Queen Caroline's lawyers, led by Brougham, into conflict with the King's will and government policy, in a case with great political and constitutional ramifications. It was on this occasion, which justified majestic eloquence and defiance, that Brougham made his controversial statement of the duties of the advocate:[35]

> an advocate, by the sacred duty which he owes his client, knows, in the discharge of that office, but one person in the world, THAT CLIENT AND NONE OTHER. To save that client by all expedient means,—to protect that client at all hazards and costs to all others, and among others to himself,—is the highest and most unquestioned of his duties; and he must not regard the alarm—the suffering—the torment—the destruction—which he may bring upon any other. Nay, separating even the duties of a patriot from those of an advocate, and casting them, if need be, to the wind, he must go on reckless of the consequences, if his fate it should unhappily be, to involve his country in confusion for his client's protection!

This statement, Brougham explained many years later, 'was anything rather than a deliberate and well-considered opinion'. It 'was a menace, and it was addressed chiefly to George IV, but also to wiser men, such as

[34] Brougham (1810) (quotations at 124 and 127); 'Mr. Erskine' in 1 Brougham (1839–45) 236, especially at 243; Brougham (1847). Cf. Brougham's descriptions of Erskine as 'the greatest of forensic heroes' and 'the Tully of our Hall' in *Recollections of the Bar and Bench* in 4 Brougham (1872–73) 366 at 406.

[35] 1 Brougham (1838) 105 (emphasis original). The 'trial' of Queen Caroline was an investigation, before the House of Lords, to determine the truth of allegations of adultery against her. It arose from the introduction into the House by the Government, at the insistence of George IV, of a Bill of Pains and Penalties to annul the royal marriage and to deprive Caroline of her title as queen. On Brougham's role in the trial and the politics surrounding it see Stewart (1985) ch. 7, and 2 Brougham (1871) ch. 16 and 17.

Castlereagh and Wellington'. It told them that if the defence seemed likely to fail then Brougham was prepared to challenge George IV's right to the throne by raising the subject of his clandestine marriage to the Catholic Mrs Fitzherbert. Brougham fashioned his statement of the advocate's duties for the needs of an extraordinary case and, in the event, his commitment to it was never put to the test.[36]

In subsequent years Brougham drew two oblique parallels between *The Queen's Case* and Erskine's defence of Thomas Paine, who was prosecuted for seditious libel following the publication of *Rights of Man*. Firstly, Erskine suffered a loss of professional status in undertaking this defence by being dismissed from his position as Attorney-General to the Prince of Wales. This Prince of Wales became King George IV, who after *The Queen's Case* inflicted a similar professional rebuff upon Brougham and two of the Queen's other counsel, Thomas Denman and John Williams, by refusing for many years to elevate them to the rank of King's Counsel. In a prefatory memoir to a new edition of Erskine's *Speeches* in 1847 Brougham said of the Prince's action against Erskine 'that the outrage on all common decency of punishing an advocate because he does his duty to his client, was then first perpetrated'. 'But', Brougham continued, placing himself in Erskine's company, this outrage 'was afterwards repeated by the same artist [i.e. George IV] in a much more celebrated instance'.[37] Secondly, Erskine justified the unpopular defence of Paine by declaring at the outset of his speech that an advocate was bound to accept all briefs, irrespective of his opinions of the merits of the client's case. In the aftermath of *Courvoisier* both Brougham and the 'Templar' who wrote to the *Morning Chronicle* sought to derive the precept of all expedient means from the duty to accept all briefs.[38]

[36] Brougham's explanation of his statement appears in a letter referred to in Forsyth (1874) 389n., and is confirmed by Brougham (1871) 405–11.

[37] Brougham (1847) (quotation at xvii). Brougham often alluded to the King's refusal to make Denman, Williams and himself King's Counsel which, because of professional etiquette relating to precedence at the Bar, had significant repercussions upon the distribution of business on circuit: see, for example, 2 Brougham (1871) 428–30; Brougham (1845a) 86; 'Mr Justice Williams' in 4 Brougham (1872–73) 315–16. Lord Lyndhurst on becoming Lord Chancellor secured the rank of King's Counsel for these three barristers.

[38] (1840) 55 P. D. 1401 (Brougham); *Morning Chronicle*, 25 June 1840. Erskine's statement, the most famous expression of the modern 'cab-rank' rule, is as follows (from 2 Erskine (1810) 90–1, emphasis original): 'From the moment that any advocate can be permitted to say, that he *will* or will *not* stand between the Crown and the subject arraigned in the Court where he daily sits to practise, from that moment the liberties of England are at an end. If the advocate refuses to defend, from what *he may think* of the charge or of the defence, he assumes the character of the Judge; nay, he assumes it before the hour of judgment; and in proportion to his rank and reputation, puts the heavy influence of, perhaps, a mistaken opinion into the scale against the accused, in whose favour the benevolent principle of English law makes all presumptions and which commands the very Judge to be his Counsel'.

Brougham referred to neither his own nor Erskine's statements of the advocate's duties in his article entitled *Rights and Duties of Advocates,* which appeared in the *Edinburgh Review* of October 1836. Instead he sought to derive the duties of the advocate from the necessity for legal representation. He saw litigation as an inquiry into 'contested truth' which, in the absence of advocates, would suffer from 'an imperfect disclosure of the facts' and work 'in favour of the parties whose natural capacity, or study of the law, or experience in litigation, surpassed that of their adversaries'. Professional advocates were necessary to clarify the facts and the law for the judge and to prevent injustice by establishing an equality between the parties.[39] From these premises Brougham delineated the representative character of the advocate:[40]

> It follows immediately from this obvious view of the matter, that the advocate cannot be said to appear at all in his own person; and that whatever he states to the judge must be considered as offered by the party whom he represents. He is that party endowed with legal knowledge, with the skill of applying it, and with the power of bringing forward the facts of the case. Therefore, whatever the party could have justly said for himself, the advocate may justly say for him.

All the advocate's zeal, ingenuity and pathos 'must be taken as the effusions of the client himself', what 'the party would have said if he had been equally gifted and equally experienced in the rhetorical art'.[41] From this conception of the representative character of the advocate Brougham deduced that the advocate is bound to accept all cases offered to him, is not responsible for the accuracy of his client's instructions or the merits of his case, and should never express a personal opinion. Brougham drew back, at least in respect of civil litigation, from the proposition that the advocate must urge whatever the exigency of the case demands, admitting three qualifications: 'he is not at liberty to maintain positions of clearly bad law, or to state as facts which are not in his instructions, or the falsehood of which he is made aware by his client. Beyond these exceptions, however, the limitation of the advocate's duty cannot be carried'. In criminal cases, however, the advocate is bound to undertake the defence, even if the client has confided its utter groundlessness, and 'do his best to make it successful'.[42]

In this article Brougham develops the representative character of the advocate, derived from adversarial premises, to maximise forensic

[39] Brougham (1836–37) 157–9 (quotation at 158). Brougham's assumption that facts are incapable of clarification by the parties and judge alone reflects the 'complex facts' argument of the contemporary Prisoners' Counsel Act debate: see Chapter 4.

[40] *Ibid*, 159. [41] *Ibid*, 164. [42] *Ibid*, quotations at 163 and 166.

licence, reaching a position only a little short of his heroic rhetoric in *The Queen's Case.* The advocate's representative character means that he may do whatever the client would do for himself, and is not responsible for the consequences. He is only restricted by a narrow duty of candour towards the court; there is no mention of any duties towards witnesses or third parties. This analysis leaves some difficult questions unanswered, especially in relation to criminal trials to which Brougham devoted only one paragraph, but its logic deserved consideration during the licence of counsel controversy. However, it appeared anonymously in the *Edinburgh Review,* and was forgotten in the controversy over defence advocacy which began a few years later.

Accordingly Brougham was identified simply with his emphatic statement in *The Queen's Case* which, stripped of its context, interpreted literally, and applied to everyday practice, was easily disparaged. This statement put treason within the duty of counsel, Disraeli observed, which to him confirmed the arrogance and reckless spirit of the Bar. It was dissected sentence by sentence by Chadwick, who called it 'extravagant pretension'. A reviewer of Chadwick's article in the *Law Magazine* noted that the statement would justify 'picking the opposite attorney's pocket of a document calculated to prejudice the accused', and said the absurdity of this result showed that the statement must be read 'subject to the general obligations of morality'. Later in the decade the *Law Magazine* was no longer prepared to infer qualifications to make Brougham's sentiments acceptable. It linked the statement with Seymour's explanation of his conduct in *Reid and M'Cabe* and denounced their views 'as unprofessional, outrageous, and detestable'.[43]

Brougham adhered to his strict view of the advocate's duty, though he did not publicly defend his statement in *The Queen's Case.* He told the House of Lords in 1840, in response to the Bishop of London's proposal to reconsider the Prisoners' Counsel Act, that defence advocacy was the privilege of the prisoner and not of the counsel; 'it was a privilege upon which the elucidation of truth...depended, and the life, liberties, and property of the subject were not worth an hour's purchase if the freest scope, he would say more, the most unrestrained licence, was not given to the Bar'.[44] Brougham's rationalisation of forensic zeal was a challenge to the profession, in the controversial years of the 1840s, to identify the limits, if there were any, on adversarial advocacy.

[43] Stammers (1838) 11; Chadwick (1841) 3–4; 'Licence of Counsel' (1841) 25 *Law Magazine* 143 (quotation at 144); 'Licence of Counsel' (1848) 39 *Law Magazine* 53 (quotation at 61).

[44] (1840) 55 P. D. 1401.

Thomas Noon Talfourd: Advocacy and Human Nature

The licence of counsel controversy and the dispute between the Oxford Circuit mess and *The Times* inspired Thomas Noon Talfourd's article *On the Principle of Advocacy as Developed in the Practice of the Bar,* which appeared in the *Law Magazine* in 1846. It is an impassioned and original plea for advocacy to be properly understood and its merits and difficulties appreciated. Talfourd wrote of his 'fervent wish' to remove misconceptions between the Bar and 'Literature', under which heading he included the press, 'for the sake of both', and emphasised the 'intimate associations' between them. 'When we consider the true relation of the Bar to Literature', he wrote, 'we feel sure that nothing can permanently place them in hostile positions. No other great occupations of human energies are so nearly allied;...no others are so entirely lighted up from *within*'.[45] Advocacy, like poetry, he argued, drew upon impulses deep within human nature, especially partisanship and sympathy.

Talfourd was well placed to reconcile the Bar and the press. He was a successful barrister, a serjeant-at-law who within three years of this article would be raised to the Bench. He had supported himself during his early years at the Bar as a law reporter for *The Times* and as a contributor to periodicals, particularly *The New Monthly Magazine,* and *The London Magazine,* where his fellow contributors included Charles Lamb, Thomas De Quincey (whom Talfourd introduced to the magazine) and Charles Phillips. His literary works as an established barrister included four verse tragedies, a memoir of Charles Lamb, and some travel writings. Talfourd's legal career and his passion for literature came together in his speech—the only forensic speech that Talfourd published—for the defence in *R v Moxon,* a prosecution for blasphemy arising from the publication of Shelley's *Queen Mab,* and in his advocacy of increased copyright protection for authors, which resulted in the Copyright Act of 1842. Law and literature came together less pleasantly for him in 1845, when the barristers of the Oxford Circuit resolved to exclude from their mess any members who acted as law reporters for newspapers. The resolution followed dissatisfaction with the manner that *The Times* reported cases on the Oxford Circuit, and it placed Talfourd in a delicate position as a leader of the Oxford Circuit and a former *Times* reporter. He resisted the resolution within the mess, but not sufficiently strongly for *The Times,* which for a period deleted his name from its reports of cases in which he appeared as

[45] Talfourd (1846) especially at 295–8 (quotation at 296, emphasis original).

counsel, and subjected him to editorial ridicule and innuendoes of hypocrisy.[46]

Talfourd's writings on legal subjects included substantial contributions to works on the criminal law and the practice of quarter sessions, and a number of articles on legal life. These articles on legal life included biographical pieces on Lord Guildford, Lord Tenterden, Lords Eldon and Stowell, a superb short piece on the transience of forensic glory entitled *Vestiges of Follett,* and a discussion, in *The London Magazine* in 1825, of the criteria for success at the Bar. Talfourd contemplated a book on the legal profession, which he never wrote, and his miscellaneous writings show a preoccupation with the intellectual and moral qualities of the successful advocate, which received their fullest expression in his 1825 *London Magazine* and 1846 *Law Magazine* articles.[47]

Talfourd believed that success in law, and advocacy in particular, required only mediocre intellectual qualities. In his article *On the Profession of the Bar* he argued, with wry humour, that at the lower end of the profession clearness of thought, and intellectual honesty and sophistication, were impediments to progress. In cross-examination 'taste, feeling, and judgment, are sometimes no trifling hindrances'. In arguing questions of law before lay magistrates an advocate might be 'greatly assisted by confusion of language, and a total want of arrangement and grammar. Mere stupidity, accompanied by a certain degree of fluency, is no inconsiderable power'. In addressing a jury the junior barrister only needed the mundane attributes of 'a certain degree of nerve, a readiness of utterance, and a sufficient acquaintance with the ordinary line of illustration used and approved on similar occasions'. Mediocrity might

[46] **Talfourd's legal career and literary work generally**: 'The Late Mr. Justice Talfourd' (1854) 51 *Law Magazine* 298; 'The Life and Writings of the Late Mr. Justice Talfourd' (1856) 25 *North British Review* 47; for an idiosyncratic example of the overlap of Talfourd's legal life and literary pursuits see Wrottesley (1948) which reproduces Talfourd's notes of evidence, taken in verse, of a trial in 1842. ***Times* law reporter**: 1 Robinson (1872) 213–14. ***The London Magazine***: 3 De Quincey (1897) ch. V, especially 126–7 and 143. ***R v Moxon:*** Talfourd (1841); 2 Townsend (1850) 356. **Talfourd and the dispute with the Press**: for references to this dispute generally, see *supra* n. 2. Talfourd's position is specifically discussed in *The Times*, 29 July 1845, 'Events of the Quarter' (1845) 33 *Law Magazine* 421, and 'Newspapers and the Bar' (1845) 34 *Law Magazine* 163.

[47] Talfourd's writings on law include the third edition of Dickenson and Talfourd (1829), where the statement of the prosecution counsel's duty of restraint, discussed in Chapter 2, appeared, and, as a student of Joseph Chitty, his contribution to Chitty's *Practical Treatise on Criminal Law* ('I wrote—actually wrote—the whole of Mr. Chitty's book on the Criminal Law—from a plan and references provided by him—and was glad and grateful for an acknowledgement of valuable assistance in the Preface': 6 January 1842, *Talfourd Papers, Memorandum 1842–1843).* For his writings on legal life, other than his two primary articles discussed in the text, see Talfourd (1820) ('Lord Guildford'); Talfourd (1821a) ('A Call to the Bar'); Talfourd (1833) ('Lord Tenterden'); Talfourd (1844) ('Lords Eldon and Stowell'); and 'Vestiges of Follett' in Talfourd (1854) at 113–24.

take a barrister to the summit of his profession, as in the case of Lord Tenterden, the Chief Justice of King's Bench from 1818 to 1832.[48]

Leading advocates, however, usually possessed considerable ability, and at this level 'the deficiencies which aided the aspiring junior will no longer prevail'. But even leaders rarely displayed 'the highest powers of the mind', because they were confined by the subject-matter of litigation which rarely gave scope for passion or imagination.[49] Talfourd, like Brougham, considered Erskine the exemplary advocate, but his view of the qualities required for success at the Bar led to a more sober assessment of Erskine's abilities and his place beside the great statesmen of his age:[50]

> To describe Mr Erskine, when at the bar, is to ascertain the highest intellectual eminence to which a barrister, under the most favourable circumstances, may safely aspire. He had no imaginative power, no originality of thought, no great comprehension of intellect, to encumber his progress...Had his mind been pregnant with greater things, teeming with beautiful images, or, indued with deep wisdom, he would have been less fitted to shed lustre on the ordinary feelings and transactions of life. If he had been able to answer Pitt [in the House of Commons] without fainting, or to support Fox without sinking into insignificance, he would not have been the delight of special juries, and the glory of the Court of King's Bench...He was, in short, the most consummate advocate of whom we have any trace; he left his profession higher than he found it; and yet, beyond its pale, he was only an incomparable companion, a lively pamphleteer, and a weak and superficial debater!

The successful advocate was also not likely to be distinguished by a high sense of principle. The advocate required 'a pliable temperament' so that he could commit himself to any position which the exigencies of his brief required. The interests of clients were not 'like the objects of moral zeal, fixed in character, but [were] liable to frequent change', so that the advocate needed 'the faculty of directing the whole power of the understanding to each shifting aspect of the cause in its minutest shadowings, without the guidance of an inflexible law'. This dexterity, Talfourd said, 'is far more wonderful, if far less noble, than a singleness of devotion to right'.[51]

A pliable temperament was wonderful because it enabled the advocate to give full expression to his sympathy for his client. Sympathy, 'a spare fund of warmth and kindness to bestow on whoever seeks it', ennobled the advocate and inspired great forensic achievement. It predisposed counsel to believe the statements in his brief and, impressed

[48] Talfourd (1825) quotations at 328 and 329; Talfourd (1833).
[49] Talfourd (1825) quotation at 330; Talfourd (1820) 255.
[50] Talfourd (1825) 335–6; see also Talfourd (1821b).
[51] Talfourd (1825) 333–4; Talfourd (1844) 38; Talfourd (1854) quotation at 120.

with the passions and hopes of his client, converted him into 'a zealous, often a passionate, partisan'. It made the advocate 'not only the representative, but the sharer, passioned for the hour', of his client's fortunes. It enabled him to throw all his energy into another's cause, and to struggle, never cease to hope, 'and to cling to it if it is hopeless as to a friend in misfortune'. This original understanding of the advocate's relationship with his client, which Talfourd reiterated over a period of nearly 30 years, achieved its most developed expression in the 1846 *Law Magazine* article.[52]

This article, entitled 'On the Principle of Advocacy as Developed in the Practice of the Bar', began with a familiar demonstration of the necessity for legal representation, by reason of the complexity of law and social relations which made it impossible for individuals to present their own causes effectively. However, in a significant departure from other defences of advocacy, such as Brougham's *Edinburgh Review* article, Talfourd conceded that the necessity for professional advocacy did not 'rescue it from disgrace' if its practice 'proved to be inconsistent with personal truth and honour'. In Brougham's analysis the utility of representation was the moral justification of advocacy, and the basis of the advocate's rights and duties. Talfourd did not take this simple course, but turned instead to human nature for the vindication of advocacy.[53]

'Human nature', Talfourd declared, 'is essentially partisan'. Of 'the great benefactors of mankind, how many have been partisans of theory, how few single-minded seekers after wisdom!' He demonstrated the partisanship of human nature by reference to literature, identifying this quality in the poetry of Wordsworth, the history of Carlyle, and the political writings of Burke. We are all, he said, advocates. In litigation partisanship affected witnesses who, 'without interest and above suspicion', developed a bias in their perspectives of events, and counsel. The statements in the brief presented to counsel, Talfourd noted, were 'always such as to induce a strong belief in the justice of the cause, and to enlist his feelings powerfully in its success. To one thus prepossessed, who can wonder that in the animation of the contest the first impression is deepened; and as the little chapter of life, with all its living interest, opens around him, *his client's case becomes part of his own being*'. Talfourd considered that such forensic zeal was conducive to the discovery of the truth but, unlike the Criminal Law Commissioners and other supporters of adversarialism during the Prisoners' Counsel Act debate, did not adopt the discovery of truth as its rationalisation.

52 Talfourd (1825) quotations at 333; Talfourd (1844) quotation at 37; Talfourd (1854).
53 Talfourd (1846) 265–9.

Forensic zeal was no more than the inevitable manifestation in the trial of the partisanship of human nature.[54]

The statements in counsel's brief which enlisted such zeal were, of course, partial, and sometimes false. It was also human nature for clients to disguise, to themselves as well as their legal advisers, any baseness in their own conduct, and to allow excuses, wishes and resentments to mould their instructions. It was not 'the habit of clients to stand confessed, before their counsel, wrongdoers and oppressors'. The complexities of counsel's relationship with his client and his imperfect factual knowledge were ignored by the critics of the profession who, Talfourd believed, assumed 'not only that all litigated questions involve a direct opposition of truth and falsehood...but that the advocate engages in the support of the worst cause with the full knowledge of its hollowness'. Talfourd used five forensic situations to demonstrate the groundlessness of this assumption, but he also acknowledged that the advocate had a duty 'to the court and to justice' to avoid deliberate misrepresentations in the presentation of his client's case.[55]

Sympathy, which Talfourd called the 'soul' of the advocate's profession, inspired the partisanship of the advocate. Talfourd described the strengths and weaknesses of the sympathetic advocate in these terms:[56]

> The chief excellence of the advocate is in proportion to the facility with which he can become a party to the most momentous concerns of strangers—admitted by their choice into a little world of anxious hopes and fears, affections and resentments—and identifying his own existence, for the time, with the sharp and giddy crisis of alien fortunes. As thus he lives in the lives of others, while it involves no indifference to personal hypocrisy or falsehood, may tend to relax the sterner fibres of the mind, and render it less capable of discerning and appreciating abstract truth. A pliancy of character may thus be fostered,...a weakness which the advocate shares with the poet, who...is open to the seductions of sentiment when he would scorn those of lucre.

This sympathy might push an advocate, in the heat of forensic struggle, perhaps surprised by unexpected developments in the trial, to 'flaws of temper', 'hurried lapses from candour', and 'expedients which deliberation would not sanction, and which are afterwards deplored in vain'. Talfourd thought that the controversial advocacy condemned in the press was more often the result of understandable excesses of feeling,

[54] *Ibid*, quotations at 271 and 275, emphasis added.

[55] *Ibid*, quotations at 274 and 269 respectively. The five forensic situations discussed by Talfourd were: (1) cases dependent on legal argument where the facts were undisputed; (2) cases depending on the truth or falsehood of allegations of fact; (3) cases dependent on inferences from facts; (4) cases involving unliquidated damages; and (5) criminal trials: *ibid*, 269–87.

[56] *Ibid*, 283.

in difficult circumstances, than any habitual or deliberate irresponsibility amongst barristers.[57]

Talfourd's portrayal of the nature of advocacy, and the strains that it might place on the advocate, was more confident than his discussion of specific trials. He dealt reluctantly with the accusation that in *Courvoisier* Phillips had imputed guilt to innocent witnesses, notwithstanding his censure earlier in the article of advocacy which endangered innocence. Assuming the accusation to be true, he said, then Phillips imputations were 'a grievous fault', but in the next sentence Talfourd palliated the fault as 'a lapse, made under peculiar circumstances of great agitation', and then quickly passed on to praise Phillips' oratorical skills and 'unblemished domestic and social life'. He justified Fitzroy Kelly's tears in *Tawell* by reference to the circumstances of the case and 'the secret of sympathy' for those who might shortly die for their crimes. Kelly's abhorrence of the death penalty, his awareness that a man's last chance of life depended upon his advocacy, and the contrast he was trying to convey to the jury between Tawell's bright circumstances just a few weeks before and his shame at the time of the trial might, argued Talfourd, 'surely call into the eyes the tears which have been scoffed at'.[58]

Talfourd's discussion of these cases, especially *Courvoisier,* exposed the shortcomings of his analysis as a response to the licence of counsel controversy. His notion of the sympathetic partisanship of the advocate did not identify any limits to forensic licence, but merely demonstrated that the best of intentions might lead to its abuse. Talfourd made it clear in this article that the advocate must hold his partisanship within bounds and, in affirming that the advocate's zeal must cease 'when his cause conflicts with the higher requisites of religion, of morality, or of patriotism', rejected the precept of all expedient means. However, neither sympathy nor any other principle in his analysis defined these bounds. Talfourd seemed to assume that the advocate must adhere in his advocacy to the standards of morality expected in his personal life, which accords with the unusually high moral sense of Talfourd's own career.[59] This approach to the moral limits of forensic licence was, however, too personal and piecemeal to satisfy the critics of the profession, and potentially too rigorous for the profession itself.

[57] Talfourd (1846) 265–9. [58] *Ibid,* 290–4, quotation at 292.

[59] 'He [Talfourd] had so strong a repugnance to concealment, evasion, and mental circuitry, that he could not avail himself of these ordinary devices, even when the cause he was fighting required them...It was interesting to watch him with an acute, low-minded junior, who took technical objections and quibbled *con amore;* he was like a Brahmin with an unclean animal upon him': 'The Late Mr. Justice Talfourd' (1854) 51 *Law Magazine* 298 at 306. See also 'Modern Orators' (1847) 37 *Law Magazine* 131 at 161.

Talfourd's article illuminated the practice of advocacy and reached, with romantic grandeur, for the noble impulses of human nature which he believed redeemed advocacy. Its imagination and compassion make Brougham's heroic rhetoric and the utilitarian criticisms of Fonblanque and Chadwick seem, respectively, shallow and mean-spirited, but they, and not Talfourd, determined the course of debate. Talfourd's article passed with little notice as the pragmatic arguments of more traditional and mundane discussions settled the professional response to the licence of counsel controversy.

Professional Ethics

In the first part of his *Foundations of the Modern Bar* Raymond Cocks explores the relationship between the literature of the Bar of the 1830s and 1840s, especially the prevalence of works about 'great men', and professional ideals. The Bar at this time, he argues, was characterised by 'a vague but strong form of individualism', a suspicion of regulations, and weak institutional control from the Inns of Court and the circuit messes. The 'indeterminate but powerful fascination' with 'great men', Cocks suggests, 'explains how the Bar managed to administer itself. Barristers saw the Bar as the scene of individual adventure, and unexciting matters like the creation of an efficient disciplinary procedure were of little interest. The ideal of the "Great Man" united the Bar'. This was an insular ideal which, though understood by members of the profession, was ill-suited to defend professional values from public criticism.[60]

The legal literature of the 1840s produced, Cocks suggests, 'two radically different portraits of the profession'. On the one hand, the 'great man' genre continued to flourish, in a profusion of books and articles throughout the decade, the most significant of which was perhaps Lord Campbell's *Lives of the Lord Chancellors.* This work was 'a defiant reassertion of the ideas associated with the traditional Bar', and Cocks demonstrates how, in his life of Lord Eldon, Campbell harnessed Eldon's fame to defend 'a traditional form of preparation for the Bar which Campbell clearly thought was in decline'.[61] Brougham wrote within the same well-established convention in legal literature in choosing the medium of 'great man' biography to explore the qualities of the ideal advocate. Alternatively, other works displayed a novel willingness to address directly questions such as legal education, discipline, and standards of advocacy 'which had previously been ignored by a profession that preferred to think more of

[60] Cocks (1983) chs. 1 to 3, especially at 26–9 (quotation at 28).
[61] *Ibid*, 57–64 (quotations at 57, 62 and 61 respectively).

individual achievement than of public standing'. These publications, which included the *Law Times* founded in 1843, were prepared to respond to public criticism, recognise the need for moderate reform, and sought to give professional organisation a modern, utilitarian direction.[62]

The licence of counsel controversy was discussed, sometimes obliquely, in the 'great man' literature of the 1840s and also, in a more pragmatic fashion, in the legal journals. These discussions show a professional consensus against the precept of all expedient means, and in favour of moral restraints on advocacy. Forensic morality was, however, a matter for the subtle pressures of professional opinion and the advocate's conscience and not, at this time, for rules. The controversy prompted some interest within the profession in the formal regulation of advocacy and the creation of procedures to discipline forensic excesses, but the acceptance of such innovations lay in the future.

The subtle pressures of conscience and professional opinion appear in an anecdote in Campbell's life of Lord Eldon. Lord Eldon, Campbell says, frequently repeated this story of a discussion he had on his first circuit, in 1776, with one of the circuit leaders called Jack Lee. The anecdote is narrated by John Scott, as Lord Eldon then was, who is troubled by the morality of Lee's advocacy:[63]

> After supper I said to him [Jack Lee], 'I have observed that throughout circuit, in all causes in which you are concerned, good, bad, indifferent, whatever their nature was, you equally exerted yourself to the uttermost to gain verdicts, stating evidence and quoting cases, as such statement and quotation should give you a chance of success, the evidence and the cases not being stated clearly, or quoted with a strict attention to accuracy and to fair and just representation. Can that', said I, 'Lee, be right? Can it be justified?'—'Oh, yes' he said, 'undoubtedly. Dr. Johnson has said that counsel were at liberty to state, as the parties themselves would state, what it was most for their interest to state'. After some interval, and when he had had his evening bowl of milk punch and two or three pipes of tobacco, he suddenly said, 'Come, Master Scott, let us go to bed. I have been thinking upon the question that you asked me, and I am not quite so sure that the conduct you represented will bring a man peace at the last'.

Lee justifies his misleading advocacy by claiming counsel may state whatever the parties themselves would state, which he attributes to Dr Johnson. Johnson's often quoted defence of advocacy does not in fact

[62] Cocks (1983), 64–77 (quotation at 69). For a contemporary acknowledgement of this division in legal literature see Kirwan (1852), which contrasted the work of William Forsyth, whose *Hortensius* is discussed *infra,* with the writings of Edward Cox, the proprietor of the *Law Times* and author of *The Advocate.*

[63] 9 Campbell (1856–57) 161–2. This anecdote endorses the traditional practical training for the Bar, as the novice barrister and the experienced circuiteer informally discuss their profession.

include this particular justification, and in any event did not appear in print until 15 years after this discussion supposedly took place. Lee's justification, however, was a commonplace of Campbell's day, appearing prominently, for example, in Lord Brougham's *Edinburgh Review* article. After reflection Lee recognises the moral dimension of advocacy for which the advocate must account, at least to himself. This accountability appears in the anecdote through private conference and personal contemplation, and not public discussion or professional regulation.[64]

A comprehensive response to the licence of counsel controversy within the 'great man' tradition was William Forsyth's 'historical sketch of the office and functions of an advocate' entitled *Hortensius*. Forsyth traced the role of the advocate in Greek, Roman and French history so that the English Bar, when he came to discuss it, appeared as the culmination of an illustrious tradition of great figures and noble action stretching back to antiquity. The final chapter considers forensic morality, to which Forsyth on one occasion applied the novel term of 'ethics'.[65] Civilised society, he reasoned, required advocates, who must be allowed 'a certain latitude...the limits of which are not easy to define, and which must be left in a great degree to [their] own good sense and discretion'. On the other hand, their representative character did not exonerate them from personal responsibility for their advocacy, because 'whenever men imagine that the quality of an act, as regards right or wrong, can be altered by the capacity in which they perform it, the most dangerous consequences will be the result'. It followed that the advocate must avoid trickery and falsehood, and in criminal cases could not claim a licence 'to sacrifice every consideration to the one object of enabling a client to escape conviction'. Forsyth alluded to the 'painful' cases of *Courvoisier* and *Reid and M'Cabe* which, he said, 'may be dismissed with the single observation, that the opinion of the bar was in entire accordance with that of the public, in condemning the line of defence adopted'. The opinions of famous lawyers and moralists, to which Forsyth made plentiful reference, established that morality was an inescapable element of advocacy, and 'one of the chief trials of the profession', demanding 'constant vigilance' from the advocate, was to maintain the balance between morality and zeal in his client's cause.[66]

If the limits of advocacy depended on the advocate's conscience then occasional errors of judgement were inevitable. The Bar recognised that to err in matters of forensic morality was human, but to persist in error, or to

[64] Boswell's *Life of Johnson*, which includes Johnson's defence of advocacy, first appeared in 1791.

[65] Forsyth (1849) ch. X. At 427 appears the only use of the term 'ethics' to describe questions of professional morality that I found in the legal literature of the 1840s.

[66] *Ibid*, quotations at 442, 431, 460, 461, and 443.

defend error, especially in an embarrassing public fashion, was unforgivable. Seymour in 1847 and Phillips in 1849 sought to defend their advocacy publicly, and alienated professional opinion by doing so. The *Law Magazine*, for example, responded to Phillips' self-justification with disdain:[67]

> The very unpleasant duty is...imposed upon us of canvassing a subject which, for many reasons, it would have been well and wise to have left in the category of those personal affairs with which the profession is not bound to concern itself. As the matter stands no such option is left to the organs of the profession...[I]t might be that a professional assent to the conclusions of Mr. Phillips would be widely inferred from silence, which we have reason to know would thus misrepresent the feelings of the English Bar.

These public self-justifications coincided with and probably contributed to the hardening of professional feeling against the precept of all expedient means. Brougham's statement was treated in professional journals with respect, and sometimes qualified approval, until Seymour's letter to *The Times* following *Reid and M'Cabe* drew stark, almost revolting, conclusions from the separation of the advocate's duties from ordinary morality. In 1841 the *Law Magazine* dealt moderately with Phillips' advocacy in *Courvoisier*, but in 1850 said bluntly that his conduct 'always was, still is, and will continue to be condemned by ninety-nine out of every hundred of the profession'.[68] Defence advocacy in criminal cases would continue to cause the Bar periodic embarrassment, but the existence of moral limits on adversarialism could no longer be questioned.[69]

[67] 'The Defence of Courvoisier, and the Plea for it' (1850) 43 *Law Magazine 26*. Similarly *The Law Times* felt obliged to respond to Seymour's letter to *The Times* because 'he has not confessed [his] error, but deliberately justifies the proceeding': (1848) 10 L. T. 277.

[68] Compare 'Events of the Quarter' (1840) 24 *Law Magazine* 238, and 'Licence of Counsel' (1841) 25 *Law Magazine* 143, with 'Licence of Counsel' (1848) 39 *Law Magazine* 53, and 'The Defence of Courvoisier, and the Plea for it' (1850) 43 *Law Magazine* 26.

[69] In 1864, at the age of 86, Lord Brougham asserted the precept of all expedient means one final time. The occasion was at a dinner to honour the distinguished French advocate M. Berryer, attended by over four hundred members of the Bar. Lord Brougham compared M. Berryer to 'our own Erskine—one of the greatest advocates, perhaps, the world ever saw', and said that '[i]n both was observed the first great quality of an advocate, to reckon everything subordinate to the interests of his client'. The Lord Chief Justice, Sir Alexander Cockburn, followed Lord Brougham and to the applause of the assembled Bar buried the precept of all expedient reasons with a simple appeal to personal honour and responsibility: 'Much as I admire the great abilities of M. Berryer, to my mind his crowning virtue—as it ought to be that of every advocate—is, that he has throughout his career conducted his cases with untarnished honour. (Loud cheers). The arms which an advocate wields he ought to use as a warrior, not as an assassin. (Cheers). He ought to uphold the interests of his clients *per fas*, but not *per nefas*. (Cheers). He ought to know how to reconcile the interests of his client with the eternal interests of truth and justice': see 2 Selborne (1896) 470–5; (1865) 40 *Law Times* 16–18 (quotations at 17). The significance of Sir Alexander Cockburn's deft contradiction of Lord Brougham was fully appreciated by those present: see 2 Selborne (1896) 473; Parker (1865) 106; 'The Moral Code of the Bar' (1865) 40 *Law Times* 574–5.

The licence of counsel controversy of the 1840s gave forensic morality a permanent place in professional literature. A paper was read on the subject before the Juridical Society in 1857, and Samuel Warren devoted a chapter to it in his successful *A Popular and Practical Introduction to Law Studies* for the first time in its third edition of 1863. The *Cornhill Magazine* published articles on forensic morality by Fitzjames Stephen and Francis Parker in 1861 and 1865, and Stephen also made it a central feature of his description of the adversarial criminal trial in his *A General View of the Criminal Law* which first appeared in 1863. These writers take pains to reconcile the representation of the client with the advocate's conscience, the administration of justice and respect for the distinct roles of advocate, judge and witness in adversarial procedure. As the client's representative the advocate was neither, on the one hand, a mere delegate, agent or mouthpiece nor, on the other, 'the arbiter and dictator of his client's rights and interests' or 'the keeper of his client's conscience'. Representation, even of the guilty, was not incompatible with responsible independence, nor zeal with fair advocacy. The advocate did not have an unrestrained licence in the conduct of his client's case, but was of necessity trusted with a wide discretion. Professional opinion, 'enlightened public opinion', judicial authority, rules of evidence and the vigilance of opposing counsel exercised a beneficial influence on the advocate's discretion but did not and could not 'afford a security against disingenuousness—against malignant insinuations, gratuitous imputations artfully introduced into speeches, or a harsh and brutal way of asking justifiable questions. In short, they strictly limit the sphere of an advocate's discretion, but they do, and must of necessity, leave it to him whether he will use that discretion like a gentleman or like a blackguard'.[70]

As early as the 1840s suggestions appeared that some form of professional regulation might prevent the abuse of advocacy. In 1841 the *Law Magazine* discussed and rejected Chadwick's suggestions for the judicial supervision of advocacy, but after *Reid and M'Cabe* endorsed this form of control. It argued 'that no better mode exists of checking these disgraceful practices than the prompt and unsparing chastisement of counsel who resort to them...Learned judges cannot better uphold the dignity and purity of public justice, than by branding such advocates with

[70] Daniel (1858), quotations at 303 and 308; 1 Warren (1863) 387–441; Stephen (1861), quotation at 455; Stephen (1863a), ch. V; Parker (1865), where the influence of 'enlightened public opinion' is discussed; and see also 'The Moral Code of the Bar' (1865) 40 *Law Times* 574–5. 1 Warren (1863) 409–11 and Parker (1865) 113 quote with approval the fine statement of the duties of the advocate of Crampton J., an Irish judge, in *The Queen v O'Connell* (1844) 7 Irish Law Rep. 312–13. Crampton J. compared the nature of the advocate's representation to that of a member of the House of Commons, which was so eloquently described by Edmund Burke in his *Speech to the Electors of Bristol* (1774).

public reprobation'. It went on to discuss briefly the regulation of advocacy by the Inns of Court and the circuit messes, and thought the Inns should punish forensic misconduct. A similar solution was often proposed at this time to ensure respect for professional etiquette which, like the abuse of advocacy, was a particular problem at the Old Bailey.[71] The Inns took no action, but the recognition of the possibility of the regulation of advocacy was a significant development. The public criticism of forensic morality during the 1840s and to a lesser extent the public responses of Phillips and Seymour turned a private question into a public and professional one, so that by the 1860s Fitzjames Stephen and Francis Parker could openly explore the potential of professional opinion and discriminating public censure to restrain unacceptable advocacy. Forensic morality had emerged from the secret domain of confidence and conscience, and begun a transformation which would lead to the rules and disciplinary procedures of modern professional ethics.

Expressions of Personal Belief

A startling new issue in forensic morality, largely passed over during the licence of counsel controversy, arose during the sensational murder trial of William Palmer in 1856 when defence counsel, Sergeant William Shee, declared his personal belief in his client's innocence. This declaration showed a degree of commitment to the client which, at first glance, associates it with the precept of all expedient means and the controversial advocacy of the 1840s. The precept of all expedient means, however, presupposed that the advocate addressed the court solely as a representative of the client, and consequently his personal beliefs or morality were irrelevant; while the essence of Shee's declaration was that it was made on his own behalf. Shee confounded the advocate's personality and the prisoner's innocence or guilt in a way that challenged accepted norms of forensic morality and threatened the division of responsibility between the judge, witnesses and counsel which was the basis of adversarial procedure. This section examines Shee's statement, and Chapter 7

[71] See, for example, (1844) 2 L. T. 301, (1844) 3 L. T. 501, 'The Bar' (1844) 32 *Law Magazine* 174. It is important to distinguish professional etiquette, subject to an established, though informal and imperfect, tradition of enforcement through the circuit messes, from forensic morality. Professional etiquette was primarily concerned with fees, the relationship between the barrister and the attorney, and circuit life. Where a brief was properly obtained, and any rules relating to the formality of appearance respected—such as the two counsel and special retainer rules—then the influence of the rules of etiquette was over. Forensic morality, like advocacy generally, was a matter for the barrister's discretion. On professional etiquette see Duman (1983) at 40–7, Shaw Lefevre (1863) 16–35, and Dicey (1867).

considers the significance of *Palmer* to the realisation of the ideal of adversarial procedure. At the outset, however, some attention must be given to *Palmer's* complex facts.

William Palmer was tried and hanged for the murder by strychnia of his racing friend, John Parsons Cook, and at the time of the trial he was also facing indictments for the murder of his wife and one of his brothers. He was further suspected of the murders of his mother-in-law, one of his illegitimate children, and another racing friend and creditor who, like Cook, died while sharing Palmer's hospitality. He had a medical training but devoted his time, in his home town of Rugeley in Staffordshire, to horses and racing. He was credited by contemporaries with complete composure, great energy and courage, and his murders and attempts to avoid prosecution display an impressive audacity and commitment to the principle that all human nature was as corrupt as his was. His *sangfroid* was well illustrated by a note he sent to his counsel during the trial suggesting that the Lord Chief Justice's unfairness to the defence might be cured by $2^1/_2$ grains of strychnine. There is perhaps no better illustration of the identification, so strongly urged by Sir Samuel Romilly, of the criminal and gaming minds. Palmer could not resist playing at high risks for high stakes, gambling in this way on horseflesh, with rapacious London money-lenders, with the companies that insured the lives of his wife and brother, finally staking his own life for the prizes of murder. His risk-taking seems to have been based—as Romilly suggested it was in criminals—on faith in his own luck, and he remained confident of an acquittal at his trial until the delivery of the verdict. Another interpretation of Palmer's career, apparent in Fitzjames Stephen's writings, is as a morality tale demonstrating a slide through vice from respectability to gambling, debt, fraud and forgery, murder and finally to a deserved death on the scaffold.

At first sight the circumstantial evidence against Palmer at his trial was overwhelming. The motive was financial gain for shortly before the murder one of Cook's horses had won at the Shrewsbury races, bringing its owner a considerable sum in prizes and bets. When Cook died a week later in Rugeley his prize money and betting book had disappeared, and the prosecution could show that Palmer had collected the bets and applied the proceeds to his own purposes. Palmer's enormous debts, the pressing money-lenders, threats of legal action and the imminent discovery of his forgeries augmented the proof of motive. Palmer had the opportunity to poison Cook, for he tended him in his illness prior to his death, and the prosecution could show that Cook's condition regularly worsened after Palmer administered food, drink or medicine to him. Palmer had access to strychnine, was proved to have purchased it on two occasions within 16 hours of Cook's death, and after his death could neither produce the strychnine nor account for its use. He had sought to obstruct the investigation of Cook's death, attempting to bribe a post-boy to overturn the jars taking Cook's stomach and intestines to London for analysis, had attempted to corrupt the coroner with communications and gifts, and had induced the local postmaster, an old school friend, to open a letter from the London analysts to Cook's stepfather. The weakness of the prosecution case, however, was that these analysts were unable to find any strychnine at all in Cook's body. The prosecution proposed a number of explanations for this result at the trial, culminating in an admission that their analysts may have been 'a pair of bunglers', and sought to counter this defect in their case by producing eminent medical witnesses to prove that Cook's paroxysms, manner of death and the state of his body in dying and death were symptomatic of strychnine poisoning.[72] The defence argued, by calling its own chemical and medical experts, that if strychnine were administered to Cook it would be detectable in his body after death, that some features of Cook's death were not consistent with a poisoning by strychnine, and that his death might be explicable by natural causes. The trial occupied 12 days and involved 82 witnesses, a substantial proportion of whom were medical or scientific experts. The prosecution engaged five counsel, led by the Attorney General, Sir Alexander Cockburn,[73] while Serjeant Shee led the four counsel for Palmer.

William Shee was a successful *nisi prius* advocate and the editor of leading works on shipping and insurance law, who would eventually crown his career by becoming the first Roman Catholic superior court judge since the Glorious Revolution. He was a genial man, particularly well liked by his brethren at the Bar, big in figure and possessed of a rather bombastic style of advocacy. He did not usually practise in the criminal courts, only having defended one person on a capital charge before Palmer, and was further disadvantaged by being retained at a late stage. During the trial Shee never matched Cockburn's grasp of the detail of the case, nor his powers of cross-examination, close reasoning with the circumstantial evidence or deadly use of the strongest parts of

[72] 'A pair of bunglers': see Knott and Watson (1952) 263.

[73] Sir Alexander Cockburn (1802–80) was called to the Bar in 1829, took silk in 1841 and served as Solicitor-General and Attorney-General before his elevation to the Bench as Chief Justice of Common Pleas in 1856. He became Lord Chief Justice of England in 1859. He was the foremost advocate of the 1850s, with a fine analytical mind, sense of purpose, ability to rise to the occasion, and a consciousness of his own power. Lord Selborne thought that '[a]s an advocate, he was only second to Erskine'; and Sergeant Ballantine called his defence of Daniel M'Naughten in 1843 'one of the most masterly arguments ever heard at the English Bar': 2 Selborne (1896) 495; Ballantine (1883) 164.

his case. Palmer himself acknowledged that his counsel had been outclassed in his remark, after the verdict was announced, to the effect that the better jockey had won.

Shee's lengthy speech on the sixth day of the trial attacked the prosecution case in a piecemeal fashion, without a coherent alternative explanation of the sequence of events and suspicious behaviour that culminated in Cook's death and Palmer's arrest.[74] The lack of focus in the defence meant too much significance was attached to proving that minute doses of strychnine were detectable in the human body, too many incompatible theories of Cook's death were proposed, and some damning circumstantial evidence against Palmer was hardly addressed at all.[75] Shee compounded these errors of judgement with two extraordinary declarations of personal belief in Palmer's innocence. At the outset of his speech he told the jury:[76]

> though, of course, like everybody else, I knew generally and loosely, very loosely indeed, the history of these transactions at Rugeley, I had formed, when the papers came into my hands, no opinion upon them, no opinion upon the guilt or the innocence of the prisoner at the bar, and my mind was perfectly free to form what I trust will be declared by you the right judgment in this case. I commence his defence, I say it all in sincerity, with an entire conviction of his innocence. I believe that there never was a truer word pronounced than the words he pronounced when he said 'not guilty' to this charge. If I fail in establishing that to your satisfaction I shall be under a great misgiving that my failure was more attributable to my own ability to do justice to this case than to any weakness in the case itself; and I will give you this proof of the sincerity with which I declare

[74] Shee's speech was arranged around a three-fold division of the evidence: firstly, the question of motive, where Shee argued that Palmer did not gain by Cook's death but rather lost a valuable source of financial support; secondly, the scientific and medical questions, and thirdly, the other circumstantial evidence against Palmer.

[75] **The detection of strychnine**: the most important point for the defence about the tests on Cook's body for strychnine was that none had been found, which was conceded by the prosecution and by itself supported the argument that strychnine had not been administered. The great length to which the defence went to show that even the minutest dose of strychnine in the human body was detectable scientifically added little to this argument and was finessed by Sir Alexander Cockburn by his concession in his reply that the prosecution analysts may have bungled. On this aspect of the defence case see also Stephen (1890) 261–5. **Defence theories of Cook's death**: Shee took the view that the defence was not bound to identify the cause of Cook's death (see Knott and Watson (1952) 157), which was strictly true but the defence would have been unanswerable if they could have definitely shown some innocent cause. Instead, a succession of medical witnesses with widely differing explanations of Cook's symptoms—general convulsions, arachnitis, epilepsy proper, epilepsy with tetanic complications, and *angina pectoris*—were called and their diversity, and weakness under cross-examination, provided material for ridicule, irony, indignation and some devastating commonsense in Cockburn's reply: see Knott and Watson (1952) 251–5. **Circumstantial evidence not properly addressed**: Palmer's purchases of strychnine are probably the best example of evidence of this class: compare Knott and Watson (1952) 181–3 (Shee) and 264–70 (Cockburn).

[76] Knott and Watson (1952) 128.

upon this evidence my conviction of his innocence, that I will meet the case of the prosecution foot to foot at every stage.

Shee repeated his declaration in the peroration after reading an old love letter from Palmer to his wife:[77]

Such, gentlemen, is the man whom it is my duty to defend. Upon the evidence which is before you I cannot believe him guilty.

The emergence of a crisp division between the judicial, testimonial and defensive functions in the criminal trial had been a steady feature of its development since the Prisoners' Counsel Act debate. The confusion of the judicial and defensive functions manifested in the maxim that the judge was counsel for the prisoner was discarded, the silencing of the prisoner and the rule forbidding counsel to refer to facts that he was not in a position to prove kept apart the testimonial and defensive functions, and full defence by counsel itself assumed a strong and independent defensive role for the prisoner's counsel. Shee's declaration played havoc with this functional separation by making the advocate before the trial assume the role of judge or jury in reaching a decision on the innocence of his client, and then at the trial testifying on the prisoner's behalf by offering his considered personal opinion in support of a not guilty verdict.

Shee's declaration also interfered with the rationale of adversarial procedure of the discovery of the truth through the contention of counsel. It placed the advocate lucky enough to believe in all honesty in his client's innocence in the privileged position of being able to declare that belief and struggle to his utmost for an acquittal. An advocate with doubts could not make such a declaration, and too close a preoccupation with his own conscience would detract from his zeal for the prisoner's defence. An advocate presented with a brief in an apparently hopeless case would face the anxiety of reconciling the dictates of his conscience with adherence to the 'cab rank' rule which bound barristers to act for any client in need of their services.[78] Declarations of personal belief also created the temptation for prosecution counsel to respond in kind to avoid conceding the defence the high ground of conscience. Sir Alexander Cockburn in *Palmer* alluded, not without menace, to the opportunity Shee's declaration offered the prosecution in its reply:[79]

[77] Knott and Watson (1952) 191. The reading of this letter, a shallow appeal to sentiment under the best of circumstances, was particularly tasteless when Palmer had been indicted for his wife's murder.

[78] Thomas Erskine's famous statement of the 'cab rank' rule is set out in n.38 above. It is premised on a distinction between the responsibilities of advocate and judge.

[79] Knott and Watson (1952) 295.

You have had from my learned friend the unusual, and I think I may say unprecedented, assurance of his conviction of his client's innocence.

Mr SERJEANT SHEE: Not unprecedented.

The ATTORNEY-GENERAL: I can only say I think it would have been better if my learned friend had abstained from so strange a declaration. What would he think of me if, imitating his example, I at this moment stated to you, upon my 'honour', as he did, what is my internal conviction from a conscientious consideration of this case. The best reproof which I can administer to my learned friend is to abstain from imitating so dangerous an example.

The benefits of adversarial procedure could only be realised if defence counsel confined himself to submissions as the prisoner's representative. Under this procedure it was the duty of the advocate, as Lord Campbell expressed it in his summing up in *Palmer*, 'to press his argument upon the jury, and not his opinion'.[80] The reality of adversarial procedure was that defence counsel was in the worst position to judge the prisoner's guilt. He was instructed, through a solicitor, by the prisoner or the prisoner's friends; his brief, as Talfourd had pointed out, was likely to induce a belief in the justice of the cause; if he were a man of feeling, as Shee undoubtedly was, his sympathies would be engaged by the prisoner's jeopardy; and under adversarial procedure he was expected to be zealous in the prisoner's defence. He was, as Talfourd had said, a partisan, not fully 'capable of discerning and appreciating abstract truth', and an advocate self-aware of this condition realised that he had to suspend or distrust his judgment on the ultimate issue. Whether or not Palmer had murdered Cook, Shee erred in believing that he could reach a meaningful conclusion on this question. This point was well made by Sir Alexander Cockburn in the prosecution reply:[81]

when my learned friend said that he had entered upon this case with an unbiased and an unprejudiced mind, who could have failed to feel that never in anything could he have been more deceived than in thinking that? For who that has to give his best energies to a defence upon such a charge as this would not shrink in his own mind from the conclusion that he was to advocate the cause of one whom he believed to have been guilty of the foulest of all imaginable crimes. I say, therefore, I think my learned friend had better have abstained from making any observations which involved the assurance of his own conviction.

In the aftermath of *Palmer* nobody doubted the sincerity of Shee's declarations, but nor was anyone prepared to step forward to justify them. Cockburn in his reply and Lord Campbell in his summing-up politely rebuked Shee, the Bar accepted the judgment of these leaders

[80] *Ibid*, 298. [81] *Ibid*, 295.

of the profession, and Shee himself, showing more discretion than Charles Phillips or Digby Seymour had done, never defended his advocacy. His popularity and a reputation uncompromised by association with the Old Bailey stifled criticism, and the partisanship of some of the defence's witnesses diverted controversy towards the medical profession. *The Examiner* condemned Shee's declaration, the legal press agreed and the matter ended there.[82]

The solidity of professional opinion against Shee begs the question of why an experienced and respected advocate would so blatantly transgress the norms of forensic morality. Shee's interruption of Cockburn's peroration in the first of the two quotations above indicates Shee thought his declaration was 'not unprecedented'. Sergeant Ballantine, who discusses the trial in his memoirs, suggests that the precedent lay in Campbell's advocacy when at the Bar. The published speech of Sir John Campbell, as he then was, in defence of Francis Medhurst on a charge of murder in 1839 begins as follows:

> GENTLEMEN OF THE JURY, although deeply and conscientiously convinced of the innocence of my client, no language could describe the anxiety with which I rise to address you.

Further, in his defence of the Prime Minister, Lord Melbourne, in a civil action for adultery, Sir John Campbell made this statement:

> But before I conclude, I am bound according to the express instructions that I have received from Lord Melbourne, to declare in his name, and in the most solemn and emphatic manner, that he is not guilty of the charge brought against him, and that neither by word or deed has he ever abused the confidence reposed in him by Mr Norton. I know well, Gentlemen, that you cannot act upon this assertion, and I do not seek to influence by it that verdict which you have sworn to find according to the evidence.

Lord Melbourne, as a party, was not at this time entitled to give evidence himself, and Campbell, in effect, testified on his behalf. Campbell acknowledged the irregularity of the statement by asking the jury not to be influenced by it, although this is a disingenuous figure because if the jury were to disregard it, then why mention it at all? Campbell did not here indicate any personal opinion, but his statement is nevertheless a precedent for Shee's declaration insofar as it involved defence counsel testifying on the ultimate issue.[83]

[82] **The rebukes of Cockburn and Campbell**: Knott and Watson (1952) 295 and 297, Cockburn saved his rebuke until his peroration so maximising its impact. **Press and legal comment**: *The Examiner*, 24 and 31 May 1856; *Law Times*, 31 May 1856; 'The Evidence in Palmer's Case' (1856) 1 *Law Magazine and Review* 332 at 350–1.

[83] Campbell (1842), quotations at 30 (*Norton v Lord Melbourne*) and 34 (*Medhurst*); Ballantine (1883) 131–2 (cf. 98).

Reports of nineteenth century speeches show that counsel often expressed personal opinions on collateral issues—the credibility of witnesses, the proof of circumstantial facts, the plausibility of a defence—and such opinions are open to the same objections, although to a lesser degree, as an opinion on the prisoner's guilt or innocence. A particularly clear example of this practice is Cockburn's treatment of the evidence of the defence witness Jeremiah Smith contradicting the prosecution evidence of Palmer's purchase and opportunity to administer strychnine. Cockburn told the jury:[84]

> As to the fact of the witness pretending that he saw him [Palmer] alight from the car, and that he went to Cook and stayed a certain time so as to cover [Palmer's movements for] the whole evening, I ask you not to believe a single word, and I do so because in my heart I do not believe a single word of it.

A more subtle expression of personal opinion occurred whenever an advocate used a first person pronoun to introduce a line of argument in phrases such as 'I consider', 'I think' or 'to my mind'. In such circumstances the argument is recommended to the jury not only by its intrinsic merit but by the advocate's approval, the significance of which would depend on his reputation and integrity. Thomas Erskine's notoriety for insinuating his admirable personality into his speeches survives in the anecdotes of newspapers that had to break off reports of his speeches when their stocks of the letter 'I' were exhausted.[85] The cases discussed in this work—particularly *Patch, Courvoisier,* and *Palmer*—all saw counsel guilty of this practice to a greater or lesser degree and it seems widespread at this time. Its effect is to subvert the distinction, referred to by Lord Campbell in his rebuke of Shee, between argument and opinion.

During the Prisoners' Counsel Act debate supporters of full defence by counsel had argued that the jury could not appreciate the significance of 'complex fact' evidence without the assistance of speeches from counsel. The jury would best discern the truth, they claimed, when skilled counsel were permitted to explain the evidence from the perspectives of both sides. No one considered, however, the extent to which forensic argument—interpreting evidence, revealing implications, drawing inferences, connecting seemingly unrelated events, doubting innocent acts and bringing together a wealth of information to a reasoned conclusion—might contaminate the truth with counsel's personal beliefs. In the aftermath of the Act expressions of counsel's beliefs appeared in

[84] Knott and Watson (1952) 267.

[85] 9 Campbell (1856–57) 92–3. The anecdotes related to public and parliamentary rather than courtroom speeches, but the trait they satirise appears in Erskine's forensic masterpieces.

criminal advocacy on collateral questions or as an inseparable element of forensic argument but did not attract notice or comment. Shee's declaration in *Palmer*—a case of complex fact evidence *par excellence*—pushed, apparently deliberately, the existing practices and precedents to their logical conclusion. Its immediate and decisive condemnation by the Lord Chief Justice and the Attorney-General, and subsequently by the legal and popular press, established beyond doubt that advocates must not express a personal opinion on the ultimate issue of the causes they represent. It also stifled the possibility of a debate within the profession which might have recognised the various manifestations of personal belief in advocacy and examined their propriety. It is probably true to say, however, that after the licence of counsel controversy of the 1840s the profession did not desire another debate on forensic morality and, having pronounced definitively on the extreme case, were content to leave the lesser manifestations of personal belief to the responsibility and discretion of individual practitioners.

7

The Adversarial Criminal Trial

The Apotheosis of Adversarial Procedure

The adversarial criminal trial is seen to come of age in *Palmer*. Twenty years after the Prisoners' Counsel Act this trial, one of the great criminal trials in the history of English law, triumphantly realised the expectations of full defence by counsel. A case of labyrinthine facts, involving a mass of circumstantial evidence, the conflicting recollections of dozens of witnesses, and questions of bewildering medical and toxicological perplexity, was reduced by the prosecution and the defence to coherent alternative versions of events to be then presented and tested in examination and cross-examination. The speeches of counsel introduced the alternative interpretations of the evidence, explained their logic, urged their credibility, and uncovered the weaknesses of their adversary's interpretation. Cross-examination and the prosecution reply exposed the fallacies of the defence, and minimised the need for judicial involvement beyond an impartial summing-up. The thoroughness of the trial manifested Palmer's guilt, and the opportunity of his professional representatives to say all that could be said in his favour eliminated all sympathy for him. In *Palmer* adversarial procedure delivered the truth, and a verdict beyond reproach.

This achievement was made possible in *Palmer* by the exceptional advocacy of Sir Alexander Cockburn, who demonstrated the standards of advocacy now possible in criminal trials. Cockburn presented the jury with a picture of Palmer's guilt in his opening which he maintained and reinforced throughout the trial. It guided the examination of witnesses, cross-examination, and is even apparent in his re-examinations, for so fine is the advocacy in this case that even Cockburn's re-examinations reward study. The reply reiterated this picture, combining it with a sweeping dismissal of the defence. Such was Cockburn's mastery of the evidence that his eight-hour reply was reportedly delivered without the assistance of a single note. The defence advocacy was much less impressive, although the zeal and ingenuity of Palmer's counsel, and the many alternative explanations of Cook's death advanced by their witnesses, baited Cockburn's genius and produced that forensic contention that in the theory of the adversarial criminal trial was the key to the discovery of the truth.

The vindication of adversary procedure in practice was accompanied by the acceptance of legal writers of the validity of its underlying rationale that the contention of counsel was conducive to the discovery of the truth. Accordingly, the proposals for further reform of criminal procedure of the 1840s and 1850s, surveyed in the next section, were largely derived from or consistent with adversarial premises. Civil litigation was the dominant paradigm for the criminal law reform of this time, so proposals for procedural change built upon rather than threatened the newly-established adversarial procedure, and promised further expansion of the responsibilities of counsel.

An excellent contemporary rationalisation of the criminal procedure of the early 1860s, which embraces its adversarial premises, is Fitzjames Stephen's *A General View of the Criminal Law.* Stephen was the leading writer on the criminal law of his generation, distinguished by his clarity of thought and expression, a preference for principle over precedent, and a strong distaste for technicality or oversubtlety in the law or in the legal life.[1] He attended Palmer's trial as a spectator and reflecting upon it towards the end of his career said that 'it made an impression on my mind which the experience of thirty-four subsequent years, during which I have witnessed, studied, and taken part, both as counsel and a judge, in many important cases, has rather strengthened than weakened. It is impossible to give an adequate idea of the manner in which it exhibited in its very best and strongest light the good side of English criminal procedure'.[2] *A General View* was Stephen's first full length work on the criminal law. It included a comparative analysis of English and French criminal procedure in order to 'throw light upon the strong and weak points of each' and to introduce his examination of the leading features of the English system, and also accounts of seven English and French trials, including *Palmer,* to demonstrate the practical consequences of the two systems.

English criminal procedure, Stephen said, was 'almost exclusively litigious', in that it took the form of a settlement of a private dispute between the prosecutor and the prisoner. This litigious character was apparent in the onus on the prosecutor and prisoner to instruct attorneys and to prepare the case for trial, in the theory of pleading, and the distinction between examination-in-chief and cross-examination ('perhaps the strongest illustration' of the litigious character of English crim-

[1] **Stephen's life and character**: see Stephen (1895); Radzinowicz (1957); Smith (1988). Stephen was an acute observer of professional practice as well as of the criminal law: see Stephen (1861); Stephen (1863b) and his criticisms of circuit mess discipline recorded in *Midland Circuit Mess Records,* Nottingham, 24 July 1867.

[2] Stephen (1890) 269.

inal law, because it assumed that a witness would 'be favourable to the side by which he is called'), and in the roles of counsel and the judge. French procedure by contrast was inquisitorial and in the form of a public inquiry. As a matter of logic, Stephen argued, the French approach was the more sensible one:[3]

> Upon the general merits of our mode of procedure, it must be observed that the inquisitorial theory of criminal procedure is beyond all question the true one. It is self-evident that a trial ought to be a public inquiry into the truth of a matter deeply affecting the public interest.

On a closer examination, however, English procedure served a public purpose because the free presentation of opposite views in the litigious form of trial tended to disclose the truth. 'The general result may', he concluded, 'be fairly expressed, by saying that an English criminal trial is a public inquiry, having for its object the discovery of truth, but thrown for the purpose of obtaining that end into the form of a litigation between the prosecutor and the prisoner'.[4]

The ultimate rationale of English criminal procedure in Stephen's analysis was the discovery of the truth through the contention of counsel. Significantly Stephen did not question nor seek to demonstrate the validity of this truth rationale of forensic contention. This rationalisation of adversary procedure, which had been so hotly disputed during the Prisoners' Counsel Act debate, had become so self-evident that Stephen offered only a commonplace in its support.[5] The life of the law is not logic, but experience and the accumulation of authority by uncritical repetition, and by these means the truth rationale had by 1863 become firmly embedded in legal thought. It would have been churlish for Stephen to doubt the premises of the procedure that had the confidence of the profession, where that confidence seemed so fully justified by the satisfaction of the public in the outcome of trials like *Palmer*.

The truth rationale generously expanded the role for advocacy in the criminal trial. It was taken, in the aftermath of the Prisoners' Counsel Act, to sanction an aggressively adversarial mentality or 'adversarialism' and so contributed to the licence of counsel controversy. It was subtly qualified by the recognition through that controversy of the need for the advocate to temper zeal with responsibility. It conferred considerable power on counsel, but the attainment of its object required counsel to

[3] Stephen (1863a) 166. [4] *Ibid*, 167.

[5] 'it may be, and probably is, the case, that in our time and country, the best manner of conducting such an inquiry [i.e. into the truth of a matter deeply affecting the public interest] is to consider the trial mainly as a litigation, and to allow each party to say all that can be said in support of their own view; just as the best means of arriving at the truth in respect of any controverted matter of opinion might be, to allow those who maintained opposite views to discuss the matter freely and in public': *ibid*, 166.

exercise this power responsibly. The truth rationale and the integrity of the Bar in this way became mutually supporting pillars of the litigious form of trial.

Stephen fully appreciated the importance of forensic morality to the efficacy of adversary procedure, emphasising that counsel were subject to 'tacit rules' which ensured the attainment of the public purpose of the discovery of the truth. There were a number of professional rules, he said, 'not reduced to any express form, but well understood and constantly acted on, which, in practice, assigned to the counsel for the Crown and for the prisoner definite duties', and he referred to the special duties of prosecution counsel and the obligations of both counsel 'not to do anything to propagate falsehood', nor 'to attempt to browbeat, or terrify, or confuse a witness' and explained their different responsibilities in addressing the jury. 'The neglect or observation of these and other rules of the same kind', he concluded, 'practically establishes a wide distinction...' between those who exercise a noble profession, and those who disgrace it...The form of English Criminal Procedure places a very wide discretion in the hands of counsel, and it depends entirely on the way in which they use it whether their functions are a public duty, or a public nuisance'.[6]

The distinctive feature of the criminal trial by the early 1860s was that it had substantially the same form as the trial of civil actions between individuals. This private form was acceptable because it secured the public purpose of a thorough investigation of the truth, which in turn depended on the responsible advocacy of counsel. The reform of criminal law and procedure was an ongoing subject of debate but this conception of the criminal trial—the litigious form, the truth rationale and professional responsibility—was by this time quite secure.

Unfinished Business

Adversary procedure matured to the form rationalised and praised by Stephen during two decades—the 1840s and 1850s—that promised much for criminal law reform. During these years there were senior lawyers in Parliament, particularly Lord Brougham and Fitzroy Kelly, prepared to promote wide-ranging reforms of the criminal law. Outside Parliament there was a group of hard-working and able lawyers ready to gather information and arguments, write pamphlets and articles, appear before select committees, serve on royal commissions, prepare countless drafts of

[6] Stephen (1863a), quotations at 167 and 168. For other discussions of forensic morality of the mid-1860s proceeding from explicit adversarial premises see Parker (1865), and 'The Moral Code of the Bar' (1865) 40 *Law Times* 574–5.

bills and otherwise provide advice and assistance so as to ensure reformers in positions of influence had the prerequisite raw material and support for a programme of legislative reform. These lawyers included Criminal Law Commissioners Thomas Starkie and Henry Bellenden Ker, whose labours culminated in draft codes of substantive criminal law in 1843 and of criminal procedure in 1845, and also Charles Spregal Greaves and John Pitt Taylor, who made their first contributions to criminal law reform in the early 1840s with a series of articles in the *Law Magazine*.[7] The cooperation of reformers and the propagation of their ideas were enhanced in 1844 with the establishment of the Society for the Promotion of the Amendment of the Law, usually called the Law Amendment Society, the primary objective of which was to bring together individuals with an interest in 'the amendment of the law, and thus render their efforts more systematic and effectual'. Lord Brougham was its guiding spirit and first president, Lords Lyndhurst and Denman accepted honorary membership, its original ordinary members included Fitzroy Kelly, William Ewart, Stephen Lushington, and Thomas Starkie, and John Pitt Taylor was active in its affairs during the 1850s. The establishment at the same time of the *Law Review*, under the editorship of the Society's treasurer, James Stewart, with Lord Brougham as its most prolific contributor, ensured the Society's activities were well-publicised to the profession.[8]

[7] On Ker and Starkie see Chapter 4; **Draft Codes of Substantive Criminal Law and Procedure**: *Seventh Report of Her Majesty's Commissioners on the Criminal Law* (1843) Parl. Papers XIX. 1 and *Eighth Report of Her Majesty's Commissioners on the Criminal Law* (1845) Parl. Papers XIV. 161. **C. S. Greaves**: Greaves (1801–81) was called to the Bar in 1827, joined the Oxford Circuit, and took silk in 1850. He was the editor of the 3rd and 4th editions (1843 and 1865 respectively) of *Russell on Crimes*, and the author of a comprehensive report on criminal procedure for Lord Cranworth in 1856 and of a work on the criminal law consolidation acts: see *A Report on Criminal Procedure by Charles Sprengal Greaves* (1856) Parl. Papers L. 79, and Greaves (1862). The lengthy introduction to the latter work shows Greaves extensive involvement in criminal law reform and a certain bitterness that so little was ultimately achieved: see especially at 1vii-1viii. It is safe to assume he was the author of the *Law Magazine* articles of the criminal law in the 1840s under the initials 'C.S.G': see Greaves (1845) and Greaves (1846); **J. Pitt Taylor**: Taylor was the author of a successful evidence text, which first appeared in 1848 and ran through eight editions in his lifetime. He was the author of the articles appearing under the initials 'J.P.T' in the *Law Magazine*: see Taylor (1842); Taylor (1843); Taylor (1844). Numerous letters from Taylor to Lord Brougham on the affairs and internal politics of the Law Amendment Society survive amongst the *Brougham Papers*. Taylor ended his career in the 1880s as a county court judge.

[8] **Foundation of the Society for Promoting the Amendment of the Law** (1844) 27 *Legal Observer* 462, 484–5 (quotation at 485); (1844) 28 *Legal Observer* 52, 157; Anderson (1992) 13–15; **Brougham's contributions to the Law Review**: see Stewart's letters to Brougham, *Brougham Papers*. Brougham contributed at least five articles to the first two issues of the *Law Review*: see Stewart to Brougham 25 October 1844 ('Lord Chief Baron Abinger', 'Lord Chancellor Eldon' and 'Legal Education'), November 1844 ('Mr Baron Garrow') and 20 December 1844 ('Lord Chancellor Eldon' and 'Inns of Court'). *Brougham Papers Nos. 38,557, 23,878,* and *32,142*. It is also likely that he wrote 'Sir John Bayley' on the grounds of its style and subject-matter.

At the same time, the widespread acceptance of the need for uniformity between civil and criminal procedure meant reforms of procedure and evidence gave impetus to changes in criminal law. The Evidence Act of 1851 authorised parties in civil proceedings to give evidence on their own behalf, and so raised the question of whether the accused in criminal proceedings should be entitled to the same privilege. C.S. Greaves in his *A Report on Criminal Procedure* for the Lord Chancellor in 1856 addressed the question of extending certain provisions of the Common Law Procedure Act 1854 to criminal cases, taking as a starting-point the proposition that '[a]s the object of proceedings, both in the Civil and Criminal Court, is to ascertain the truth by means of a judge and jury, it would appear but reasonable to suppose that the course to be adopted ought to be the same in both courts'.[9] A further impetus for procedural reform came from the increasing length and complexity of criminal trials, so that the very thoroughness of adversary procedure created a need for its refinement.

The grand aspiration for the reform of the criminal law was its complete codification. In May 1844, the same month as the Law Amendment Society selected its inaugural set of officers, Lord Brougham made a powerful plea for codification, with rhetorical flashes reminiscent of his epic 1828 speech, in introducing a bill based on the Commissioners' draft code. Over the next decade law reform, and codification in particular, gathered momentum, so much so that in early 1853 the normally cautious Lord Cranworth, on assuming office as Lord Chancellor, was so affected by the spirit of the times to pledge himself to initiate codification on a sweeping scale:[10]

> To simplify our statutes and improve their style would be something—would be a great deal. But I look further. I can see there is no reason why this proposed step should not, at some future time—some years hence—constitute the foundation of that which I have always looked forward to as most desirable—heretobefore I have feared it to be unattainable—a Code Victoria, that shall put us on the same footing that a neighbouring nation has attained by that code which will immortalise its author long after his triumphs and his failures—his victories and his defeats—have passed into oblivion.

Lord Cranworth placed the management of this task in the hands of the veteran Bellenden Ker and a Statute Law Board, subsequently replaced by the Statute Law Commission, but his vision quickly foundered on logistical difficulties, legislative suspicion, and professional hostility. Meanwhile, the proposal to codify the criminal law had been referred to another Criminal Law Commission, which produced five reports between 1845 and 1849, was championed again by Lord Brougham in bills of 1848 and

[9] *A Report on Criminal Procedure by Charles Sprengal Greaves* (1856) Parl. Papers L. 79 (quotation at 110).

[10] (1853) 124 P. D. 58–66 (quotation at 65–6).

1849, to be eventually placed in the hands of C. S. Greaves and J. J. Lonsdale in 1852 to be broken down into a series of bills on specific legal topics. Lord Cranworth made the mistake of referring the first two of these bills, on offences against the person and larceny, to the judges, who seized the opportunity to disparage them. At this point the proposal become entangled in the débâcle of the Statute Law Commission, codification gave way to consolidation, and only after further legislative misadventures were seven consolidation acts finally passed in 1861.[11] Fitzjames Stephen subsequently resumed the struggle to codify the criminal law in the late 1870s, but his efforts only bore legislative fruit in the colonies.[12]

Improvements to criminal procedure promoted in the mid-century period included the introduction of criminal appeals, a second speech for defence counsel, the right of the accused to give evidence, and the creation of public prosecutors. The role of expert witnesses and of the jury in criminal trials were also critically examined.[13] Legislative change, however, remained slow and piecemeal despite the climate of reform and the commitment of reformers, and the most important reforms to criminal procedure—the introduction of appeals and the accused's right to give evidence—had to wait until the turn of the century.

The attempt to introduce new trials or appeals in criminal cases is perhaps the most instructive of the mid-century disappointments for criminal law reformers. It began in May 1844 when Fitzroy Kelly moved in the House of Commons for leave to bring in a bill to allow appeals in criminal cases. Kelly[14] described his bill as 'a very simple measure' that sought to assimilate 'the practice of the Criminal to that of the Civil

[11] The 1845–49 Commission reconsidered and revised the work of the original Commission. Bellenden Ker and Starkie were members of this Commission (with Andrew Amos, Sir Edward Ryan and Vaughan Richards), which ended on Starkie's death in 1849. On the work of the Criminal Law Commission and the fate of codification see Chapter 4; Cross (1978); Cornish and Clark (1989) 598–607; Greaves (1862) 'Introduction'; and 'State of the Criminal Law Digests' (1851) 14 *Law Review* 184–90; **Judicial disparagement of bills on larceny and offences against the person**: see Cross (1978) 9–10. The Judges' comments appear in *Copies of the Lord Chancellor's Letters to the Judges on the Criminal Law Bills of the last Session and Copies of their Answers thereto* (1854) Parl. Papers LIII. 389. Greaves and Lonsdale published a reply, and Lord Brougham wrote two articles questioning the capacity of the judiciary to comment meaningfully on law reform: see Greaves and Lonsdale (1854), Brougham (1853–54) and Brougham (1854). Codification joins the amelioration of capital punishment, full defence by counsel and criminal appeals—discussed *infra*—as criminal law reforms of this era forcefully opposed by the judiciary.

[12] 5 Radzinowicz (1948–86) 738–40; Cornish and Clark (1989) 600–1.

[13] See, for example, Stephen (1859).

[14] Fitzroy Kelly (1796–1880) was called to the Bar in 1824, appointed King's Counsel in 1834, and first returned to Parliament in 1837. He was junior counsel for the prosecution in *Corder*, and his defence of the murderer Tawell in 1845 attracted censure during the licence of counsel controversy. He was an ardent supporter of criminal law reform and codification. He enjoyed short periods in office as Solicitor-General and Attorney-General before his appointment as Chief Baron of the Exchequer in 1866.

Law, giving, as nearly as possible, the same remedy to persons in criminal cases against an erroneous verdict or a wrong charge, as the English Law gave in civil cases'.[15] Kelly withdrew his bill on the Government indicating its willingness to investigate the introduction of criminal appeals. Shortly afterwards the *Eighth Report* of the Criminal Law Commissioners endorsed criminal appeals, and Thomas Starkie and C.S. Greaves drew attention to the defectiveness of the existing procedure in articles in the *Law Review* and the *Law Magazine*. The government's failure to act on this question led William Ewart in 1848 to introduce another bill to allow appeals in criminal cases.[16]

The history of appeals has many similarities with the struggle for full defence by counsel of the previous decade. Both measures drew support from opponents of capital punishment and the Benthamite Criminal Law Commissioners, and faced their most powerful opposition from the judiciary. The practice in civil cases was a prominent argument in favour of both measures, often expressed rhetorically in the question of why should a man be entitled to counsel or an appeal in a case involving a few pounds of property, but not when his life was at stake? The simple and complex facts views of evidence appears in discussion of both measures; Mr Baron Parke, for example, stated in opposition to appeals that 'in Questions of Criminal Law the Decision upon Matters of Fact and also upon Matters of Law is vastly more easy than in Civil Cases', while the Criminal Law Commissioners took the opposite view:[17]

Questions of civil right are for the most part dependent on facts, the effect rather than the existence of which is disputed. Criminal questions, on the contrary, frequently depend on transactions of a hidden and secret nature, the truth of which it is oftentimes difficult to unravel, and, in consequence, resort must often be had to a chain of presumptive or circumstantial evidence. Looking therefore to

[15] There were three means to review criminal convictions at this time. Firstly, there was a long-established practice of petitions to the Crown for the exercise of the royal prerogative of mercy. Secondly, the trial judge, in his discretion, could agree to refer a point of law for the opinion of the 15 judges. There references were not heard by any formally constituted Court, argument by counsel was permitted only at the judges' discretion, no judgments were delivered, and a decision in a prisoner's favour after conviction was implemented by the indirect means of a recommendation for pardon. Thirdly, and rarely, a writ of error lay for defects apparent on the face of the record: see generally Greaves (1845). By contrast the litigant dissatisfied with the decision in a civil case could formally bring it before a full court at Westminster, for argument and decision, by the procedures of a writ of error, a motion for a new trial or a bill of exceptions.

[16] *Eighth Report of Her Majesty's Commissioners on the Criminal Law* (1845) Parl. Papers XIV 161; Starkie (1844–45) 444–6, and 457–8; Greaves (1845). Ewart questioned the Government on its intentions in 1846 and 1847 before introducing in 1848 the bill: see (1846) 83 P. D. 642; (1847) 95 P. D. 527; (1847–48) 96 P. D. 1299.

[17] *Eighth Report of Her Majesty's Commissioners on the Criminal Law* (1845) Parl. Papers XIV. 161 at 180. The quotation from Parke B. is from the *Report From the Select Committee of the House of Lords on the Criminal Law Administration Amendment Bill* (1847–48) Parl. Papers XVI. 425.

the nature of the inquiry, it is quite as likely that error or mistake should occur in the investigation of a criminal charge as on that of a mere civil claim.

Both measures increased the role of counsel, reduced judicial discretion and by promising more satisfactory trial outcomes diminished the importance of the prerogative of mercy. As Fitzroy Kelly recognised, a bill allowing criminal appeals was a logical successor to the Prisoners' Counsel Act.[18]

The judges responded to the prospect of a court of criminal appeal by preparing their own alternative measure. The Criminal Law Administration Amendment Bill was prepared by Barons Parke and Alderson, at the invitation of the Home Secretary, and introduced in the House of Lords by the Lord Chief Justice, Lord Campbell, a month after Ewart's bill appeared in the Commons. It regularised the existing practice by establishing a Court of Crown Cases Reserved to which judges at their discretion could refer difficult points of law. Counsel would be heard and judgments delivered in open court, but appeals on questions of fact or evidence remained impossible. Any wider appeal, the judges maintained, was unnecessary and would protract criminal cases to the prejudice of the repression of crime, which depended upon the speedy and certain punishment of guilt.[19] This Bill quickly passed through Parliament and became law in August 1848, to be called the Crown Cases Act.[20]

The Crown Cases Act did not silence calls for a comparable right of appeal in criminal as in civil cases. Further bills relating to criminal appeals were introduced in the Commons in 1853, 1858 and July 1859 but made no progress. However, the trial, conviction, respite and pardon of Thomas Smethurst between August and November 1859 then provided a clear example for reformers of the necessity for an appeal process, both to examine possible errors in the handling of facts at a trial and to consider new evidence discovered after the trial. Smethurst was tried for the murder of Isabella Bankes—whom he had bigamously married in December 1858—by poisoning. The leading prosecution toxicologist, Dr Taylor,[21] confidently told the depositions hearing that a

[18] (1844) 75 P. D. 11 at 12.

[19] See *Report from the Select Committee of the House of Lords on the Criminal Law Administration Amendment Bill, supra*, especially at 4 and 5 (Parke B.), and 49 (Lord Brougham); (1847–48) 97 P. D. 964–5 and (1847–48) 100 P. D. 465–6 (both Lord Campbell L.C.J.).

[20] 11 & 12 Vict., c. 78.

[21] Dr Alfred Swain Taylor, Professor of Chemistry at Guy's Hospital and author of the leading work on poisons held his opinions firmly, took contradiction personally and did not shy from acrimonious professional debate. He was also the leading expert witness for the prosecution in *Palmer*, where speculative statements in his depositions and comments on the evidence in *The Lancet* prior to the trial were seized upon by Sergeant Shee in his speech to the jury. Taylor's deposition in *Palmer* and his letter in *The Lancet* appear in Old Bailey Sessions Papers (1855–56), vol. 44 at 116–17 and 117–19 respectively. For Shee's comments on Taylor's evidence in his speech see Knott and Watson (1952) 131–2, 153–75, *passim*.

'watery-looking mixture' in a medicine bottle found in Smethurst's possession contained arsenic and the regular administration of small doses of this mixture would produce the symptoms and slow death by exhaustion experienced by Miss Bankes. However, between the depositions hearing and the trial Taylor discovered that he had inadvertently introduced arsenic into the medicine bottle by the process adopted to test for its presence. He admitted his error immediately, but it was blamed for creating a prejudice against Smethurst and was the first in a series of unsatisfactory features of the evidence which led many to doubt whether Smethurst's guilt was adequately proven. The guilty verdict immediately produced a rush of letters to the papers, and sustained discussion in medical journals. *The Lancet* considered that great suspicion attached to Smethurst but 'the mistakes and contradictions in the chemical portions of the trial...and the possibility that the death of Miss BANKES may have arisen from natural causes, all concur to render the certainty of the guilt of the condemned man anything but unequivocal'.[22]

Smethurst challenged the verdict in a petition to the Home Secretary, Sir George Cornwall Lewis, dated 30 August 1859. The Home Secretary also received over two hundred other communications relating to the case, including memorials from medical practitioners, members of the Bar, expert witnesses for the defence and Smethurst's counsel. Smethurst's sentence of death was respited and the Home Secretary referred all communications relating to the case to the trial judge, Sir Frederick Pollock. Pollock produced a one hundred page review of the evidence and communications received since the trial, which concluded that while the evidence at the trial justified the verdict 'the medical communications which have since reached you [Sir George Lewis], put the matter in a very different light and tend very strong to shew that the medical part of the inquiry did not go to the Jury in so favourable a way as it might and indeed ought to have done...The effect of this according to the Practice of the Home Office would be to save the life of the Prisoner'. Pollock did not, however, believe that Smethurst deserved a full pardon and advised Sir George Lewis that if this course was being considered then 'I think it ought to be founded on the Judgment of *medical and scientific persons selected by yourself*'. The Home Secretary adopted this suggestion and referred the case to the leading surgeon of the day, Sir Benjamin Brodie, who in a short report, which did not confine itself to the medical aspects of the case, concluded that 'the impression in my own mind is that there is not absolute and complete evidence of

[22] For letters to *The Times* regarding Smethurst's trial see Parry (1931) 206–32; for *The Lancet* editorials on this trial see 27 August (quotation at 220), 17 September and 26 November 1859.

Smethurst's guilt'. Sir George Lewis then decided to grant Smethurst a free pardon.[23]

Smethurst's trial was thus reviewed, and the verdict of the jury overturned, in private correspondence between the Home Secretary, the trial judge and an expert whose opinion was never publicly stated nor tested in cross-examination. Whatever merit the prerogative of mercy had in mitigating punishment on humanitarian grounds, or had once enjoyed in the calculations of the capital felony process, *Smethurst* demonstrated that it was ill-adapted for the review of several days' evidence on complex medical and scientific questions, evaluating additional evidence of the same nature, and deciding whether the jury's verdict was justified. The new phenomenon in the criminal law of 'monster trials' placed unprecedented pressures on counsel and expert witnesses, and the fallibility of professional men, in a procedure so heavily reliant upon them to uncover the truth of crimes, created an independent need for a thorough, public, and professional appeal procedure.[24]

In the aftermath of Smethurst's pardon his case appeared prominently in professional writing on criminal appeals, and in debate over the Appeal in Criminal Cases Bill introduced into the House of Commons in January 1860. Sir George Lewis led the opposition to this bill in a lengthy speech displaying paternalistic echos of the capital felony process as well as a desire not to augment lawyerly cost and formality in criminal procedure.[25] The drafting of this bill troubled many legal members, and it failed at its second reading without a division. The struggle for criminal appeals had produced a stalemate where the inadequacy of the existing procedure was hardly disputed, but change could not be

[23] **Communications with the Home Secretary**: Smethurst's petition and memorials to the Home Secretary from 'Thirty Medical Practitioners', 'Members of the Bar', and 'Three Medical Witnesses for the Defence' are included in the appendices to Parry (1931). The letter from Smethurst's counsel, Sergeant Parry and Hardinge Giffard is discussed in Pollock's report at 59–60; **Sir Frederick Pollock's report**: *Report on the Papers relating to the Case of Thomas Smethurst, by Sir Frederick Pollock*, Forster Collection, 48. F. 52, National Art Library, Victoria and Albert Museum (quotations at 64–5, 66 and 99–100 (emphasis original) respectively; **Sir Benjamin Brodie's report**: Parry (1931) 191–2. Note also the subsequent correspondence between Sir George Cornwall Lewis and Sir Frederick Pollock set out in Parry (1931) at 193 and 194.

[24] The expression 'monster trials' is from Stephen (1859) at 236.

[25] See (1860) 156 P. D. 414–15 and particularly at 422: 'Let the House remember that the appeal to the Home Office is cheap, direct, rapid, and unaccompanied with any official forms; and that whatever importance they may attribute to the cross-examination of witnesses, or to the technical rules of a court of justice, it is of essential advantage to the poor prisoner who has no means of feeing counsel for motions to obtain writs of *certiorari* that his access to the Home Office should be easy and unencumbered with forms and expenses. However gloomy and secret may be the procedure of the Home Office, let it be observed that from those gloomy and secret recesses no bill of costs ever emerges, and that the poorest prisoner in the country may, at the cost of a sheet of writing paper, obtain a revision of his sentence'.

effected.[26] The creation of the Court of Criminal Appeal had to wait until 1907.[27]

The proposal to introduce public prosecutors repeats this pattern of reformist determination and legislative inertia, and the result of little progress. Lord Brougham, encouraged by Charles Phillips, took steps towards creating a public prosecutor at the Central Criminal Court as early as 1834.[28] The proposal was subsequently endorsed by the Criminal Law Commissioners in their *Eighth Report* and was a concern of many of the respondents to the Commissions' questionnaire on procedure.[29] In evidence before the select committee of the House of Lords on criminal appeals in 1848 Lord Lyndhurst and Fitzroy Kelly agreed that the need for public prosecutors had been increased by the introduction of full defence by counsel, for such officers would relieve the judges of the responsibility of neutralising the effect of speeches of defence counsel.[30] The first bill to create public prosecutors was introduced in 1854, but no legislative success was achieved until the creation of the office of Director of Public Prosecutions, with responsibility limited to exceptional cases, by the Prosecution of Offences Act of 1879.[31]

There was at this time minor legislative amelioration of the difficulties for defence counsel of the practice relating to the order of speeches. The Criminal Procedure Act 1865[32] conferred on the prisoner's counsel a closing address at the conclusion of the defence evidence in addition to his opening speech, thereby extending to criminal trials an innovation made in civil procedure 11 years earlier.[33] The second speech meant that

[26] The stalemate over criminal appeals is well illustrated by Stephen's analysis. He describes the status quo as 'strange and unsatisfactory in the extreme', but goes on to find the arguments against new trials or appeals in criminal cases to be convincing. He proceeds to propose a curious hybrid institution, akin perhaps to a modern commission of inquiry, consisting of the Home Secretary, the trial judge and one other judge, to investigate unsatisfactory verdicts or new evidence discovered after conviction: see Stephen (1863a) 223–32.

[27] Criminal Appeal Act (7 Edw. VII, c. 23); see Cornish and Clark (1989) 619–23.

[28] See Brougham (1851) 431, and Phillips to Brougham, *Brougham Papers No. 28, 437* (3 July 1834), *No. 36, 815* (26 August 1834), and O'Connell to Phillips, *No. 26, 362* (attachment, 5 September 1834).

[29] The responses to the Commissions' questionnaire are set out in Appendix A of the *Eighth Report of Her Majesty's Commissioners on the Criminal Law* (1845) Parl. Papers XIV. 161. On these responses see Cornish (1978), especially at 307–10. John Pitt Taylor published his responses as an article in the *Law Magazine*: (see Taylor (1844)), which appears as Appendix C to the *Eighth Report*.

[30] *Report from the Select Committee of the House of Lords on the Criminal Law Administration Amendment Bill* (1847–48) Parl. Papers XVI. 425 particularly questions 202 and 203 (Fitzroy Kelly) and 307 and 308 (Lord Lyndhurst). Lord Brougham made a similar comment shortly after the Prisoners' Counsel Act was passed: see Lord Brougham to Lord Lyndhurst, 20 December 1836, *Lyndhurst Papers No. 121* (quoted in Chapter 5).

[31] 42 & 43 Vict., c. 22. On the struggle to introduce public prosecutors see generally Kurland and Waters (1959).

[32] 28 & 29 Vict., c. 18.

[33] By section 18 of the Common Law Procedure Act 1854 (17 & 18 Vict., c. 125).

the prisoner's counsel was able to comment on the actual rather than anticipated testimony of defence witnesses and on the prosecution cross-examination, but it made no alteration to the prosecution right of reply. The restrictive clauses of the 1837 Practice Memorandum relating to both the depositions and the prosecution reply remained unchanged, despite criticism in the responses to the Criminal Law Commissioners' procedural questionnaire and C.S. Greaves' 1856 *A Report on Criminal Procedure*.[34]

The development of adversary procedure in the wake of the Prisoners' Counsel Act silenced the prisoner's voice in the courtroom. The speech of counsel deprived prisoners of their statement to the jury, and the practice relating to the last word encouraged defence counsel to dispense entirely with evidence on the prisoner's behalf. The statutory recognition in 1848 of the prisoner's rights to a caution and to remain silent at the taking of the depositions,[35] and a strict judicial attitude towards the admissibility of confessions, further reduced the likelihood of a prisoner's own account of events being heard at the trial. Prisoners who wished to give evidence in their own defence were not permitted to do so, though they might, like Smethurst, have much to say after conviction.[36] Fitzjames Stephen complained that the silence of prisoners encouraged 'sham defences', where counsel met the prosecution case with hypothetical explanations compatible with innocence rather than the prisoner's own story. The conclusion seemed inescapable that the silence of prisoners was not conducive to the discovery of the truth. Jeremy Bentham suggested a robust remedy to this evil early in the century by arguing that prisoners should be both competent and compellable witnesses at their trials.[37]

Perhaps the most startling feature of the debate on criminal procedure in the two decades after the Prisoners' Counsel Act is the absence of any suggestion that full defence by counsel, the desuetude of prisoners' statements, and the increasingly thorough pursuit of truth in adversary

[34] *Eighth Report of Her Majesty's Commissioners on the Criminal Law* (1845) Parl. Papers XIV. 161 at 311 (M. D. Hill Q.C.); 409–10 (C. S. Greaves); 457 (J. P. Cobbett); 496–7 (J. L. Adolphus); *A Report on Criminal Procedure by Charles Sprengal Greaves* (1856) Parl. Papers L. 79 at 111–13.

[35] Indictable Offences Act 1848 (10 & 11 Vict., c. 42), s. 18.

[36] Smethurst made a lengthy statement between the delivery of the verdict and sentence: see Parry (1931) 135–44.

[37] *Rationale of Judicial Evidence* in 6 and 7 Bentham (1843) *passim*. See for example at 6 Bentham (1843) 204: 'In the character of objections to competency, no objections ought to be allowed [except on the grounds of the avoidance of vexation, expense and delay]. Willing or unwilling witnesses of all descriptions ought to be heard...the unwilling not to be excused on any such grounds...as those of family-peace-disturbing, trust-betraying, self-convicting or accusing, self disgracing, or in any other way self-prejudicing evidence'. Bentham was also prepared to infer guilt from a defendant's 'obstinate silence': see 7 Bentham (1843) 455.

procedure might necessitate reconsideration of the prohibition on prisoners' evidence. Neither the Criminal Law Commissioners nor C.S. Greaves in his comprehensive *A Report on Criminal Procedure* considered this possibility. Even Stephen, so sensitive to the discovery of the truth as the ultimate purpose of criminal procedure, sought to reveal prisoners' own accounts of events through their pre-trial interrogation rather than by enabling or compelling them to enter the witness box at their trials. When Lord Brougham and Fitzroy Kelly proposed during the late 1850s and early 1860s that prisoners be permitted to give evidence in their own defences, the impetus came not from the changes that had already occurred, or were mooted, in criminal procedure, but from civil procedure. The Evidence Act 1851 permitted parties in civil proceedings to give evidence, and the success of this measure, the argument ran, justified its extension to criminal cases.[38] The proposal attracted little support, and not until the Criminal Evidence Act of 1898 did prisoners in all cases become competent, though not compellable, to give evidence on their own behalf.[39]

Advocacy and Legal Change

The Prisoners' Counsel Act stands at the head of a series of nineteenth and early twentieth century legislation on criminal procedure that includes the Crown Cases Act, the Criminal Procedure Act, the Prosecution of Offences Act, the Criminal Evidence Act, and the Criminal Appeal Act. Its enactment within 15 years of its first proposal appears relatively trouble-free beside the history of criminal appeals or the futile Victorian efforts to codify the criminal law. Its introduction of full defence by counsel wrought an immediate and far-reaching transformation of criminal procedure, and also changed advocacy and the substantive criminal law. It ushered in a form of trial that maintained public confidence for over half a century, and it is arguable that even the Criminal Evidence Act and the Criminal Appeal Act at the turn of the century did not remodel criminal procedure to a comparable degree. There is much greater difference in character between the form of trial of *Corder* in 1828 and of *Palmer* in 1856, than between *Palmer* and the great criminal trials of the Edwardian era. The Prisoners' Counsel Act transformed the rough-and-ready procedure of the eighteenth and early nineteenth centuries into the scrupulous adversarial trial of today.

[38] Kelly sets out the proposal's pedigree from civil procedure at (1865) 153 P. D. 308–9; see also 'Evidence of Parties in Criminal Cases' (1858) 5 *Law Magazine and Law Review* 101–8 and Bruce (1865).

[39] 61 & 62 Vict., c. 36.

The Prisoners' Counsel Act has not received the attention it deserves from modern scholars. The eighteenth century criminal trial has received more attention than the nineteenth, and the emphasis on the impact of early practitioners in the criminal courts and the first steps in the direction of a more litigious form of trial, without sufficient regard to what was to follow, has led to the over-hasty identification of the late eighteenth century criminal trial as adversarial. This view is untenable because throughout the eighteenth century and up until 1836 the felony counsel restriction entrenched a major inequality between counsel and kept defence advocacy within narrow bounds, giving the felony trial a quite different character from civil trials of the same period. The felony counsel restriction barred the litigious development of the criminal trial, and in brushing it aside the Prisoners' Counsel Act both completed the trend of the procedural developments of the previous century and commenced the new era of the adversarial criminal trial.

The professional response to the Prisoners' Counsel Act as much as the Act itself created the adversarial criminal trial. The Prisoners' Counsel Act rough cast a new procedure from which a generation of lawyers and judges hammered and buffed a sharp adversarial shape. The legislative and judicial craftsmanship—the Act itself and the judicial implementation of the Act through practice direction and precedent—do not by themselves explain the work of transformation. Beyond the legislator and judge a welter of day-to-day activity impressed its mark on the malleable stuff of procedure. The interpretation of the Prisoners' Counsel Act by the Bar, through for example its adaptation of the tactical management of defences and forensic morality to the demands of full defence by counsel, influenced the character of criminal procedure, the conduct of trials and, no doubt, their outcomes. The practice of advocacy—the artisanship of the barrister—is revealed by the history of the Prisoners' Counsel Act as a diffuse but unmistakable determinant of legal development.

The contribution of advocacy to the development of the law usually occurs through legal argument, where a submission of counsel is accepted by the judge and becomes law. Both nineteenth century and modern scholars have recognised that the law of criminal evidence owes much in this way to the effort, ingenuity and sometimes desperation of counsel.[40] However, the skills of the advocate employed in the forensic

[40] 'The allowing persons accused of treason or felony the right of being defended by counsel, the necessary consequence of which was that objections to the admissibility of evidence were much more frequently taken, the attention of the judges was more directed to the subject of evidence, their judgments were better considered, and their decisions better remembered': Best (1849) 133 (footnote omitted); the recent work of Beattie and Langbein affirms this link between the appearance of counsel and the development of the law of criminal evidence; Beattie (1986) 362 *et seq*; Langbein (1994): 'The privilege against self incrimination at common law was the work of defense counsel' at 1047 and *passim*.

struggle to achieve favourable findings of fact—the examination and cross-examination of witnesses, the jury address and tact—might percolate through legal argument and judicial decision and so also influence the development of the law. The degree of case analysis that the establishment of this connection requires makes its demonstration highly problematic, but an unusually clear example of legal development in this way is provided by the clarification of the law of insanity in 1843. Prior to the introduction of full defence by counsel an insane prisoner had to address the jury himself, by a sad irony of the felony counsel restriction, to establish the fact of his own insanity. The Prisoners' Counsel Act enabled counsel for the first time to precede the evidence of insanity with a speech that could draw out the implications of the evidence and build arguments upon it in such a way as to raise novel legal questions. The strength of Alexander Cockburn's address to the jury in *M'Naughten* in 1843 and the expert evidence that followed it led the judge, Sir Nicholas Tindal, to stop the trial and ask the jury to acquit the prisoner. The apparent ease with which M'Naughten had escaped the consequences of a carefully executed murder prompted debate in Parliament, raised the possibility of legislation to tighten the law, and finally resulted in the summoning of the judges to the House of Lords to make their famous statement of the law of insanity in the M'Naughten Rules. The M'Naughten Rules were judicial legislation brought about by the increased sophistication of defence advocacy.[41]

The introduction of the jury address may also have affected the law relating to confessions during the 1840s. The public suspicion of the police at this time made any police misconduct in the investigation of a crime a potent topic in the jury address, with which counsel might discredit police evidence and enlist the jury's sympathy for the prisoner. Phillips' defence of Courvoisier, with its amplified rhetoric of scorn, indignation and fear at the actions of police 'miscreants' and 'bloodhounds', demonstrates this style of advocacy. The opportunities for defence counsel to divert the jury's attention from the guilt of the prisoner to the behaviour of the police were substantially reduced by a rule excluding all confessions to which any suspicion at all attached. There are indications from the evidence collected by the Criminal Law Commissioners and published as an Appendix to their *Eighth Report* of increased strictness in excluding confessions after the introduction of full defence by counsel in 1836. One of the Commission's respondents made an explicit connection between the new defence speech and the law of

[41] **M'Naughten's trial**: Bousfield and Merrett (1843); *The Times*, 6 March 1843. The difference made by counsel is best appreciated by comparing *M'Naughten* with Bellingham's trial in 1812. **Parliamentary debate**: (1843) 67 P. D. 288, 353, and 424; (1843) 68 P. D. 888. **The M'Naughten Rules**: (1843) 10 Cl & Finn. 200.

confessions arguing that all confessions should be excluded because this, 'by disarming counsel for prisoners of many of the topics most popular and attractive with juries, would, in effect, greatly conduce to the conviction of the really guilty'.[42]

The influence of advocacy on the shape of procedure and the development of the law in this way makes it a proper and long overdue subject for jurisprudential study. Advocacy can be classified as a cause of law, and as a species of professional opinion. In mid-nineteenth century terms, as analysed by John Austin, it joins the work of legal writers, the established practice of conveyancers, and the general opinion of the profession as a significant influence on judges.[43]

These forms of professional opinion, in Austin's analysis, both positively influenced the direction of the law and also acted as a check on wayward or arbitrary judicial behaviour. That could compel the judiciary 'by a sort of moral necessity' to adopt a rule of law. He saw this power of professional opinion as raising the profession into a form of partnership with the Bench in the administration of justice:[44]

> The judiciary law made by the tribunals, is, in effect, the *joint product* of the legal profession, or rather of the most experienced and most skillful part of it: the joint product of the tribunals themselves, and of the private lawyers who by their cunning in the law have gotten the ear of the judicial legislators...[I]t *is not the product of judge alone,* but it is the joint product of Judge and Co. So great is the influence of the general opinion of the profession that it frequently forces upon the Courts the adoption of a rule of law, by a sort of moral necessity...What a howl would be set up (and not unjustly) if the Courts were to disregard the established practice of conveyancers; although until sanctioned by judicial decisions, it is not strictly law.

The contribution of advocacy to the administration of justice during the mid-nineteenth century was, as it is today, the facilitation of the discovery of the truth, the improvement of the law, and the prevention of judicial error. The mundane demands of legal life—attracting briefs and chasing verdicts—were no doubt of more concern to barristers on

[42] *Eighth Report of Her Majesty's Commissioners on the Criminal Law* (1845) Parl. Papers XIV. 161, Answer 241; Cornish (1978) 311–14.

[43] Austin identified three forms of professional opinion and practice that routinely operated upon legislators and judges. First, 'the opinions of private lawyers eminent for their knowledge and ability', such as leading text writers, were often adopted as law. Secondly, there were the practices of established conveyancers; much of the law of real property was, Austin said, 'notoriously taken from opinions and practices, which have grown up, and are daily growing up, amongst conveyancers'. Thirdly, there were the expectations of the profession in respect of unresolved points of law. Here the 'authority of lawyers, numerous and experienced, has great weight': Austin (1879) 560–5. On the expectations of the profession see also *ibid*, 674 (Lecture XXXIX). On the authority of leading conveyancers at this time see Anderson (1992) 6.

[44] 2 Austin (1879) 667 (Lecture XXXVIII, emphasis added).

a day-to-day basis, but their zealous representation of prosecutors and prisoners through countless trials, steered by professional ethics, enriched the administration of justice. The drama and moral ambiguity of forensic contention meant that the zeal and commitment of the advocate, his hour's passion for a virtual stranger and for a fee was, and always will be, easily maligned. That is why Talfourd took pains to prove the advocate might as readily be inspired by sympathy, trust, and the noblest impulses of human nature as by baser motives. Yet above the fascinating human and professional dimensions of advocacy was its incremental role in revealing the truth of crimes, modifying criminal law and procedure and softly checking judicial idiosyncrasy. The great development in criminal procedure of the mid-nineteenth century, initiated by the Prisoners' Counsel Act, was the full realisation of these benefits of advocacy.

Appendix 1

Legislation

1.1 The Prisoners' Counsel Act (6 & 7 Will. 4, c. 114)

An Act for enabling Persons indicted of Felony to make their Defence by Counsel or Attorney.

[20th *August* 1836]

Whereas it is just and reasonable that Persons accused of Offences against the Law should be enabled to make their full Answer and Defence to all that is alleged against them: Be it therefore enacted by the King's most Excellent Majesty, by and with the Advice and Consent of the Lords Spiritual and Temporal, and Commons, in this present Parliament assembled, and by the Authority of the same, That from and after the First Day of *October* next all Persons tried for Felonies shall be admitted, after the Close of the Case for the Prosecution, to make full Answer and Defence thereto, by Counsel learned in the Law, or by Attorney in Courts where Attornies practise as Counsel.

II. And be it further declared and enacted, That in all Cases of summary Conviction Persons accused shall be admitted to make their full Answer and Defence, and to have all Witnesses examined and cross-examined by Counsel or Attorney.

III. And be it further enacted, That all Persons who after the passing of this Act shall be held to bail or committed to Prison for any Offence against the Law shall be entitled to require and have, on Demand, (from the Person who shall have the lawful Custody thereof, and who is hereby required to deliver the same,) Copies of the Examinations of the Witnesses respectively upon whose Depositions they have been so held to bail or committed to Prison, on Payment of a reasonable Sum for the same, not exceeding Three Halfpence for each Folio of Ninety Words: Provided always, that if such Demand shall not be made before the Day appointed for the Commencement of the Assize or Sessions at which the Trial of the Person on whose Behalf such Demand shall be made is to take place, such Person shall not be entitled to have any Copy of such Examination of Witnesses, unless the Judge or other Person to preside at such Trial shall be of opinion that such Copy may be made and delivered without Delay or Inconvenience to such Trial; but it shall nevertheless be competent for such Judge or other Person so to preside at such Trial, if he shall think fit, to postpone such Trial on account of such Copy of the Examination of Witnesses not having been previously had by the Party charged.

IV. And be it further enacted, That all Persons under Trial shall be entitled, at the Time of their Trial, to inspect, without Fee or Reward, all Depositions (or Copies thereof) which have been taken against them, and returned into the Court before which such Trial shall be had.

V. And be it further enacted, That this Act may be amended, altered, or replaced by any Act or Acts to be passed in this present Session of Parliament; and that nothing herein contained shall extend to *Scotland*.

1.2 The Last Word Clause

This clause was passed by the House of Commons in 1836 (as clause 2 of the Prisioners' Counsel Bill) and was then deleted by the House of Lords:

'And be it further Enacted, That in all such cases of Felony, and likewise in all cases of Treason, Misprison of Treason and Misdemeanour, if, after the close of the case for the person or persons accused, the Counsel for the prosecution shall make any reply, the Counsel for the person or persons accused shall be admitted to answer it.'

1.3 Practice Memorandum (from (1837) 17 Law Magazine 470)

'At a meeting of twelve of the Judges, for the purpose of choosing the spring circuits of 1837, (Littledale, J., Bosanquet, J., and Coleridge, J., being absent from indisposition), a discussion took place as to some points which were thought likely to occur at the assizes, in consequence of the recent act for allowing prisioners, indicted for felony, to make full defence by counsel; and the following seemed to be the course of practice which the judges present thought it would be most advisable to adopt:—

1. That where a witness for the crown has made a deposition before a magistrate, he cannot, upon his cross-examination by the prisioner's counsel, be asked whether he did or did not, in his deposition, make such or such a statement, until the deposition itself has been read, in order to manifest whether such statement is or is not contained therein; and that such deposition must read as part of the evidence of the cross-examining counsel.

2. That, after such deposition has been read, the prisioner's counsel may proceed in his cross-examination of the witness as to any supposed contradiction or variance between the testimony of the witness in Court and his former deposition; after which the counsel for the prosecution may re-examine the witness, and, after the prisioner's counsel has addressed the jury, will be entitled to the reply. And in case the counsel for the prisoner comments upon any supposed variance or contradiction, without having read the deposition, the Court may direct it to be read, and the counsel for the prosecution will be entitled to the reply upon it.

3. That the witness cannot, in cross-examination, be compelled to answer,

whether he did or did not make such or such a statement before the magistrate, until after his deposition has been read, and it appears that it contains no mention of such statement. In that event the counsel for the prisoner may proceed with his cross-examination; and if the witness admits such statement to have been made, he may comment upon such omission, or upon the effect of it upon the other part of his testimony; or if the witness denies that he made such statement, the counsel for the prisoner may then, if such statement by material to the matter in issue, call witnesses to prove that he made such statement. But in either event, the reading of the deposition is the prisoner's evidence, and the counsel for the prosecution will be entitled to reply.

4. If the only evidence called, on the part of the prisoner, is evidence to character, although the counsel for the prosecution is entitled to reply, it will be a matter for his discretion whether he will use it or not. Cases may occur in which it may be fit and proper so to do.

5. In cases of public prosecutions for felony, instituted by the Crown, the law officers of the Crown, and those who represent them, are, in strictness, entitled to the reply, although no evidence is produced on the part of the prisoner.'

Appendix 2

Conviction Rates England and Wales 1805–1840

Year	*Committals*	*Convictions*	*Conviction Rate (%)*
1805	4605	2783	60.43
1806	4346	2515	57.87
1807	4446	2567	57.74
1808	4735	2723	57.51
1809	5330	3238	60.75
1810	5146	3158	61.37
1811	5337	3163	59.27
1812	6576	3913	59.50
1813	7164	4422	61.76
1814	6390	4025	62.99
1815	7818	4883	62.46
1816	9091	5797	63.77
1817	13932	9056	65.00
1818	13597	8958	66.03
1819	14254		
1820	13710	9318	67.96
1821	13115	8788	67.01
1822	12241	8209	67.06
1823	12263	8204	66.90
1824	13698	9425	68.81
1825	14437	9964	69.02
1826	16147	11095	68.71
1827	17924	12567	70.11
1828	16564	11723	70.77
1829	18675	13261	71.01
1830	18107	12805	70.72
1831	19647	13830	70.39
1832	20829	14947	71.76
1833	20072	14446	71.97
1834	20168	14443	71.61

Source: *Report from the Select Committee on the Criminal Law* (1819) P. P. VIII 1, Appendix No 1; *Committals. Summary Statements 1820–26* (1836–27) P. P. XIX 183; *Committals England and Wales 1825–1831* (1931–32) P. P. XXXIII 1; *Comparative Number Committed for Trial in England and Wales, 1828–1834* (1835) P. P. XLV 21.

Year	*Committals*	*Convictions*	*Conviction Rate (%)*
1834	22451	15995	71.24
1835	20731	14729	71.05
1836	20984	14771	70.39
1837	23612	17090	72.38
1838	23094	16785	72.68
1839	24443	17832	72.95
1840	27187	19927	73.30

Sources: *Tables Showing the Number of Criminal Offenders in England and Wales* (1835) P. P. XLV 43; (1836) P. P. XLI 11; (1837) P. P. XLVI 9; (1837–38) P. P. XLIII 1; (1839) P. P. XXXVIII 241; (1840) P. P. XXXVIII 331; (1841) P. P. XVIII 255.

Notes

1. Committal and conviction figures are for indictable offences in England and Wales. The conviction rate is the proportion of convictions to committals, expressed as a percentage rounded to two decimal points. Conviction figures could not be located for 1819.

2. There was a reorganisation of the returns of criminal statistics in 1833, which expanded the list of indictable offences included in the returns. The second table is based on the new and more comprehensive statistics. In 1834 figures were published for the old and new lists of offences, hence the two different sets of figures for this year. On these returns and their interpretation see Gatrell and Hadden (1972).

Appendix 3

The Defence Speech in R v Courvoisier

Notes

1. This is the text of the speech of Charles Phillips for Courvoisier as reported in *The Times* of 22 June 1840. Newspapers provide the only contemporary transcripts of the trial and *The Times* report was preferred to other newspaper accounts by Phillips and by the victim's family in a privately printed account of the trial: see *The Times*, 20 November 1849, and Poland (1918). Contemporary commentators on Phillips' defence also usually relied on this report: see, for example, Warren (1850).

2. *The Times* recorded Phillips' words in reported rather than direct speech, which involved changes to pronouns, verbs and often tenses. The best alternative report is in the *Morning Herald* of 22 June 1840, which largely retains the first person expression.

3. The speech has been divided here into seventeen sections, labelled 3.1 to 3.17 and with descriptive headings. These divisions and headings are not part of *The Times* report, but are inserted here to provide a means of reference to this appendix in the text, and incidentally to show the choice and arrangment of topics within the speech. Some topics discussed primarily at one point in the speech are, of course, alluded to in other places.

4. A few obvious spelling errors in this report, and two literary quotations in the speech (in 3.12 and 3.13, from *Hamlet* Act I Scene 5 and *The Traveller* of Oliver Goldsmith respectively) have been corrected.

The Times, 22 June 1840

Mr C. PHILLIPS addressed the jury for the prisoner.

3.1 Exordium

He supposed he need scarcely say, that after 20 years' experience in courts of criminal justice, he had seldom risen to address a jury under more painful and more anxious sensations. There were certain circumstances in this case revealed before the magistrates which has caused him much anxiety, and he left them to conjecture how much that anxiety must be increased by the production, without any notice whatever, of evidence by which the life of the unhappy man at the bar might be placed in the greatest peril. He said 'might', because he did not consider even that additional proof, for reasons which he should state to them, by any means conclusive. He felt that in the situation in which he stood he should have their kindest sympathies; he should also have the sympathy of his associates. They were embarked together in a common cause; they had incurred together a common responsibility: the life of a fellow-creature was intrusted to their keeping; and so surely as they dealt with that life unjustly, so surely would they have to answer for it to the God who made them. He had not merely the facts of this case to combat; the odious prejudices which the various preliminary investigations must have engendered filled him with apprehension. The horrid nature of the crime itself, the rank of the deceased, the numerous connexions mouring their bereavement, the opinions promulgated before the prisoner could be heard, the fact that his case had not been left to the ordinary instruments of justice, but that speculation had been stimulated by the offer of a Government reward, as if the grave knew any aristocracy,—these things did fill him with apprehension. And when he looked around him on that crowded court, and saw the intensity of the public gaze, and almost heard the throb of popular indignation, and when he turned himself to the dock where the wretched object of this outburst stood, alone amid this multitude, far from his native land, far from the friends that loved, and the associates that in his hour of danger would have crowded round him—a poor, solitary, isolated, helpless foreigner—he did own that he should feel his spirits fainting fast within him, were it not for the anchor by which he held, an anchor that was centred in the breasts of the jury. He relied upon their integrity, upon their sense of justice; he participated in that generous reliance which the prisoner showed, when he refused all foreign interference, and trusted his life to a jury of Englishmen. He thought the prisoner was right, he had no fear in appealing to such a tribunal. He knew that the case, whatever it was, would by such a tribunal be fairly, fully, impartially heard, and justly decided. He should proceed, then, to consider the most extraordinary and unheard-of circumstances of this case, and, having done so, he should submit that in such a case, wrapped up in clouds, in mystery, and darkness, there was not only nothing upon which they could safely convict the prisoner, but that here and there probabilities started up which might make them suspect that he had been made the victim of an unjust and depraved conspiracy.

3.2 The Effect of the Prisoners' Counsel Act

He had much to complain of the opening address of his friend Mr Adolphus, not personally indeed, for in a case like this he should be unworthy of the gown he wore if he did not forget all personal considerations. He complained of it on the part of the accused, but he confessed there was nothing here which he had not expected, nothing which he had not long ago anticipated. It was no new notion of his, as the learned Judges knew, that the consequence of an act of Parliament now in operation would be to make a court of criminal jurisdiction the arena of angry passions, and to place the life of a fellow-creature in peril or in safety, just in proportion to the skill and talent of his advocate. He should be glad to know from the learned Judges who presided there, whether it was not startling to them, after the experience of their early life, when such a thought never entered into the head of any advocate, to find the defence of a prisoner anticipated—to find that defence answered by anticipation—to find appeals to passion and prejudice where everything should be decided by the coolest reason. He appealed to them to think for one instant in what a situation this placed the advocate of the accused.

3.3 The Prosecution Opening I: 'foreigners always murder when they rob'

Let them consider how the case had been met. 'This man is a foreigner,' said Mr Adolphus, 'and foreigners always murder when they rob.' That expression filled him with horror. In the name of the human race he protested against it. All men who did not belong to this country were foreigners, and it was a libel upon the human race to utter such a sentiment. He declared most solemnly that when he heard it uttered his countenance sank; he was ashamed to look up, for fear that he should meet the glance of some of those representatives of foreign countries who had filled the court; he was ashamed to see what their sensations much have been, when they heard an English advocate utter such a slander on their nations. But it was not ture. Let them maintain the character of England, high and noble as it stood, but let them not seek to erect a character upon the ruined reputations of other countries; it was a bad compliment to us; we needed not detraction. Mr Adolphus was a historian, and history ought to have taught him the character of Courvoisier's countrymen,—ought to have taught him that if there were in any corner of the world a nation free from crime, it was that Switzerland of which he was a native. Let the jury search their memories and see if they could recollect an instance of a Swiss murderer. They rob, he said, and murder when they rob! He (Mr C. Phillips) believed that instances of robbery were very rare in that country—he was sure that instances of murder were still more rare. And yet a man who ought to have addressed the jury cooly and calmly set out by insisting that because the man at the bar was a foreigner, he was a murderer! He had had the experience of five or six days in observing the manner in which the jury had attended to the cases, and he believed from his heart and soul that the attempt to excite a prejudice in their minds upon any such ground would be entirely frustrated. Let him beseech the jury—for that was the way to test the generosity of the expression—to imagine for one instant that they were in a court of criminal justice in Paris or Madrid, and saw an unhappy fellow-countryman arraigned on trial for his life—to imagine the advocate whose bounden duty it was to state the facts on which he founded his accusation calmly, dispassionately, and truly, rising and saying to the jury, 'Gentleman, this man comes from the country of Patch and Greenacre, and Thurtell; and Englishmen murder when they rob!' With what burning indignation would their soul be filled! Could they restrain their indignation at the attempt to make an individual the victim, not merely of others' crimes, but of a foul calumny upon his country?

3.4 The Prosecution Opening II: Motive and the Failure to Escape

There was another topic of Mr Adolphus's address to which he wished to direct their attention, equally unfair, but infinitely more absurd. Mr Adolphus had told them, forsooth, that it was not necessary for a man to have a motive. Mr Adolphus knew, that if he were to ransack the annals of his 30 or 40 years experience, he could find no instance in which a man committed a crime without a motive, and he knew equally well, that if he were to torture his ingenuity to the quick, he could attribute no motive to Courvoisier for an attempt of this nature, and then he told them that it was not necessary to have a motive! Why, his friend forgot that he was addressing a jury of adult men—men of the world—men of reasoning minds—men who must know that the most trifling action of human life had its spring from some motive or other. But his friend knew that no motive could be attributed to the prisoner for such a crime, and therefore he broached the monstrous doctrine that crime, ay, even the blackest crime, that of murder, might be commited without a motive! What motive, for instance, said his friend, had the man who fired the other day at the Queen? How did he (Mr C. Phillips) know what motive that man had? For aught he knew, and he hoped and trusted that it would appear so, that unhappy man was a maniac; his belief was that the man was so, for he could not conceive that any man in his senses, not actuated by a morbid craving after notoriety, would have attempted to commit the crime. Why, to lift the hand against youth, beauty, innocence, virtue, and talent, all centred in the person of her who sat enthroned, not merely in artificial state, but in the hearts of her loyal subjects—how could such a crime be committed by any reasoning man, by any man who was not, if not actually mad, at least upon the very verge of madness? He (Mr C. Phillips) knew that there must be motives to the commission of crime; he could not have practised so long before criminal tribunals without being convinced of that. There were motives of hatred that might prompt to crime; there were motives of jealousy that might inflame men to madness; there were motives of revenge that might tempt men to murder; there were motives of avarice and plunder that might instigate men to the perpetration of wickedness; but try by that test the conduct of Courvoisier. What motives had he of hatred? He was living with a master that loved him, and whom he loved; he was that master's confidential servant, who accompanied him in his journeys, saw him to his repose at night, and was trusted with his schemes. Was their any hatred that could instigate such a person to murder? Of motives of jealousy there was not the slightest whisper. Was there motives of revenge? For what? For kindness always received? Motives of plunder? Why should Courvoisier commit the crime of murder from motives of avarice? He could fancy a midnight depradator getting into the house, he could fancy that depradator, alarmed in his progress, terrified at his discovery, and driven, to madness from fear for his safety, committing the last dreadful crime to save him from detection. But was it necessary for Courvoisier to break into the house of which he was an inmate, to rob where he had daily and hourly opportunity to plunder,—the suspicion not cast upon him at all—but, if cast upon him, shared with others? In these days of speedy progress he had opportunities of escaping with that plunder six or eight hours before detection, and carrying it perhaps 200 miles from the place where it was appropriated, Nay, more, if Courvoisier were the man who committed this offence, did they think that he was in his senses? Did they think that he could be in his senses, and remain in the house after its commission, to be certainly detected? What did the experience of his learned friend opposite (Mr Bodkin), who had done credit to himself by his conduct during this trial, suggest to him in reference to this subject? When a man committed the pettiest crime in the street, what did self preservation prompt him, nay, imperatively command him, to do? To fly. There was a chance that he might outstrip his pursuers—might he be pursued at all—might not be suspected. But here was a man committing, according to those who conducted the prosecution, a most dreadful crime, remaining in the home after its commission, as if to be detected; committing the crime without motive, with the chance, nay, almost the certainty, of escape, and not seeking to avail himself of the opportunity! This was not a case in which they had clear proofs before them; it was a case of circumstances only, as the counsel for the presecution had told them, and therefore every minute observation with which it might be his unpleasant duty to trouble them would, he was sure, be taken into consideration. It was not his case; it was their own case. His duty performed, not upon his feeble breath, thank God, would the irrevocable doom depend; upon theirs it would, and therefore, when the arduous task committed to his friends and himself was performed, their consciences would be clear. He had demonstrated to them what the counsel for the prosecution was obliged to admit—that not only no adequate, but no assignable, motive for the murder on the part of the prisoner could be discovered. Did this man, then, commit the murder without motive? The counsel for the prosecution was driven to declare that there was no necessity for a motive to the commission of crime. That, it appeared to him, was a contradiction to all experience—a contradiction to common sense.

3.5 The Burden of Proof

But the counsel for the prosecution had undertaken to prove that the crime was committed by the prisoner. He believed it would be laid down by the learned Judges as a doctrine not to be controverted, that it was the duty of the prosecutors to bring home to the prisoner, without any reasonable doubt whatever, the commission of this offence. It was not his business to prove who did it; that was the task they had undertakem. Unless that was proved, he would beseech the jury to be cautious how they imbrued their hand in this man's blood. The omniscient God alone knew who did this crime; he was not called on to rend asunder the dark mantle of the night, and throw light upon this deed of darkness. They were bound to show the prisoner's guilt, not by inference, by reasoning, by that subtle and refined ingenuity which he was shocked to hear exercised in the opening address of his friend, but to prove by downright, clear, open, palpable demonstration. How did they seek to do this?

3.6 Sarah Mancer

What said Mr Adolphus and his witness Sarah Mancer? Here he would beg the jury not to suppose for a moment in the course of the narrative with which he must trouble them, that he sought to cast the crime upon either of the female servants. It was not at all necessary to his case to do so; he wished not to asperse them. God forbid that any breath of his should send tainted into the world persons perhaps depending for their subsistence upon their character. It was not his duty, nor his interest, nor his policy, to do so. The first imputation upon the prisoner by Mr Adolphus was his agitation. Let them try that by the test of their own hearts and consciences. The prisoner had seen his master retire to his peaceful bed, and was alarmed in the morning by the housemaid, who was up before him, with a cry of robbery, and some dark, mysterious suggestion of murder. 'Let us go,' said she, 'and see where my Lord is.' He did confess that that expression struck him as extraordinary. If she had said 'Let us go and tell my Lord that the house is plundered,' that would have been natural; but why should she suspect anything had happened to his Lordship? She saw her fellow-servant safe, no taint of blood about the house, and where did she expect to find her master? Why, in his bed-room, to be sure. What was there to lead to a suspicion he was hurt? Courvoisier was safe, the cook was safe, and why should she suspect that her master was not safe too? If he had heard the character of that nobleman rightly, there was never a man who breathed who had less reason to suspect or dread a foe.

3.7 Courvoisier's Behaviour on the Discovery of the Murder

But Courvoisier did as he was desired. He preceded the woman down stairs, as was his custom; he was the first person who entered the bed-room; and what did he do. The jury would see whether there was anything unnatural in it. The room was in darkness, every window was closed; what would any one of the jury have done on such an occasion? The prisoner walked up to the window, which he was in the habit of opening; he opened a shutter, and then this female servant saw a speck of blood on the pillow, and ran screaming out of the room. He had put a question to the witness respecting the account she had given before the coroner. The depositions taken before the coroner were now before the learned judges, and perhaps they would consider it their bounded duty to tell the jury whether that woman swore before the coroner as she did before the court. His conscience was clear; he had discharged his duty throwing out that suggestion. The question he had put to the witness was this—'Upon the oath you have taken, did you not tell the coroner that you saw—instead of some blood on the pillow—his Lordship murdered on the bed?' That was matter for the jury to consider; he would not pass on. The windows were opened, the daylight was let in upon the dreadful spectacle, and could they expect Courvoisier, or any human being, who did not disguise within a human shape the heart of a wild beast, to remain unmoved at the exhibition? To see rank, age, a nobleman of 73, in the enjoyment of good health, having respectable friends around him, having as much happiness as wealth, rank, and respectability could procure him, weltering in his blood—how did the jury think they could have borne the spectacle? Mr Adolphus said they must show no agitation at such a sight, and if they did, it was to be taken as a proof of guilt! What would have been said if that man had remaind calm, and looked on unmoved? Would they not have thought, and thought justly, that the man who was unmoved, who did not shudder with agitation at such a sight, was himself capable of committing the deed? But when Mr Adolphus called on them to mark the agitation of the prisoner as a proof of his guilt, what became of the women who showed the very same feelings? He thought the better of those women for doing so: God forbid that he should insinuate it was proof of their guilt; it would appear to him, on the contrary, to be a proof of their innocence. He wished his friend had been where he (Mr C. Phillips) happened to be by accident, in Hyde Park, some days since, when the murderous attempt on the life of our Queen was made. He wished his friend could have seen the countenances of the bystanders when it became known; how the stoutest man stood appalled, and every face betrayed the most painful agitation. If that were proof of guilt, there was not a man in the park who should not have been condemned for murder. Agitation, indeed! Thank God he had not yet met with that demon in the shape of man who could look on murder without agitation. Then his friend said that the prisoner had given no assistance. That was not true; he had given such assistance as he could when his agitation had in some degree subsided. It could not be expected that a man whose nerves were unstrung by such a sight could immediately settle to habits of business. But it had been proved that the prisoner did what was the most natural of all things for him to do. Lord W. Russell had a son, the sole remnant of his admirable family, a friend of his (Mr C. Phillips's) own, with whose great loss he most deeply sympathized. The prisoner sat down, and instantly began to write to this gentleman to tell him what had occurred; he was in the act of doing so, when the maid-servant accosted him—feminine exclamation!—with 'What the Devil are you doing?' and told him that Mr Russell must be sent for. The prisoner rushed down stairs, and in the agitation of the moment stopped the first man, in order to send him to Mr Russell. 'What do you mean by sending such a man as that?' said the witness to him. In the name of Heaven, was that a time to look minutely at the exterior of the messenger! Would not any human being who had sense enough to recollect the number of the house in which Mr Russell lived do as well as the profoundest philosopher in the country? Everything the prisoner attempted to do was objected to, and yet it was made a complaint against him that he did nothing! Helping the deceased was out of the question, and, except to have medical testimony of the cause of death, and the absence of proofs of self-destruction, it was useless to call in any human being. Suppose Courvoisier had himself gone out for this purpose, having, as had been mentioned, horses at his command, what was there to prevent him, if he were conscious of guilt, from escaping? But no, he made no such attempt; he remained in the house,

3.8 Truthfulness under Police Questioning

and there it was remarkable that throughout the whole of the examination to which he had been subjected by the police he had not answered a single question incorrectly. His answers were given without hesitation, and on every point they turned out to be true. He was subjected to the strictest scrutiny, and tortured by every interrogatory their ingenuity could suggest. Attempts were made to intimidate him by base expressions; he was asked by one man, 'Dare you look me in the face?' and yet the fellow who asked him that told the jury he did not mean to intimidate the prisoner! Every answer he gave was given truly, but that only increased their suspicion. Was it not remarkable that the cause of the prisoner's being taken into custody at all proved to be quite groundless? The locket that was found upon his person the police supposed to be the property of the deceased. Courvoisier declared that it was his own. That was found to be true. The former valet, Ellis, an honest man, he believed, had been applied to and told them that he could not swear the locket was his Lordship's. The search went on, and Lord W. Russell's locket was found in the pantry. Had the true locket not been found, what would have been the consequence? It would have been said that Lord W. Russell's locket was found in the pocket of the prisoner; and what answer could have been given to that, Ellis not being able to say positively whether it was so or not? Thus, it was found that the prisoner had told the whole truth, and nothing but the truth. Then the impression of Lord Russell's seal, his family crest, 'the goat,' was found in Courvoisier's possession; that too was fixed on as a proof of guilt. The man alone, it was argued, who had stolen the seal could have its impression. 'No,' said Courvoisier, 'Mr William Russell gave me that impression; send for him and he will prove it.' But it did not suit the gentlemen who conducted this case at Bow-street to pursue that course, when the life of a fellow-creature was at stake. He must, however, do one honourable man justice; there was a solicitor, the worthy representative of the Russell family, Mr Wing, who, hearing the assertion of the prisoner, went to Mr William Russell, and that young man, still agonized with grief and stricken with horror—still mouring over his murdered father's grave—had no object but to do justice. He told Mr Wing that what Courvoisier said was the truth, and Mr Wing, with a nobleness of humanity, did not drive the prisoner to the peril of calling witnesses and hazarding a reply, but at once exonerated him from the proof by the admission of the fact. These were two instances, and he would not fatigue the jury with many, in which it could be proved that Courvoisier had told nothing but the truth. Suppose it could have been proved he had told a falsehood instead. His learned friend Mr Adolphus would have a right to say it was to cover his guilt; but having told the truth when interrogated, he (Mr Phillips) had a right to say it was proof of his innocence. There was another circumstance: he was asked if he was in the habit of chaining and locking the front door. Yes, he said, he was. But it was found unlocked, unchained, unfastened, and the natural suspicion of the police, who suspected every thing, was, that it had not been fastened on the night of the 5th. But the cook was called, who said she heard him chaining, locking, and bolting it. Here was another instance in which the prisoner told the truth; nor had the prosecutor been able to show a single case in which he told a falsehood. He was asked about the different things; he was required to identify them: 'These,' said he, 'are his Lordship's rings and coins, &c.' There was no hesitation, no tardiness in his explanations. So far there could not be stronger indications of innocence in any man. Then his learned friend said there was a candle found on a table opposite the bed, and a book on the floor, the *Memoirs of Sir Samuel Romilly*; but the candle, it was said, had been so placed that it was impossible for his Lordship to have read by it. A policeman, however, was called who swore it was near enough for any one in bed to read by. What his learned friend meant he did not know, but if he meant anything, the insinuation was not true, being disproved by his own witness.

3.9 The Contents of the Courvoisier's Trunk

Then, said his learned friend, the prisoner's trunk had been examined, and to be sure nothing was found in it; but do you think, said he, that the prisoner would have been fool enough to put the evidence of his guilt into his own trunk! He (Mr Phillips) did not think he would. He must have been either a fool or a mad man to have done it. It was searched by Inspector Tedman on the morning of the 6th—an officer who had given his evidence most fairly—his object being, as he stated, to ascertain if any stolen property or suspicious article could be found in it. He searched it minutely, taking out and unfolding article by article, but without detecting anything to criminate or make him suspect the prisoner. Of course not, said his learned friend; Courvoisier was not such a fool as to put into his own trunk the evidence of his guilt. Well, but that trunk having been minutely searched by Tedman, what in fairness to the prisoner should have been done with it? What would a practised policeman of the old school have done—one of those who, after years of experience and drudgery, were dismissed to poverty in the street, to make way for the regiment? Having once satisfied himself, as Tedman had done, that there was nothing in the trunk to criminate the prisoner, he would instantly, for the interests of justice and the interest of the prisoner, if the interests of a prisoner ever entered into the calculations of a policeman, he would instantly have locked and sealed that trunk, and sent it to a place of safety, where no miscreant, speculating on his share of £450 reward, could have tampered with it in order to ensure the conviction of the unfortunate man at the bar. But it was left in the room open, accessible to the female servants and the whole gang of policemen. And then what did they do? Having examined it on the 6th, they went to it again on the 8th. The same policeman Tedman, who had examined it on the 6th, again examined it again on the 13th. Why? He gave an honest reason for it. Courvoisier's uncle went to the house of Lord William with a message from the prisoner, who had been committed on the 10th. He sent for a shirt on the 13th. The man who was supposed to be conscious of having perpetrated this horrid deed sent his uncle to get linen out of his trunk, which was in the custody of the police, did he know that in that very trunk evidence of the murder was to be found? Tedman unfolded a shirt the same way he had done on the 6th, and then out dropped the gloves spotted with blood. Who put them there between the 6th and the 14th?

3.10 The Police Conspiracy

His learned friend demanded who murdered Lord William Russell; he (Mr Phillips) was not bound to show that; but he had a right to know who placed these bloody gloves in the prisoner's trunk between the 6th and the 14th of May, after the first minute examination by Tedman, and when the prisoner had been already three days in goal? Had there not been practice here? 'Thus bad begins, but worse remains behind.' This man it was evidently determined should be made the victim so some foul contrivance. Collier, who, for reasons best known to himself, would not go to the trunk without a witness (and, to make sure of his witness, took a brother policeman)—Collier went to the trunk after it had been already three times examined, and found, as he had stated, on the very top of the things, two handkerchiefs spotted with blood, which he took care to inform the jury, lest the fact of being found there should not be considered sufficient, had the prisoner's initials upon them. So as to the shirt front, or frill; who put these thing into the trunk, and for what purpose? They were not there on the 6th. It was clear that Courvoisier had not put them there; it was physically impossible; he was in his dungeon at the time, three miles distant. Some villains must have been at work here to provide proofs of guilt against the prisoner, and endeavour to make the jury instrumental in rendering him the victim, not of his own guilt, but of their machinations. He was not wrong in saying there existed a strong suspision, if not actual proof, that the trunk had been practised on.

3.11 The Interrogation of Courvoisier

The next evidence to which he would call their attention was that of Inspector Pearce—he who would not intimidate a poor wretch in the fangs of the police, trembling for his life—he who would make no suggestion to extort the confession that might hang a prisoner! Finding some things, forsooth, in Courvoisier's pantry, he produced them before him, and if there had been one taint of guilt within him he must have been taken by surprise, thunder-struck, and unable to answer. It would have required no speech to intimidate him, the silent proofs of his guilt would have been sufficient, and his manner would at once have indicated what he felt. But the policeman was too cunning; his manner in court under the control of the bench, and under the eye of the jury, was very different from what it must have been when he had his anticipated victim alone. 'Look here, Sir,' said he to Courvoisier, 'dare you look me in the face?' Merciful God! was there any exhibition on earth so likely to strike him dumb with horror as the proofs of the murder lying before him, and that miscreant challenging him to look him in the face? He did look him in the face, and answered him, 'I see them, I know nothing about them; my conscience is clear, I am innocent.' The learned counsel animadverted in very strong terms upon the testimony of this witness, charging him with an attempt to intimidate the prisoner, and thereby to extort from him a confession of the murder. He also condemned the conduct of Mr Mayne and Mr Hobler in permitting Pearce to hold that interview with the prisoner. Such treatment was worthy only of the Inquisition.

3.12 Blood Money

Yet the fellow who did all this told the jury he expected to share in the plunder—the £450 reward—which was to be divided over the coffin of Courvoisier! He had hoped the days of blood money were passed. There was the humbug of a reward in Templeman's case, but he lay five long weeks in his grave until a nobleman had fallen, and then decency required that the advertisement of £450 for the conviction of his murderer should be coupled with a smaller reward for the apprehension of the commoner's assassin. Those rewards might be offered by the government from the purest of motives. They might induce men to hunt out evidence, but the effect also was to make them invent, fabricate, colour, distort, and exaggerate it to attain the end they had in view. Next came Baldwin, who had done his best in the work of conspiracy to earn the wages of blood. He swore well and to the purpose—he did all he could to send a fellow-creature 'unhouseled, disappointed, unaneled' before his God. That man enquivocated and shuffled, and lied on his oath as long as he could, pretending never to have heard of the reward because he was no scholar, although every wall in London was blazoned with it. But he was obliged at last to admit that he had heard the reward read as a general order in the station-house. Was there no practice here? It stood detected at once. After this, and after the case of Gould, he could consider any Government that offered rewards accessory to murder.

3.13 Other Circumstantial Evidence against Courvoisier

The learned counsel went on to contend, that if Courvoisier had committed the murder, his own pantry would have been the last place he would have resorted to for the concealment of the stolen goods. Nor were the expressions he had used, as given in the evidence, to be taken necessarily as a proof of guilt. The slightest expressions had been fastened upon—'I wish I had only old Billy's money, I would not be long in this country,' was construed into a proof that he had meditated murder. Yet it was not an unnatural wish for a foreigner to express, toiling for his daily sustenance, yet longing to revisit his fatherland, rugged though it be—'I wish I had the wealth of such an one, I would not be long away from my own country!' Ambition's vision, glory's bauble, wealth's reality, were all nothing as compared with his native land. Not all the enchantments of creation, not all the splendour of scenery, not all that gratification of any kind could produce could make the Swiss forget his native land:

'Dear is that shed to which his soul conforms,
And dear that hill which lifts him to the storms;
And, as a child, when scaring sounds molest,
Clings close and closer to the mother's breast,
So the loud torrent, and the whirlwind's roar,
But bind him to his native mountains more.'

There never dropped from human lips a more innocent or natural expression, 'I wish I had old Billy's money, I would soon be in my own country.' Then as to the money that was found, he also told the truth. Was that like a guilty man? But was there no other evidence of contrivance in this case? There was a gold watch, half-a-dozen rings, and a number of other valuable articles left behind, while a woman's silver thimble, worth 1s. 6d., was said to be stolen. Who put that thimble in the passage? Much value the thimble would be to the prisoner! These were suspicious circumstances which should make the jury believe that the prisoner had been practised on. Over every portion of the case doubt and darkness rested, and they would come to a conclusion against this man at the peril of their souls. Was it possible to believe that, if the prisoner had committed the murder, he would have hit upon such contrivances—that he would so far have economized his property as to put a sixpenny pair of gloves, and the front of his shirt, in his box, which he must have anticipated would be subject to inspection? There was another circumstance which the jury could not fail to have remarked. The police said, that nobody could go in or out of the house without observation. This he did not believe, and it was, in fact, disproved by the evidence; because there was no doubt that Courvoisier went out for beer, and none of the police saw him. As for their vigilance, let the jury look to the history of the last six months. They had the victim before them: where were the perpetrators? There was one circumstance not unimportant in this case. Courvoisier was apprehended in the house. That house is searched, Courvoisier's linen, his person, and his box are searched; the police, according to their account, so watched the house, that nobody could have gone out. Was it not singular, then, that in no part of the property belonging to Courvoisier, or on his person, was one spot of blood discovered? If he murdered the man, did the jury think it possible that he should have no taint of blood, either on his person or clothes? Would there not have been an appearance of bloody water if he had washed himself; and would there not have been stains of blood under the nails, which, like the damned spot on Lady Macbeth's hand, no water could wash out? When was it, too, that any articles, even the slightest suspicion, were found in the prisoner's box? Not until the 14th May, at a time when the prisoner was far removed from the house, and confined to a dungeon. The jury were aware that a great many observations had been made on the subject of the walls and the back area door. On seeing these marks Courvoisier observed that whoever committed the murder must have come in at a certain place; and such was the impression of Tedman and two other policemem, though, on re-examination, they found that this could not have been the case. Did they give Courvoisier an opportunity of correcting his error also? They took means to correct their own error; but he was bound by an observation he made at the moment, and in which they all concurred at the first superficial glance.

3.14 The Location of Courvoisier's Room,

Mark the situation of the premises. He (Mr Phillips) wished it had been possible for the jury to have seen the house; it had, however, been described by witnesses with great accuracy. Was it not odd, that after all the pains and trouble gone to by the prosecution, a model of that part of the premises where the persons in the house slept should not have been produced? Would not the jury have liked to see a model of the chambers of the servants? For what reason was it that they had been left out of the model produced in court? The room in which Courvoisier slept was an important room. Did not observation arise from its position? The two maid-servants slept in the attic, and there was a staircase leading down from the attic to the floor on which Lord William Russell's bed-room was placed. At the bottom of the staircase there was a door, which closed. If that door had been shut it would have been difficult for the servants to hear anything occurring below. Courvoisier's room immediately adjoined the room in which the maid-servants slept; and on one side of this partition was Courvoisier's bed, and on the other the cook's bed. She had told the jury that if Courvoisier moved about in his shoes in the bed-room, she could have heard him. Now, one thing was certain that Courvoisier was in his bed-room during the night, because he was found in it in the morning. Was it not, then, remarkable that the cook, who, contradicting the housemaid, swore she was not asleep when the latter rose in the morning, and who did not believe she had drunk anything drugged, during the whole of the night, when the house must have been the scene of so much confusion, did not insinuate that she heard the slightest sound or noise of any kind proceeding from Courvoisier's room, in which the prisoner must have been during some part of the night, because, as he (Mr Phillips) had before stated, he was found there in the morning? And let the jury recollect that Courvoisier's sleeping room was divided by the cook's bed-room only by a thin lath and plaster partition.

3.15 The Last Minute Evidence

He (Mr Phillips) had now described to the jury this case as it had been laid before the magistrates, and as up to the close of the last day he was prepared to meet it. He (Mr Phillips) now came to a portion in the case of which he had reason loudly to complain. Strange to say, that although this murder had been rumoured about the whole metropolis for so many weeks past, yet up to the night of Thursday last nothing was known about the missing plate. He (Mr Phillips) had his strong suspicions about it. He thought that nothing could be more shameful than that after the arrival in that court of Cumming, who admitted that he knew that he (Mr Phillips) was of counsel for the prisoner, no intimation of the nature of his evidence should have been given to the prisoner. He (Mr Phillips) admitted that the names of other witnesses not examined before the magistrates had been very fairly communicated to the prisoner's counsel. He (Mr Phillips) thought that a night at least should have been given to allow inquiries to be made into the character of the persons coming up against the prisoner. This new evidence had sprung upon them like a mine under their feet. He (Mr Phillips) knew nothing about Mrs Piolaine; how should he? The prosecution had taken care that he should know nothing about her. Let the jury examine her testimony. If that woman did not tell the truth distinctly, the persons who were called to corroborate her prove nothing at all. He (Mr Phillips) hoped the jury knew something of Leicester-place. If they did, they knew the character of this hotel, with a billiard room attached to it, where, unlike at a respectable hotel, any stranger, not being a guest, might enter and gamble. This was the residence of Mrs Piolaine, who, though she heard of the murder on the day after it occurred, did not for three long weeks, whilst her husband remaining in the country, speak a word respecting it to the partner of her bed. He (Mr Phillips) asked this question, did the jury in the whole course of their existence, ever hear of such a singular circumstance. It was not until the middle of this long investigation, and after the prisoner had undergone the agonizing ordeal of standing a whole day in that dock, that this new evidence was brought into court, though it had been proved that a reward of £50 for some time previously had been offered for the discovery of this plate. He again said that it had sprung like a mine under them, and the prisoner ought at least to have had one night afforded to him to make inquiries on the subject. What was Mrs Piolaine's evidence? A French paper, forsooth, was read to her, and then, in some unaccountable manner, it puts her in mind of a parcel having been left with her by Courvoisier, whom she had never known by that name, but by the name of Jean. How on earth could a French paper have directed her suspicions against the prisoner? He (Mr Phillips) had no right to speculate upon what that paper contained, but how could a French paper have made her suspect a man of whom she had never heard?

Mr Baron PARKE here observed, that if the learned counsel wished to raise a doubt of contradiction on the point, he might have called for the paper and examined its contents.

Mr PHILLIPS continued.—He had a right to say that there was little to no proof how that paper directed her suspicions against Courvoisier. Neither was there any proof that she ever knew Courvoisier to be a servant of Lord William Russell. All this part of the case depended on the evidence of that woman. That was an important part of the case. It was attempted to be proved that this property was brought to her by Courvoisier a week or fortnight before the murder. She knew nothing about the man. She did not know him when he came in. She opened the parcel at last, and then sent for about half-a-dozen persons, who in a most extraordinary manner signed every one of them a kind of round-robin of an inventory. Still it was perfectly consistent to suppose that Courvoisier was not the man who brought this property to her. The prosecution had told them that they would identify the property in the parcel as Lord William Russell's. They went further. They said they would identify the clothes as being those of the prisoner. They called the housemaid and Ellis; but they could only say that they had seen the prisoner in a jacket similar to the one found in the paper parcel. The prosecutors went further, and they called the prisoner's washerwoman, but she swore that she frequently washed the prisoner's socks, and that they were marked, not like those in the paper parcel, on the heel, but at the top, and the letters also were different, for whereas the socks in the parcel were marked with the letter C., those she washed were marked C.B.

3.16 Robbery, Not Murder

But, supposing all this was admitted (and he was sure the jury would pay attention to what he was saying, and could they find their way out of this case consistently with the ends of justice without shedding the prisoner's blood they would be glad to do so), and that this mysterious evidence about the plate was as clear as it was doubtful, that the clothes in the parcel belonged to Courvoisier, and that the parcel itself was deposited by the prisoner with Mrs Piolaine—supposing all this admitted, was it conclusive of murder? This was a question upon which his Lordship would give his most valuable opinion; but he

(Mr Phillips) might venture to say, that though this evidence, if true, would be conclusive of robbery, and of that robbery the prisoner might hereafter be convicted, if guilty, and upon conviction, transported to undergo a lingering death in exile in Norfolk Island; yet it was by no means conclusive of murder. Therefore, in acquitting the prisoner of murder, they would have still this reflection, that if guilty of the robbery, he would be liable to a heavy and dreadful punishment. With respect to the commission of the murder, the jury might have a strong suspicion, or even a moral conviction; but it was not a strong suspicion or a moral conviction that a man was to be declared guilty of murder. If, notwithstanding that suspicion they felt bound to acquit the prisoner, he was still answerable to the laws of this country for the robbery, if guilty; and, even supposing him guilty of the murder, which indeed was known to Almighty God alone, and of which for the sake of his eternal soul, he (Mr Phillips) hoped he was innocent, it was far better that in the dreadful solitude of exile he should, though not in the sight of man, yet alone before the presence of God, atone by a lingering repentance for the deed, than that he should now be sent in the dawning of his manhood to an ignominious death in a case where the truth was not clear.

3.17 Peroration

And having now travelled through this case of mystery and darkness, his anxious task was done— that of the jury was about to begin. Might God direct their judgement! One of the attributes of the Almighty was that day given to them—the issue of life and death was in their hands. To them was given to restore this man once more to the enjoyments of existence and the dignity of freedom, or to consign him to an ignominious fate, and brand upon his grave a murderer's epitaph. His had been a painful and an awful task, but still more awful was their responsibility. To violate the living temple which the Lord had made, to quench the fire that His breath had given, was an awful and tremendous responsibility. The word once gone forth was irrevocable. Speak not the word lightly. Speak it not on suspicion, however strong, on moral conviction however cogent, on inference, doubt, or anything but a clear, irresistible, bright, noonday certainty. He spoke to them in no spirit of hostile admonition. Heaven knew he did not. He spoke to them in the spirit of a friend and fellow-Christian, and in that spirit he told them, that, if they pronounced the word lightly, its memory would never die within them. It would accompany them in their walks, it would follow them in their solitary retirements like a shadow, it would haunt them in their sleep and hover round their bed, it would take the shape of an accusing spirit, and confront and condemn them before the judgment seat of their God. So let them beware how they acted.

Bibliography

Notes

1. **Citation practice**: the books, treatises and articles listed in this bibliography are referred to in the text by their author's name and their year of publication.

2. **Nineteenth-century articles**: nineteenth-century articles are listed separately where their authors are known. Where their authors are not known they are referred to in the text by their full titles and journal references.

3. **Authorship**: the attributions of authorship for articles which originally appeared anonymously are based upon *The Wellesley Index to Victorian Periodicals* (5 volumes, Toronto, 1966–89), supplemented by the following sources:

(a) *Henry Brougham's articles on Phillips' speeches*: Brougham (1815) and (1817) are described by *The Wellesley Index* as 'possibly Henry Brougham'. This attribution, justified by style and subject-matter, is further confirmed by the references to Brougham in the notice of these articles in 'Speech Delivered by an Eminent Barrister' (1818) *Blackwood's Edinburgh Magazine.*

(b) *Lord Brougham's articles in the Law Review*: Some of Lord Brougham's articles in the *Law Review* (including Brougham (1845a)) appear in his *Works* (Brougham (1872–73)). His authorship of many other early contributions to the *Law Review* (including Brougham (1845b)) is confirmed by his correspondence with its editor, James Stewart, amongst the *Brougham Papers*, University College Library, London.

(c) *The writings of Thomas Noon Talfourd:* Talfourd's legal writings are identified in two biographical articles published after his death: see 'The Late Mr. Justice Talfourd' (1854) 51 *Law Magazine* 298, and 'The Life and Writings of the Late Mr. Justice Talfourd' (1856) 25 *North British Review* 47.

(d) *Samuel Warren's Law Magazine article:* Warren's article on *Courvoisier* (Warren (1850)) appears in his *Miscellanies Critical, Imaginative and Juridical*, and is also referred to in a letter from Lord Brougham to Charles Phillips, undated, *Brougham Papers, undated and uncatalogued letters 1849–1858.*

(e) *Thomas Starkie*: Starkie's obituary in the *Law Review* ('Mr Starkie' (1849) 10 *Law Review* 201–4) lists his contributions to that publication including Starkie (1844–45).

(f) *John Pitt Taylor*: Taylor (1842), Taylor (1843) and Taylor (1844) appear in the *Law Magazine* under the initials 'J.P.T.' Taylor (1844) appears as Appendix C to the *Eighth Report* of the Criminal Law Commissioners where John Pitt Taylor is named as its author.

(g) *Charles Sprengal Greaves*: Greaves (1845) and Greaves (1846) appear in the *Law Magazine* under the initials 'C.S.G.' and it is safe to attribute them to Greaves.

Manuscript Sources

Brougham Papers, University College Library, London.
Judges' Report, Norfolk Summer Circuit, 1828, Public Records Office, London, HO 13/6.
Lyndhurst Papers, Trinity College Library, Cambridge.
Midland Circuit Records in Oxford and Midland Circuit Mess Records, six volumes, 1773–1909, Bodleian Library, Oxford.
Minutes of the Norfolk Circuit Bar Mess in private possession, copy furnished courtesy of Professor R. Cocks, Faculty of Law, University of Keele.
Peel Papers, British Museum, London.
R v Corder, Prosecution Briefs, Suffolk County Records Office, Bury St. Edmunds, 568/1 (Kelly) and 568/2 (Andrews).
Report on the Papers relating to the Case of Thomas Smethurst, by Sir Frederick Pollock, Chief Baron, Forster Collection, 48. F. 52, National Art Library, Victoria and Albert Museum.
Talfourd Papers, Reading Public Library, Reading.

Secondary Sources

Anon. (1730), *A Complete Collection of State Trials and Proceedings Upon High Treason*, 2nd edition, 6 volumes (London, 1730).
Amicus Curiae (1819), *Criticisms of the Bar; including Strictures on the Principal Counsel Practising in the Courts of King's Bench, Common Pleas, Chancery, and Exchequer* (London, 1819).
Anderson, J. S. (1992), *Lawyers and the Making of English Land Law 1832–1940* (Oxford, 1992).
Atlay, J. B. (1899), *Famous Trials of the Century* (London, 1899).
Austin, J. (1879), *Lectures on Jurisprudence or the Philosophy of Positive Law*, 2 volumes, 4th edition, ed. Campbell (London, 1879).
Bacon, F. (1819), *The Works of Francis Bacon, Lord Verulam*, 10 volumes (London, 1819).
Bagehot, W. (1889), *Biographical Studies*, 2nd edition (London, 1889).
Baker, J. H. (1977a), 'Criminal Courts and Procedure at Common Law 1550–1800' in J. S. Cockburn ed. *Crime in England 1500–1800* (London, 1977).
—— (1977b), 'University College and Legal Education 1826–1976' (1977) 30 *Current Legal Problems* 1–13.
Ballantine, Sjt. W. (1883), *Some Experiences of a Barrister's Life*, 8th edition (London, 1883).
Beattie, J. M. (1986), *Crime and the Courts in England 1660–1800* (Oxford, 1986).
—— (1991), 'Scales of Justice: Defence Counsel and the English Criminal Trial in the Eighteenth and Nineteenth Centuries' (1991) 9 *Law & Hist. Rev.* 221–67.
Beccaria, C. (1963), *On Crimes and Punishments* (trans. H. Paolucci, New York, 1963).
Bentham, J. (1843), *The Works of Jeremy Bentham*, 11 volumes, ed. Bowring (Edinburgh, 1843).
Best, W. M. (1849), *A Treatise on the Principles of Evidence and Practice as to Proofs in Courts of Common Law* (London, 1849).

—— (1858), 'The Common Law of England; with an Examination of some False Principles of Law Reform' in *Papers Read Before the Juridical Society 1855–1858* (London, 1858) 399–434.
Blackstone, W. (1765–69), *Commentaries on the Laws of England*, 4 volumes (Oxford, 1765–69).
Bousfield, R. M. and Merrett, R. (1843), *Report of the Trial of Daniel M'Naughten* (London, 1843).
Brougham, H. (1810), 'Erskine's Speeches' (1810) 16 *Edinburgh Review* 102–27.
—— (1812a), 'Speeches of Lord Erskine' (1812) 19 *Edinburgh Review* 339–63.
—— (1812b), 'Sir Samuel Romilly on English Criminal Law' (1812) 19 *Edinburgh Review* 389–415.
—— (1815), 'Irish Oratory' (1815) 25 *Edinburgh Review* 389–98.
—— (1817), 'Speeches of Mr. Phillips' (1817) 29 *Edinburgh Review* 52–70.
Brougham, Lord (1836–37), 'Rights and Duties of Advocates' (1836–37) 64 *Edinburgh Review* 155–68.
—— (1838), *Speeches of Henry Lord Brougham*, 4 volumes (Edinburgh, 1838).
—— (1839–45), *Historical Sketches of Statesmen who Flourished in the Time of George III*, 3 volumes (London, 1839–45).
—— (1845a), 'Lord Abinger' (1845) 1 *Law Review* 79.
—— (1845b), 'Mr. Baron Garrow' (1845) 1 *Law Review* 318–28.
—— (1847), Prefatory Memoir contributed to volume 1 of *The Speeches of the Right Honourable Lord Erskine*, 4 volumes (London, 1847).
—— (1851), 'Extract of a letter to Lord Denman from Lord Brougham' (1851) 14 *Law Review* 425–34.
—— (1853–54), 'Criminal Law Digest' (1853–54) 94 *Quarterly Review* 461–6.
—— (1854), 'The Judges on Codification' (1854) 99 *Edinburgh Review* 573–81.
—— (1871), *The Life and Times of Henry Lord Brougham*, 3 volumes (Edinburgh and London, 1871).
—— (1872–73), *Works of Henry, Lord Brougham*, 11 volumes (Edinburgh, 1872–73).
Bruce, W. (1865), *The Examination of the Accused in Criminal Cases* (London, 1865).
Burn, R. (1764), *The Justice of the Peace and the Parish Officer*, 8th edition, 2 volumes (London, 1764).
Calvert, F. (1836), *Letter to the Right Hon. Lord Dacre, Chairman of the Quarter Sessions of Hertfordshire, on the Prisoners' Counsel Bill* (London, 1836).
Campbell, Lord (1842), *Speeches of Lord Campbell at the Bar and in the House of Commons* (Edinburgh, 1842).
—— (1856–57), *Lives of the Lord Chancellors and Keepers of the Great Seal of England*, 4th edition, 10 volumes (London, 1856–57).
Carr, Sir C. (1955), *A Victorian Law Reformer's Correspondence* (Selden Society Annual Lecture, London, 1955).
Chadwick, E. (1841), 'Licence of Counsel: Criminal Procedure' (1841) 35 *The Westminster Review* 1.
Cock, R. (1976), 'The Bar at the Assizes: Barristers on three Nineteenth Century Circuits' (1976) 6 *Kingston Law Rev.* 36–52.
Cockburn, J. S. (1972), *A History of the English Assizes 1558–1714* (London, 1972).
Cocks, R. (1983), *The Foundations of the Modern Bar* (London, 1983).

Coke, Sir E. (1644), *The Third Part of the Institutes of the Laws of England* (London, 1644).

Collins, P. (1994), *Dickens and Crime*, 3rd edition (London, 1994).

Cornish, W. R. and Clark, G. de N. (1989), *Law and Society in England 1750–1950* (London, 1989).

Cornish, W. R. (1978), 'Defects in Prosecuting—Professional Views in 1845' in Glazebrook ed. *Reshaping the Criminal Law* (London, 1978) 305–16.

Cottu, C. (1820), *On the Administration of the Criminal Code in England and Wales and the Spirit of English Government* (1820) 16 *The Pamphleteer* 1 (translation).

Cowen, Z and Carter, P. B. (1956), 'Unsworn Statements by Accused Persons' in Cowen and Carter *Essays on the Law of Evidence* (Oxford, 1956) 204.

Cox, E. W. (1852), *The Advocate* (London, 1852).

Cross, R. (1978), 'The Reports of the Criminal Law Commissioners (1833–1849) and the Abortive Bills of 1853' in Glazebrook ed. *Reshaping the Criminal Law* (London, 1978) 5–20.

Curtis, J. (1828), 'An Authentic and Faithful History of the Mysterious Murder of Maria Marten &c.' (London, 1828).

Daniel, W. T. S. (1858), 'On Advocacy as Connected with the Administration of Justice' in *Papers Read before the Juridical Society 1855–1858* (London, 1858) 293–312.

Davies, Sir J. (1628), *Le primer reports des cases et matters en ley resolued et adiudges en les Courts del Roy en Ireland* (London, 1628).

De Fonblanque, E. B. (1874), *The Life and Labours of Albany Fonblanque* (London, 1874).

Denman, Lord (1851), 'Letters of Lord Denman to Lord Brougham on County Courts and Evidence of Parties' (1851) 14 *Law Review* 347–353.

De Quincey, T. (1897), *De Quincey's Collected Writings*, ed. D. Masson, 14 volumes (London, 1897).

Dicey, A. V. (1867), 'Legal Etiquette' (1867) 2 *Fortnightly Review* (NS) 169.

—— (1905), *Lectures on the Relation Between Law & Public Opinion in England During the Nineteenth Century* (London, 1905).

Dickenson, W. and Talfourd, T. N. (1829), *A Practical Guide to the Quarter Sessions and Other Sessions of the Peace, Adapted to the Use of Young Magistrates, and Professional Gentlemen, at the Commencement of their Practice*, 3rd edition (London, 1829).

Downer, L. J. ed. (1972), *Leges Henrici Primi* (Oxford, 1972).

Duman, D. (1983), *The English and Colonial Bars in the Nineteenth Century* (London, 1983).

Erskine, Lord. (1810), *The Speeches of the Hon. Thomas Erskine*, 4 volumes (London, 1810).

Finer, S. E. (1952), *The Life and Times of Sir Edwin Chadwick* (London, 1952).

—— (1972), 'The Transmission of Benthamite Ideas 1820–50' in G. Sutherland ed. *Studies in the Growth of Nineteenth Century Government* (London, 1972) 11–32.

Fisher, D. H. (1971), *Historians' Fallacies: Towards a Logic of Historical Thought* (London, 1971).

Forsyth, W. (1849), *Hortensius: or The Advocate* (London, 1849).

—— (1858), 'The Speeches of Lord Brougham' (1858) 107 *Edinburgh Review* 443–64.

—— (1874), *Hortensius. An Historical Essay on the Office and Duties of an Advocate*, 2nd edition (London, 1874).

Foucault, M. (1977), *Discipline and Punish* (trans. Sheridan, 1977).

Frank, J. (1949), *Courts on Trial* (New Jersey, 1949).

Gatrell, V. A. C. (1994), *The Hanging Tree* (Oxford, 1994).

—— and Hadden, T. B. (1972), 'Criminal Statistics and their Interpretation' in E. A. Wrigley ed. *Nineteenth Century Society* (Cambridge, 1972).

George, M. D. (1992), *London Life in the Eighteenth Century* (Penguin Books, 1992).

Grant, J. (1837), *The Bench and the Bar*, 2 volumes (London, 1837).

Greaves, C.S. (1845), 'The Bill to Provide an Appeal in Criminal Cases' (1845) 33 *Law Magazine* 129–52.

—— (1846), 'Eighth Report of the Criminal Law Commissioners' (1846) 33 *Law Magazine* 1–40.

—— (1862), *The Criminal Law Consolidation and Amendment Acts*, 2nd edition (London, 1862).

—— and Lonsdale, J. J. (1854), *A letter to the Lord Chancellor, containing observations on the answers of the Judges to the Lord Chancellor's letter on the Criminal Law Bills of the last session of Parliament* (London, 1854).

Green, T. A. (1985), *Verdict According to Conscience: Perspectives on the English Criminal Trial Jury, 1200–1800* (Chicago, 1985).

Gurney, J. (1806), *The Trial of Richard Patch for the Wilful Murder of Issac Blight etc.* (London, 1806).

Hardcastle, M. S. (1881), *Life of John, Lord Campbell*, 2 volumes (London, 1881).

Hawkins, Sir W. (1724), *A Treatise of the Pleas of the Crown*, 2nd edition (London, 1724).

Hawles, J. (1689), *Remarks upon the Trials of Fitzharris, Colledge, etc* (London, 1689).

Hay, D. (1975), 'Property, Authority and the Criminal Law' in D. Hay et al. *Albion's Fatal Tree* (Allen Lane, 1975) 17–63.

—— (1984), 'The Criminal Prosecution in England and its Historians' (1984) 47 *Modern Law Review* 1–29.

Hazlitt, W. (1930–34), *The Complete Works of William Hazlitt*, ed. E. P. Howe, 21 volumes (London and Toronto, 1930–34).

Henderson, E. (1871), *Recollections of the Public Career and Private Life of the Late John Adolphus* (London, 1871).

Holdsworth, W. S. (1923), (1924), (1952), *The History of English Law*, vol. 2, 3rd edition (London, 1923), vol. 5 (London, 1924), and vol. 13 (London, 1952).

Holmes, O. W. (1897), 'The Path of Law' (1897) 10 *Harv. Law Rev.* 457–78.

Hostettler, J. A. (1982), 'Counsel for the Defence' (1982) 11 *Anglo-American Law Rev.* 74–88.

—— (1992), *The Politics of Criminal Law Reform in the Nineteenth Century* (Chichester, 1992).

House, M., Storey, G. and Tillotson, K. eds. (1965–93), *The Letters of Charles Dickens*, 7 volumes (Oxford, 1965–93).

Howell, T. B. and Howell, T. J. eds. (1809–26), *A Complete Collection of State Trials*, 33 volumes (London, 1809–26).

Irving, H. B. ed. (1912), *Trial of Mrs Maybrick* (Edinburgh, 1912).

'JPT' (1821), *An Extempore Essay on the Oratorical Style of Charles Phillips Esq.* (London, 1821).

Kaye, J. M. ed. (1966), *Placita Corone*, Selden Society, supplementary vol. 4 (London, 1966).

King, P. (1984), 'Decision-Makers and Decision-Making in the English Criminal Trial, 1750–1800' (1984) 27 *The Historical Journal* 25–58.

Kinghorn, J. (1880), 'The Decline of Circuit Life' (1880) 5 *Law Magazine and Rev. (4th Series)* 335–77.

Kirwan, A. V. (1845), 'The Late Sir William Follett' (1845) 32 *Fraser's Magazine* 165–74.

—— (1852), 'Advocates and Juries' (1852) 46 *Fraser's Magazine* 571.

Knight, C. (1873), *Passages of a Working Life During Half a Century*, 3 volumes (London, 1873).

Knott, G. H. and Watson, E. R. eds. (1952), *Trial of William Palmer* (London, 1952).

Kurland, P. B. and Waters, D. W. M. (1959), 'Public Prosecutions in England, 1854–79: An Essay in English Legislative History' (1959) 9 *Duke Law Journal* 493–562.

Lacquer, T. W. (1989), 'Crowds, Carnival and the State in English Executions, 1604–1868' in Brier *et al.* ed. *The First Modern Society* (Cambridge, 1989) 309–55.

Landsman, S. (1990), 'The Rise of the Contentious Spirit: Adversary Procedure in Eighteenth Century England' (1990) 75 *Cornell Law Rev.* 498–609.

Langbein, J. H. (1978), 'The Criminal Trial Before Lawyers' (1978) 45 *Univ. of Chicago Law Rev.* 263–316.

—— (1983a), 'Shaping the Eighteenth Century Criminal Trial: A View from the Ryder Sources' (1983) 50 *Univ. of Chicago Law Rev.* 1–136.

—— (1983b), 'Albion's Fatal Flaws' (1983) 98 *Past & Present* 96–120.

—— (1994), 'The Historical Origins of the Privilege Against Self Incrimination at Common Law' (1994) 92 *Mich. Law Rev.* 1047–85.

—— (1996), 'Historical Foundations of the Law of Evidence: A View from the Ryder Sources' (1996) 96 *Columbia Law Rev.* 1168–1202.

Linebaugh, P. (1975), 'The Tyburn Riots Against the Surgeons' in D. Hay *et al. Albion's Fatal Tree* (Allen Lane, 1975) 65–117.

—— (1985), '(Marxist) Social History and (Conservative) Legal History: A Reply to Professor Langbein' (1985) 60 *N.Y.U. Law Rev.* 212.

—— (1991), *The London Hanged* (London, 1991).

Lobban, M. (1991), *The Common Law and English Jurisprudence 1760–1850* (Oxford, 1991).

Mackintosh, R. J. (ed.) (1835), *Memoirs of the Life of the Right Honourable Sir James MacKintosh*, 2 volumes (London, 1835).

Madan, M. (1785), *Thoughts on Executive Justice with Respect to our Criminal Laws, Particularly on the Circuits* (London, 1785).

Maine, H. S. (1861), *Ancient Law: Its Connection with the Early History of Society, and its Relation to Modern Ideas* (London, 1861).

Maitland, F. W. (1885), *Justice and Police* (London, 1885).

—— (1911), 'Why the History of English Law is not Written' in H. A. L. Fisher ed. *The Collected Papers of Frederic William Maitland*, 3 volumes (Cambridge, 1911) vol. 1, 480–97.

Martin, Sir T. (1884), *A Life of Lord Lyndhurst*, 2nd edition (London, 1884).

McGowen, R. (1983), 'The Image of Justice and the Criminal Law in Early Nineteenth Century England' (1983) 32 *Buffalo Law Rev.* 89.

Medd, P. (1968), *Romilly* (London, 1968).

Milsom, S. C. F. ed. (1963), *Novae Narrationes*, Selden Society, vol. 80 (London, 1963).

—— (1981), *Historical Foundations of the Common Law*, 2nd edition (London, 1981).

Paley, W. (1820), 'The Principles of Moral and Political Philosophy' in *The Works of William Paley*, 4 volumes (Edinburgh, 1820).

Parker (1865), 'The Profession of Advocacy' (1865) 12 *Cornhill Magazine* 105–15.

Parry, L. A. ed. (1931), *Trial of Dr Smethurst* (Edinburgh and London, 1931).

Perkin, H. (1969), *The Origins of Modern English Society 1780–1880* (London, 1969).

Phifer, J. R. (1980), 'Law, Politics and Violence: The Treason Trials Act of 1696' (1980) 12 *Albion* 235–256.

Philips, D. (1980), 'A New Engine of Power and Authority: The Institutionalization of Law-Enforcement in England 1780–1830' in V. A. C. Gatrell *et al* ed. *'Crime and the Law: the Social History of Crime in Western Europe since 1500'* (London, 1980) 155–89.

Phillips, C. (1857), *Curran and His Contemporaries*, 5th edition (Edinburgh and London, 1857).

Plucknett, T. F. T. (1951), 'Maitland's View of Law and History' (1951) 67 *Law Quarterly Rev.* 179–94.

—— and Barton, J. L. ed. (1974), *St. German's Doctor and Student*, Selden Society, vol. 91 (London, 1974).

Poland, Sir H. ed. (1918), *Report of the Trial of Courvoisier for the Murder of Lord William Russell* (London, 1918).

Pollock Sir F. and Maitland F. W. (1898), *The History of English Law Before the Time of Edward I*, 2nd edition (Cambridge, 1898).

Post, J. B. (1984), 'The Admissibility of Defence Counsel in English Criminal Procedure' (1984) 5 *Jnl. Legal Hist. (Special Issue)* 23–32.

Pue, W. W. (1990), 'Moral Panic at the English Bar: Paternal vs. Commercial Ideologies of Legal Practice in the 1860s' (1990) 15 *Law and Social Inquiry* 49–118.

Pulton, F. (1610), *De Pace Regnis et Regni* (London, 1610).

Radzinowicz, L. (1948–86), *A History of the Criminal Law and its Administration from 1750*, 5 volumes (London, 1948–86).

—— (1957), *Sir James Fitzjames Stephen and his Contribution to the Development of the Criminal Law* (Selden Society Lecture, 1957).

Rezneck, S. (1930), 'The Statute of 1696: A Pioneer Measure in the Reform of Judicial Procedure in England' (1930) 2 *Jnl. Modern Hist.* 5–26.

Richardson, R. (1987), *Death, Dissection and the Destitute* (London and New York, 1987).

Robinson, H. C. (1872), *Diary, Reminiscences and Correspondence of Henry Crabb Robinson* ed. T. Sadler, 2 volumes, 3rd edition (London and New York, 1872).

Rolt, Sir J. (1939), *The Memoirs of the Right Honourable Sir John Rolt* (London, 1939).

Romilly, S. (1786), *Observations on a Late Publication Intituled Thoughts on Executive Justice* (London, 1786).

—— (1792), *Letters Containing an Account of the Late Revolution in France and Observations on the Constitution, Laws, Manners and Institutions of the English* (London, 1792).

Romilly, Sir S. (1840), *Memoirs of the Life of Sir Samuel Romilly Written by Himself with a selection of correspondence edited by his sons*, 3 volumes (London, 1840).

Ross, D (transl.) (1990), *Aristotle, The Nichomachean Ethics* (Oxford, 1990).

Rudé, G. (1964), *The Crowd in History* (New York, 1964).

Rutter, I. C. (1960–61), 'A Jurisprudence of Lawyers' Operations' (1960–61) 13 *Journal of Legal Education* 301.

Scarlett, P. C. (1877), *A Memoir of the Right Honourable James, Lord Abinger* (London, 1877).

Selborne, Lord (1896), *Memorials: Part I. Family and Personal 1766–1865*, 2 volumes (London, 1896).

Shapiro, A. H. (1993), 'Political Theory and the Growth of Defensive Safeguards in Criminal Procedure: The Origins of the Treason Trials Act 1696' (1993) 11 *Law & History Rev.* 215–55.

Sharpe, J. A. (1985), '"Last Dying Speeches": Religion, Ideology and Public Execution in Seventeenth Century England' (1985) 107 *Past and Present* 144–67.

Shaw Lefevre, G. (1863), 'The Discipline of the Bar' (1863) 15 *Law Magazine* 1–42.

Slater, M. (1928), *Maria Marten...a traditional acting version here for the first time printed and published by...M Slater* (London, 1928)

Smith, K. J. M. (1988), *James Fitzjames Stephen: Portait of a Victorian Rationalist* (Cambridge, 1988).

Smith, Rev. S. (1822), 'Prisons' (1822) 36 *Edinburgh Review* 359.

—— (1826–27), 'Counsel For Prisoners' (1826–27) 45 *Edinburgh Review* 74–95.

Smith, Sir T. (1583), *De Republica Anglorum* (London, 1583).

Stammers, J. (1838), *The Case of the Queen v D'Israeli with an Argument in Vindication of the Practice of the Bar* (London, 1838).

Starkie, T. (1844–45), 'On the Consolidation of the Criminal Law' (1844–45) 1 *Law Review* 438–65.

Staunford, Sir W. (1557), *Les Plees Del Coron* (1557).

Stephen, J. F. (1859), On Trial by Jury, and the Evidence of Experts' in *Papers Read Before the Juridical Society 1858–63* (London, 1863) 236–49.

—— (1861), 'The Morality of Advocacy' (1861) 3 *Cornhill Magazine* 447–59.

—— (1863a), *A General View of the Criminal Law* (London, 1863).

—— (1863b), 'Professional Etiquette' (1863) *Cornhill Magazine* 101–11.

Stephen, Sir J. F. (1883), *A History of the Criminal Law of England*, 3 volumes (London, 1883).

—— (1890), *A General View of the Criminal Law*, 2nd edition (London, 1890).

Stephen, Sir L. (1895), *A Life of Sir James Fitzjames Stephen* (London, 1895).

Stewart, R. (1985), *Henry Brougham 1778–1868 His Public Career* (London, 1985).

Talfourd, T. N. (1820), 'North's Life of Lord Guildford' (1820) 2 *Retrospective Review* 238–56.

—— (1821a), 'A Call to the Bar' (1821) 1 *New Monthly Magazine and Literary Journal* 533–6.

—— (1821b), 'On Pulpit Oratory' (1821) 3 *London Magazine* 182.

—— (1825), 'On the Profession of the Bar' (1825) 1 *London Magazine (New Series)* 323–38.

—— (1833), 'Lord Tenterden' in 'Events of the Quarter' (1833) 9 *Law Magazine* 234–6.

—— (1841), *Speech for the Defendant in the Prosecution of The Queen v Moxon* (London, 1841).

—— (1844), 'Lord Eldon and Lord Stowell' (1844) 75 *Quarterly Review* 32–54.

—— (1846), 'On the Principle of Advocacy as Developed in the Practice of the Bar' (1846) 35 *Law Magazine* 1.

Talfourd, Sir T. N. (1854), *Supplement to 'Vacation Rambles'* (London, 1854).

Taylor, J. P. (1842), 'Defects of the Criminal Law' (1842) 28 *Law Magazine* 1–35.

—— (1843), 'The Seventh Criminal Law Report' (1843) 30 *Law Magazine* 1–48.

—— (1844), 'Defects of Criminal Procedure' (1844) 31 *Law Magazine* 241–75.

Thackeray, W. M. (1840), 'Going to See a Man Hanged' (1840) 20 *Fraser's Magazine* 150–8.

Townsend, W. C. (1850), *Modern State Trials*, 2 volumes (London, 1850).

Twining, W. (1980), 'Goodbye to Lewis Eliot. The Academic Lawyer as Scholar' (1980) 15 *Jnl. Soc. Public Teachers of Law* 2.

—— (1984) 'Taking Facts Seriously' (1984) 34 *Journal of Legal Education* 22.

—— (1986) 'Cannibalism and Legal Literature' (1986) 6 *Oxford Journal of Legal Studies* 423–30.

Wakefield, E. G. (1831), *Facts Relating to the Punishment of Death in the Metropolis* (London, 1831).

Warren, S. (1850), 'The Practice of Advocacy—Mr. Charles Phillips, and his Defence of Courvoisier' (1850) 11 *Law Review* 376–436.

—— (1855), *Miscellanies Critical, Imaginative and Juridical*, 2 volumes (Edinburgh and London, 1855).

—— (1863), *A Popular and Practical Introduction to Law Studies*, 3rd edition (London, 1863).

Watkins, J. (1815), *The Important Results of an Elaborate Investigation into the Mysterious Case of Elizabeth Fenning* (London, 1815).

Wrottesley, Sir F. (1948), 'Mr. Justice Talfourd and the Cannock Chase Mining Case of 1842' in *Collections For a History of Staffordshire* (Staffordshire Record Society, 1948).

Index